SHAMROCK'S STORY

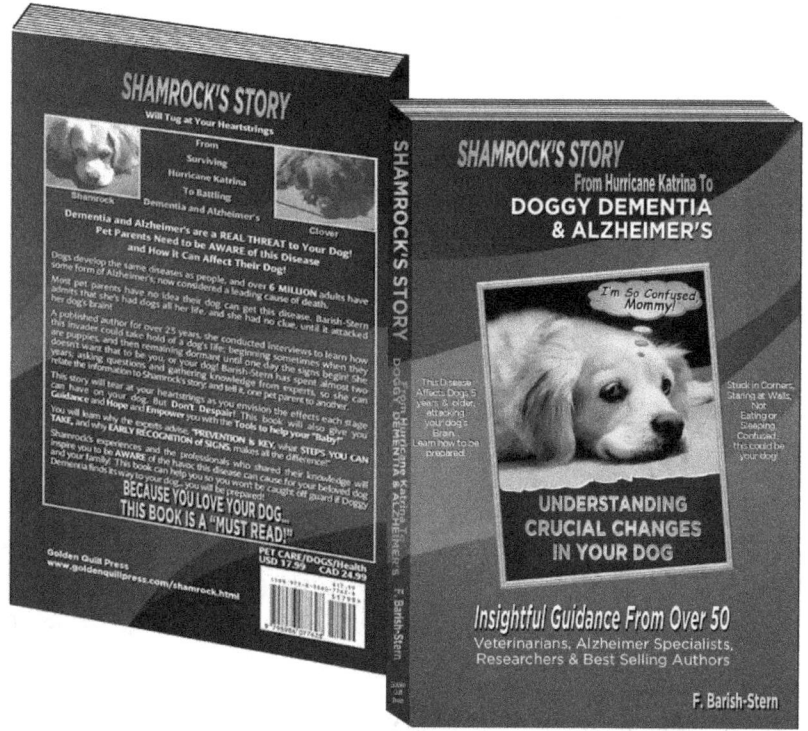

Working with writers since 1998

Other Books By F. Barish-Stern

Tell it to the Future - Have I Got a Story For You - About The Twentieth Century

Tell it to the Future - Book 1 - 1900's - 1930's

Tell it to the Future – Book 2 - 1940's -1960's

Tell it to the Future – Book 3 - 1970-2000

New Horizon's

Code 47 to BREV Force – Cracko

Code 47 to BREV Force – QuizMaster MixMatcher

Code 47 to BREV Force – Controller the Final Battle

From an Idea to Your Finished Story

How to Write Your Book - Book 1 Let's Get Started:

How To Write Your Book - Book 2 Writing on the Super-Highway:

How To Write your Book - Book 3: From An Idea...to Your Finished Story

How To Write Your Book - From An Idea to your Published Story

See an additional list of Books published by Golden Quill Press at back of this book

SHAMROCK'S STORY

FROM HURRICANE KATRINA TO DOGGY DEMENTIA & ALZHEIMER'S

Understanding Crucial Changes In Your Dog!

Insightful Guidance From Over 50 Veterinarians, Alzheimer Specialists, Researchers, & Best-Selling Authors

F. Barish-Stern

Golden Quill Press

The purpose of this book is solely as an informational source for canine cognitive issues. It is not meant to diagnose, treat, or cure any specific dog, nor as a substitute for consulting your veterinarian or healthcare provider but instead to be general information. The author discloses that she is not a medical practitioner, or healthcare provider and her information is strictly from personal experiences.

Neither the author, the publisher nor the contributors shall be liable or responsible for any loss or damage allegedly arising from any information or suggestions contained in this book.

If you follow any of the recommendations in this book, you agree to assume any and all risks, and release and discharge the publisher, author and any contributors from any and all claims or causes of action, known or unknown, arising out of the contents of this book.

The publisher and the author have made every effort to ensure that the information contained in this book is accurate, however the publisher, the author and the contributors, assume no responsibility for errors, inaccuracies, omissions or any other inconsistencies herein, and therefore disclaim any liability to any party, for any loss, damage, or issue caused by errors or omissions, whether such errors or omissions result from negligence, accident, or any other cause.

This book provides content related to canine cognitive issues. As such, use of this book implies your acceptance of this disclaimer.

Copyright © 2022 F. Barish-Stern

All rights reserved, except for appropriate quotes in reviews and scholarly works. Printed in the United States of America. No part of this publication may be reproduced, stored in a retrieval system, or transmitted in any form, or by any means, electronic, mechanical, photocopying, recording or other without the written permission of the publisher.

Published by Golden Quill Press, A division of Barish-Stern Ltd. Virginia
ISBN 979-8-9860776-2-8
Printed in the United States of America
Interior Design – Golden Quill Press and Kenneth A. Bray – Art on Gold Creations, Virginia
Cover Design By Kenneth A. Bray – Portraits on Gold

Dedication

For Shamrock

My Sweet "Baby Girl!"

and

Her Daddy

Who Was There At Every Step Of This Journey!

Acknowledgements

There are always so many people that are involved in the writing of a book and this book is no exception.

In this book's back-matter section you will find "Thank You" acknowledgements to all the veterinarians, neurologists, nutritionists, researchers, scientists, specialists, and companies, who contributed to the vital information in this book.

I also need to express my personal thanks to two very special people who are always there for me, in my writing pursuits.

To my business partner and dear friend, I thank Bobbi Madry for her encouragement and belief in me and my work, and her editing contribution to this book.

And one "Thank You" I cannot leave out, is to my husband… I could not have gone through this journey without his support, and the contributions he made to this book

Contents

Introduction

SHAMROCK'S STORY	1
DEMENTIA & ALZHEIMER'S - What Is It?	14
What Every Parent Needs To Know	15
Causes of Doggy Dementia	29
Signs & Symptoms	33
Diagnosis	43
DISHA (A) (L)	50
DEMENTIA & ALZHEIMER'S - Prevention	57
Flea & Tick, Heartworm, Spay & Neuter, Vaccines	58
Diet & Supplements	78
SHAMROCK'S STORY - Canine Cognitive Dysfunction	123
DEMENTIA & ALZHEIMER'S - Treatments & Therapies	134
Treatments & Therapies - Who Does What?	135
Dog/Human Connection Possible Future Treatments	197
DEMENTIA & ALZHEIMER'S - Latter Stages	224
End of Life Care	225
SHAMROCK – THE FINAL STORY	245
Recommendations, References, Resources	250
Thank You & Biographies	256
Author's Biography	284
To My Readers And Other Dog Lovers	285
Company History	286
Books By Golden Quill Press	287

Introduction

When I was researching dogs and cognitive issues for this book, I was amazed by some of the statistics. I learned that there are almost 900 million dogs in the world, and approximately 63 million American households have dogs. It was nice to see that 96% of pet parents consider their dogs family members. (Okay, I hoped that would be 100%, but I suppose I need to be reasonable). One thing I really connected with was how much money is spent to keep our dogs healthy; a little less than one half of all the money spent on dogs is for veterinary care or medical needs. For me, and so many other pet parents, I'll wager to say it is even more.

I concluded that with the millions of dogs and the amount of money spent, we really love our dogs and want them to have long, happy, healthy lives, but as they age disease can become a major factor.

It is important to understand old age in dogs. Many people believe if a dog is over 13 years of age, you should be glad the dog has lived that long and expect your beloved pet to die soon! I have learned from speaking with veterinarians that, "OLD AGE IS NOT A DISEASE," it is just a fact of life.

When I was a child, if people reached the age of sixty, they were considered really old! But today sixty is a prime time of life, even a new beginning for many people. Sixty in human years is approximately eight to eleven in dog years, and by that age most dogs are still very much in their prime.

In order to provide the best healthcare possible for our dogs, we need to stay informed. Fortunately, today, we have a better understanding of life expectancy, and scientists are continuing to explore ways for both humans and dogs, to live longer, better lives. So, the old assumption that "old" is another way to say, "don't bother," or "give up," or just "be glad your dog lived this long," should be thrown out with age old practices that suggested snake oil and voodoo dolls as cures.

Dementia and Alzheimer's are very scary words for people, but these words should have the same effect for pet parents. After having nine dogs, I didn't make the connection, any more than the many dog lovers I spoke with. Most responses were, "I have never heard of dogs getting dementia or Alzheimer's!" Today, with more dogs living longer lives, this needs to be a disease that is on every pet parent's radar!

Statistics are changing constantly, but current studies have shown this disease affects approximately 22% of dogs over 9 years of age, 28% of dogs over 11, and accelerates to over 68% for dogs 15-16 years of age. Dementia and Alzheimer's are now much too prevalent for anyone to ignore, especially pet parents. In many cases these cognitive diseases can come with a difficult and long-term prognosis, therefore, the earlier we recognize the signs and symptoms, the better

Veterinary medicine and scientists are learning new information every day, but in order to have a chance of fighting this disease pet parents must become the first line of defense. They must understand how to prevent the disease and how to recognize the early signs. That way parents can get their dogs diagnosed sooner and started on treatments that may be able to halt further progression of the disease.

That was my motivation for writing this story about Shamrock's journey through the stages of dementia and Alzheimer's. I am not a medical professional, and I don't want to offer my opinions as fact, therefore I needed to learn about the disease to relay information that would help other dogs and their pet parents.

That goal led me to discussions with over 50 veterinarians, Alzheimer's specialists, neurologists, researchers, and others that provided me with a better understanding of this disease. They all kindly shared their expertise to help me inform pet parents and other professionals about their experiences and knowledge regarding signs, symptoms, diagnosis, treatments, and possible ways to prevent this disease.

If this book can help one dog, one pet parent, one veterinarian, or anyone regarding this dreaded disease, then I have completed my mission in Shamrock's name!

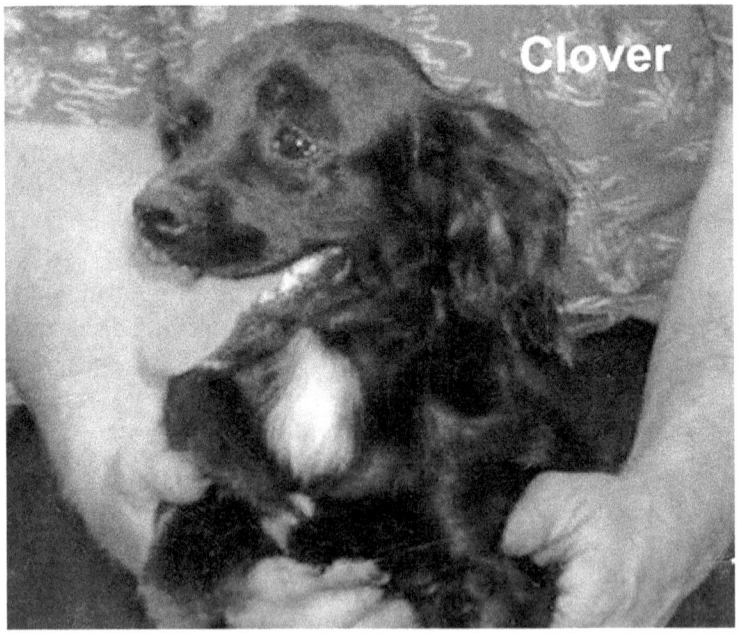

*First Picture - Shamrock & Clover
Approximately 8 months old*

SHAMROCK'S STORY

What a joy when we take puppies into our homes...

and into our hearts....

They become an integral part of our family....

They become our Babies

and give back so much love!

SHAMROCK'S STORY

Our Girl's

From Hurricane Katrina

I am a dog lover! I have been totally in love with dogs since I was a child and have had nine dogs so far in my life.

On August 29, 2005, Hurricane Katrina hit New Orleans, Louisiana, as a Category 3 hurricane. It was horrific and considered among the worst natural disasters in United States history.

Along with the reports of damage from the hurricane, I was hearing about the issues for families not being able to take their dogs with them to shelters. I couldn't begin to imagine the heartbreak and anguish for the pet family and the dogs.

I hadn't had a dog since my last, "baby," Suzanne, died when she was almost 20 years old, so I figured, maybe this was the time. My husband was also a dog lover, and he was ready to welcome one into our home. I began to search the internet to learn how we could adopt a rescued dog in need of a new home.

One such search led to "Pet Finder" an on-line directory that is a searchable database of animals in need of homes. It was exhausting and heartbreaking as my eyes scanned hundreds of those sad, but beautiful faces... I would have taken them all, but I knew that I needed to narrow down my choice.

FROM HURRICANE KATRINA

Finally, I found a dog I fell in love with. Her name was Shamrock, and she was about seven months old. I knew she was the perfect one for me just from her picture and description. As I continued reading her story, I learned she was rescued with her litter mate, Clover. They were found huddled together under a garbage dumpster; hungry and frightened. I felt so bad for them and since I was used to having two dogs at a time, I took a deep breath and asked my husband what he thought. Without hesitation we both realized this precious pair were the ones for us.

Shamrock and Clover were being cared for by a rescue called, "Soulful Hearts," and I contacted the owner, Georgeanne for additional information. She told me a little more about their personalities that wasn't in the profile, and it made me even more sure that they were the perfect puppies for us. They were now living on her farm, and played well with the other animals, but Georgeanne sensed they were basically house dogs. She told me there was a waiting list, but if I was committed to taking both dogs, she could give me first choice.

I inquired about what the next step would be to foster these two beautiful little girls. The application I had to fill out was quite extensive, including recommendations from previous veterinarians, and personal references. For their safety I would also be required to puppy proof my house and have a fully fenced in yard.

I filled out the paperwork, but because these dogs were rescued from Hurricane Katrina, there was one other condition that I needed to be aware of.

Georgeanne told me that once residents of the hurricane devastated areas returned, there might be a possibility that the dog's family would still be alive and would try to find them. Based on that, we could only foster them, and if no one came forward after a period of 18 months, only then could we become their adopted parents. We were already in love just from their pictures and stories so whatever the conditions were, we knew we wanted to take care of them.

We realized the heartbreak if their family reclaimed them, but as pet lovers we also knew if situations were reversed, we would want our "babies" returned. Finally, we got our application approval and awaited their arrival.

SHAMROCK'S STORY

On October 21, 2005, after driving six hours Georgeanne finally arrived with our new puppies. In accordance with the rescue fostering guidelines, she inspected our home, before entrusting them into our care. When she finished, she let the pups out of their crates and they jumped out of the car, as if they knew this was their new home. Shamrock immediately went to the bathroom on my husband's office floor. She looked so embarrassed, but we weren't upset. They had been in the back of a car for hours and had no idea where they were being taken. We had expected one or both of them might have an accident, but Shamrock's expression just pulled at my heart strings.

Georgeanne officially introduced us. Shamrock was a beige and white Springer Spaniel mix, around 20 pounds, and Clover was a black Cocker Spaniel mix, approximately 15 pounds. She told me her children gave them those names because they seemed to be the luckiest dogs to have survived the hurricane. We sat in the living room and finished the remaining paperwork, while my husband helped Shamrock and Clover get acquainted with their new surroundings.

I can honestly say it was love at first sight! They were the cutest puppies I had ever seen, and Georgeanne told me her veterinarian believed, based on their teeth and their growth progression during the six weeks she had them, that they were approximately eight months old now. She had just had them spayed, dewormed, given up to date vaccines and treated for heartworm, so we were good to go! Both puppies were so well behaved, and I just couldn't help reaching out to cuddle them.

When she was about to leave, to deliver a puppy named Louie, to his new home, we thanked Georgeanne for taking such good care of Shamrock and Clover. After she left my husband and I hugged our new babies...now, they were really home!

Though they had been examined and treated by Georgeanna's veterinarian I wanted to establish a relationship with someone local. The veterinarians I had for my other dogs were holistic and I felt lucky to find one, not too far from my home.

Both dogs were in good health, with Shamrock having some minor issues, which Georgeanne had told us about. She had what was diagnosed as a "Cherry Eye." In simple terms, the eye was red and bulging in the corner, but, as the report from the other

FROM HURRICANE KATRINA

veterinarian stated, the eye just needed to be watched. Shamrock also had some stomach issues which may have been a slight infection from eating the garbage and drinking the contaminated water from Hurricane Katrina.

Clover seemed to be unaffected, even though she was the runt. However, about a month later, she stopped eating for a few days and then with some change in diet and mild stomach treatment, she started eating again and got better. The only other problem that plagued Clover was due to her long, floppy ears. They needed to be cleaned often, which she hated and sometimes she did get minor ear infections.

During the long 18 months of fostering Shamrock and Clover, we knew a hurricane survivor could come forward, but we decided to cross that bridge, if it ever occurred; and be happy for them. Until then we needed to take the best care possible of our girls.

Several months later Shamrock developed a small tumor on her paw and our veterinarian, Dr. Caputo, treated it homeopathically. Finally, there was no further evidence of the tumor, and we were able to celebrate her recovery just about the time the 18-month fostering period was over. Since no one had inquired about Shamrock and Clover, our adoption process was complete. We breathed a big sigh, hugged "our" girls and finally we were all truly a family.

Since all the veterinarians agreed on approximately when they were born, we decided that February 14th, Valentine's Day would be Shamrock and Clover's official birthday... as they truly brought so much love into our lives!

They were so good and so easy to train; we spent hours with them, playing, walking and were so glad to have them as our family.

SHAMROCK'S STORY

Clover & Shamrock Celebrate Their 2nd Birthday!

From Daily Life...to Unexpected Turns

Shamrock and Clover loved to run and play and as you could imagine, they were inseparable. Clover was more the baby, very affectionate and always wanting to be hugged, petted, and loved. But Shamrock seemed more like the mother than the sister. She doted on Clover and let her do anything; sleep on her, take her toys, or even beat her in a run up the long driveway.

They both loved being in the car and particularly loved to visit family and friends, and everyone loved them. But it was always Clover who wanted all the attention, and Shamrock always backed away to allow her to get it

When we walked in a park, Clover would wag her tail, stop, and sit up, just so everyone would watch and come over to pet her. She seemed almost upset if they didn't pay attention to her. Shamrock let her sister have the glory and didn't seem to care; she was just out for a walk; to sniff and enjoy!

I was aware there could be issues that might come up from their having gone through Hurricane Katrina and I had them tested regularly to be sure they were in good health. One day, Dr. Caputo sold her practice and the new doctor, was a more "Traditional" veterinarian. At first, I wasn't sure what to do, but I decided to make their annual appointment. Dr. Kyle Faust was wonderful with them, he spent a lot of time getting to know them, examining them, and answered all my questions; he seemed to care a great deal about the health of both my babies.

Despite the best care and all the regular tests, in 2015, during a visit to our family, Clover, at 10 years of age, without any previous indications, and in less than 24 hours, succumbed to liver cancer. It was such a shock! We grieved with Shamrock and our family.

Only once before had I had such a shock with one of my other dogs. Her name was Sammy. In 1977, my brother-in-law found her in one of his abandoned apartments. She had been abused and left chained to a stove in the middle of winter. Sammy was a full breed German Shephard, only about a year old, and he asked if I would take her in with my other older dog, Missy. The "Dog Lover" in me couldn't say no! I never regretted that decision.

Sammy was sweet and beautiful. I worked hard to get her to a normal weight, back to full health; feeling loved and protected. She was a very happy dog and best of all, she was so good with my children. But when she was five, on a Labor Day weekend, with a house full of people, she was sitting in her favorite corner, suddenly yelped, flipped over, and died. The veterinarian said she had a massive fatal heart attack. Shocks like that leave you realizing how much you want to protect your dogs and be as aware, or at least, as much as you can, of anything that might hurt them.

After Clover died, we doted even more on Shamrock. She seemed to be okay, but it took time. But, three years later, at 13 years old, she started to show some, what I thought were, minor changes. She no longer wagged her tail. Over the next year there were other subtle things; she stopped sitting in her spot on the couch where she could watch the entire neighborhood. Before, she would watch for any car to drive up the long driveway to the house, but Shamrock no longer seemed interested. And very suddenly she stopped her occasional barking, now she remained totally silent.

When I discussed these issues with Dr. Faust, he did an extensive exam and ran tests, but couldn't find any substantial reasons for these changes. He asked me if she seemed lonely or depressed, without her sister. He also suggested that she was getting older; and "habits can change." Since there were no physical signs and all her tests were fine, he could find nothing to treat. Shamrock still seemed to be a "happy" girl, therefore, Dr. Faust suggested we just watch her more closely and let him know if there were any other changes.

A month or so later, she did develop some limping. Dr. Faust took a full series of x-rays but found only some minor issues, but nothing that really explained the limping. Because she was a Springer Spaniel, these minor changes were expected. He referred Shamrock to Virginia Tech Veterinary Hospital, Orthopedics department, just to be sure he wasn't missing something.

At Virginia Tech my husband and I waited for hours while the doctors did very thorough examinations, and extensive testing...it was a very tense waiting. The specialists told us they didn't see any signs of significant issues or evidence of pain. They explained their findings, "Dogs don't always show their pain!" They concurred with Dr. Faust's initial concerns about arthritis and prescribed gabapentin for Shamrock. We were told that medication would help with any pain or anxiety she might be experiencing. In addition, the specialists recommended seeing a veterinarian that specialized in massage and manipulation techniques.

We took Shamrock home, totally relieved that she didn't have any serious ailments. I scheduled an appointment with a veterinarian who was also a physical therapist and specialized in manipulation therapy.

She handled Shamrock in a soothing manner and showed me stretching techniques I could use daily to help her with relaxation. I had always believed in the power of Yoga for myself, so I discussed adding those types of movements with the doctor. She felt it might be extremely helpful to add, but suggested I allow Shamrock's responses to lead the way.

"Doga" is Yoga for dogs and is based on stretching movements and gentle massage techniques which Shamrock loved. I created a workout for her; performed to a background of soothing Classical Music. Sometimes I could feel her totally relaxing, almost to a point of sleep. It was a wonderful quiet time between us. She responded so well that the limping went away. I was thrilled and decided to perform both the manual manipulation and "Doga" with her every day.

FROM HURRICANE KATRINA

Fortunately, after that there were no real changes. With Valentine's Day fast approaching, it had been five years since Clover died from liver cancer and with the issues Shamrock had experienced, we were so happy to celebrate her 15th birthday. I put out a doggy approved birthday cupcake and candle and put her prettiest bandana around her neck. There was one final touch to our birthday celebration; we set a place in memory of Clover at the table. My husband and I felt so incredibly blessed, but little did we know that we would be entering the most difficult period with our beloved baby.

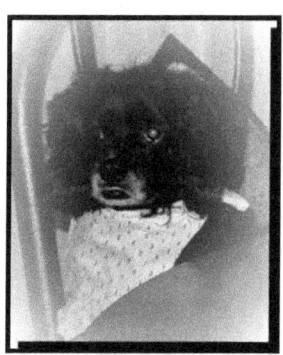

In Memory of Clover

Happy 15th Birthday Shamrock

SHAMROCK'S STORY

Mommy, I'm not a Happy Camper!

The Year That Just Kept Hitting Back

Have you ever heard the expression, "Hit me again, I'm still standing?" Well, it has been one of my go-to statements, all my life... so here we go!

This is where things began to drastically change. After she turned 15 years old, Shamrock started having symptoms that I had never experienced with any of my other dogs, even those who lived to almost 20 years of age. Her behavior became erratic, and, at times, even abnormally strange! She would have no interest in her food, didn't want any affection, or to be held, and stopped showing affection, like cuddling or licking faces. She would sleep intermittently and want to go out constantly, but when she got outside, she didn't want to come back in. She also paced constantly, sometimes for hours.

I made an appointment to see Dr. Faust. After discussing what was going on, he examined her, did more blood work, took x-rays, but nothing really explained these strange symptoms. He had been treating Shamrock for an eyelid mass and with her previous paw tumor, he felt it would be wise to have her evaluated for a possible brain tumor. That shook the life out of me. He suggested taking her again to Virginia Tech, but this time to see a neurologist, which was understandably extremely more stressful.

During the 45-minute drive to Virginia Tech, my husband and I noticed Shamrock shaking. We tried to calm her with long petting strokes and treats to distract her, but we just couldn't understand as she always loved being in the car. She usually looked out the window or went to sleep, but now she just shook!

The Virginia Tech doctors spoke with us before a nurse took Shamrock for testing. My thoughts focused on what they might find.

My husband and I waited for hours, for the doctors. They didn't have any definitive answers that might explain her behavior, but they suggested the only additional test might be an MRI, which cost about $3,000.00. The money wasn't the only issue; at age 15, was it a good idea to put her under anesthesia, which could be dangerous? And if a tumor was discovered, what about the dangers of an operation on her brain? None of that sounded good!

The neurologists pointed out that if a tumor was found, based on her examination and tests, it would probably be benign. If that were the case, then why take the risks and put her through any possible pain or suffering? Their only reply was that and MRI would conclusively eliminate one more possible cause of her symptoms. My husband and I realized that there were no good answers for Shamrock.

The neurologist's other conclusion was that Shamrock's symptoms were possibly signs of aging, depression or, "cognitive decline!" I had to stop and wonder if I heard the doctor right! I had never heard the words "cognitive decline," associated with dogs. My first reaction was to think, *NO WAY!* My husband was much calmer at that point and asked for an explanation.

The neurologist told us, "Shamrock was definitely more anxious, her panting and anxiety were unchanged whether she was resting in a cage, being examined, or wandering around the exam room." She also told us that no overt cause of Shamrock's clinical signs (panting, restlessness, disturbed sleep-wake cycle, decreased interest in normal activities), were found during her examination.

SHAMROCK'S STORY

The only good news was that they did not feel she was experiencing any pain. Therefore, their conclusion was, "We suspect, based on her history, examination and testing that Shamrock has signs consistent with 'canine cognitive dysfunction'." They added in their report that her owner, meaning me, was uncertain about this diagnosis.

That was because I had always heard dementia was a slow process and not something that happened to dogs. There were so many thoughts running through my head, for Shamrock's sake, I knew I had to consider that maybe my information was just out of date!

I glanced at my husband, and he took my hand. We realized we would have to deal with this devastating news, together, and so we did.

We began by asking without the MRI, what could we do?

The neurologist recommended supplements; a month of fluoxetine, (Prozac for dogs), supplementary omega-3 fatty acids, increasing gentle physical exercise, social interactions, and "brain training" such as using "feeding puzzles."

I knew nothing about brain training or puzzles for dogs and asked for an explanation.

She described them as a mat or toy filled with treats hidden to make it harder to find. She also told us that these "puzzles" stimulate the brain and make them work to find the treats.

I had also asked about alternative options for anxiety, and they suggested Adaptil calming products, Calming Care probiotic, Thundershirt or wrap, or Zylkene, a supplement to help reduce stress.

We went home and followed her instructions, (except for the social interaction with other dogs because we had stopped her vaccinations), but overtime, with all our efforts, we did not witness any sustained changes in Shamrock's behavior.

Dr. Faust proposed trying Benadryl to help calm Shamrock enough to sleep, but it made her more anxious, so we switched to Gaba which is supposed to help reduce feelings of fear and anxiety; happily, that worked much better.

A month after our visit to Virginia Tech, I was becoming increasingly aware that Shamrock was exhibiting signs similar to what I had seen with my uncle. At age 90 he started to have

FROM HURRICANE KATRINA

episodes of restlessness, disturbed sleep, decreased interest in normal activities, and some confusion. The biggest change I saw in him was, that he went from being the calmest person I had ever known, (he never even raised his voice), to being easily agitated, argumentative and even combative.

The similarities made me start to think... could this be what was happening to Shamrock?

DEMENTIA & ALZHEIMER'S

What Is It?

A feared and dreaded human disease,

that must be acknowledged

and dealt with as a threat to our dogs...

canine cognitive disease

DEMENTIA & ALZHEIMTER'S - What Is It?

What Every Pet Parent Needs to Know!

If you could give your dog a better quality of life, and possibly a longer life, what would you give to achieve that goal? I know I would give anything and everything. And that is why I sought out clinical advice from experts, in very diverse practices and specialties, to learn what could be done for dogs regarding dementia and Alzheimer's.

I spent months learning about this disease: how it begins, what are the potential causes and most of all what can be done to possibly prevent it. But the question I wanted answered most was what could be done once it has a grip on your dog.

This is a devastating disease in humans and unfortunately many of us have watched loved ones become lost in their abyss.

Can you imagine your dog who can't even tell you what's going on, having to deal with this darkness? I couldn't! I have had nine dogs; different breeds and sizes, and most of them lived beyond their teens, and into their twenties, but not one had cognitive issues. And if I was clueless, what about people who never had dogs or had less experience raising dogs from pups.

I saw first-hand what dementia and Alzheimer's could do to people and looking at my sweet baby girl, something inside me was crying out to question and understand this disease better. But I also realized there was more I wanted to know; so other pet parents and dogs might not go through what Shamrock and our family have.

I am not a doctor, nor do I have any desire to give my opinions; I am just a pet parent, telling a story. To do that, my goal became to obtain the best and most up to date information about this disease. Therefore, I reached out to hundreds of veterinarians, researchers, neurologists, and doctors of all specialties of veterinary and human medicine and started doing interviews and asking questions to gain that knowledge. These discussions started out as basics: do you see, diagnose and treat dogs that have dementia or Alzheimer's? But before long these questions evolved into the comprehensive information discussed in this book. I learned about the importance of early recognition of signs and what first signs might look like, what to do, what to feed, supplements and so much more.

And the more I learned, the more, specific the interviews became. Because of the complexity of this disease, I found the discussions building around topics I never thought would have had anything to do with dementia. Topics of "Prevention," such as: spay and neuter, commercial versus raw and home cooked diets, supplements, vaccines, flea and tick treatments, medicines versus holistic treatments, CBD oils and products, and even teeth cleaning.

When I first started this journey, I believed this book was only for parents with older dogs that were starting to show signs of the disease, but as I became more immersed in the vast amount of information, I realized if we start prevention from the puppy stage, we may never get to the need for diagnosis and treatment. The other surprise was the human connection. I had no idea that dogs got so many of the same diseases that people do, including dementia and Alzheimer's.

I have spoken with many dog lovers, only to find that, like me, they have never associated dementia or Alzheimer's with dogs and would have no idea how to recognize early signs or help their beloved pets. Even when they see signs, pet parents usually don't understand them. They also become confused with other issues, or just believe the "old" saying, "It's' just 'old' age!"

Because of this lack of knowledge many pet parents may do nothing until it is too late! There is a lot of frustration surrounding this disease and, in some cases, when pet parents are confronted with their "baby's" growing cognitive issues, they feel so alone and hopeless; unable to help their dog, that some out of desperation, opt for euthanasia.

I wrote this book to give pet parents options to use against cognitive disease. These insights cover a wide spectrum of ideas that can provide hope and numerous possibilities. My greatest desire is

DEMENTIA & ALZHEIMTER'S - What Is It?

that this information will help one dog and their family from enduring the horrors of this disease.

So now, let's turn to the experts regarding this disease and continue, *Shamrock's Story...From Hurricane Katrina to Doggy Dementia & Alzheimer's.*

What Is Canine Cognitive Decline?
The Interviews and Articles

The complexity of the information regarding, dementia and Alzheimer's in dogs spans a variety of opinions and practices. That information has been accumulated from the over 50 veterinarians I interviewed and the hundreds of doctors and other professionals I have spoken with. During my research I have also been supplied with, and discovered, some 200 documents on this topic. But the easiest way for me to present this to pet parents is to tell you how it relates to Shamrock and her journey.

What you are about to read are not my opinions, but statements from veterinarians of many different specialties, education and thinking. Their statements on related topics may differ, but this book is not an endorsement of any information, only an educational tool which provides knowledge about this disease, for you, the pet parent.

The reason I started this journey to interview as many sources about this disease as possible, was because I thought I knew about dogs and diseases they could get. I raised nine dogs, and yet, I was totally blind-sided by this disease.

What I am sharing with you, the reader is what I have learned about cognitive issues in dogs. This is information I never knew before, but have now become aware of, and want to share. This book is a road map to help you better understand these issues that can affect your dog.

While reading this book it is extremely important, that you keep in mind that everyone I spoke with agreed; all recommendations or advice should be discussed with your veterinarian before you make any changes for your dog.

SHAMROCK'S STORY

Veterinary Options To Consider

When asked about a doctor for their pet, most pet parents think, "Veterinarian," they rarely ask, "What kind?" or "Which specialty?" unless there is a specific need. But in truth, there are many, many distinct categories of veterinarians and many different and diverse methods for treating animals.

To better understand the veterinary statements in this book, it is important to understand their veterinary practices and their concepts regarding cognitive issues in dogs.

The following list includes the diverse veterinary choices available to pet parents and their opinions expressed in this book.

Major Categories

Conventional /Traditional – probably what most people think about when they consider a "veterinarian." This specialty uses tools similar to what your general physicians might such as blood work and x-rays to determine if illnesses are present. They may also prescribe medicines and recommend or perform surgery.

So, what else is there? In this book I have interviewed veterinarians who practice in many different areas of veterinary medicine. Here is a breakdown of their special areas, the type of veterinary medicine they practice, and their approach to doggy dementia

Holistic - From a holistic point of view, each pet is different and must be tested individually and not all dogs respond the same. Every aspect of the dog's life is looked at: physical, emotional and mental. Holistic can also include many therapies such as acupuncture and herbal therapies

Homeopathic - is a natural approach to treating a pet based on the belief that the body has the ability to cure itself with the help of remedies introduced into the system that help stimulate that ability. Similar to holistic, homeopathic treats the patient, instead of just looking at their signs or symptoms

Integrative - combines traditional and holistic practices. Veterinarians may approach dementia from different directions, but those I spoke to, felt the best way to effectively treat this disease is to use the tools of each, traditional and holistic, to combat each stage of the disease

TCVM - Traditional Chinese Veterinary Medicine – was developed in China to establish balance and harmony in the body.

DEMENTIA & ALZHEIMTER'S - What Is It?

Veterinarians are trained in understanding the life force called "Qi" which controls life functions and has many modalities to use to diagnose and treat pets including, acupuncture, herbal and food therapy, massage/acupressure therapy.

Of course, there are many sub-categories that veterinarians use in diagnosing and treating pets, but this list should give you a basic understanding of the veterinarians interviewed for this book.

Behavioral Researcher – discovers, teaches, and writes about dog behavior and the connections of humans and dogs

Behaviorist - diagnoses a pet based on their behavior for evaluating and treating the pet's condition

Cannabist- specializes in CBD Oil- therapies and products

Cannabist Researcher - expert on cannabidiol research in veterinary medicine

House call practice - is based on the idea of visiting the pet in their home, rather than the pet having an office visit. This is a great tool, especially for viewing the pet in their own environment at the onset of, and through this disease

Nutritionist - specializes in animal nutrition to determine the best way to understand the animals' dietary needs

Neurologist - specializes in treating pets affected by diseases of the nervous system: including the brain, which might include, seizures, tumors, cancers, and cognitive disorders

Oncology – specializes in cancer care and end of life care – (included due to issues of tumors in cognitive decline)

Orthopedic – specializes in pain management and physical therapy

Sports Medicine – specializes in dog training, and rehabilitation

Other Doctors to be aware of throughout this book

Physicians – (doctor's that are not veterinarians). There are also interviews with Alzheimer Specialists, and others who are currently involved with human Alzheimer patients and researchers in this field.

Also, throughout this book you will read the advice of many best-selling authors and doctors who have published in their fields.

Dementia And Alzheimer's In Dogs
From Cognitive Decline To Cognitive Dysfunction

The discussions I had with over 50 veterinarians was like any other exploration...first you begin at the beginning...and then go from there! This disease is not cut and dry and so there needs to be a real understanding of the topic before you can get to the "nitty gritty." When I spoke with these veterinarians, they gave me broad statements concerning dogs, and cognitive decline, dementia, and Alzheimer's. Then we got down to specifics. These in-depth discussions will help you, the reader, get a better grasp on all aspects of this disease and the importance of all the issues raised.

Believe it or not, there are so many terms used to categorize cognitive issues in dogs, that I decided the best place to begin was with a total understanding of these terms

What Is Cognitive Decline?

Cognitive decline is the gradual deterioration of mental abilities which can be an advanced stage of normal aging. The signs are generally mild at the beginning, and therefore in older dogs, attributed to normal aging.

What Is Doggy Dementia or Canine Cognitive Dysfunction

When the cognitive decline signs increase it is recognized as canine cognitive dysfunction, (CCD). This term is used to describe doggy dementia, which is a decline in cognitive abilities that affect functioning and behavior and includes issues with memory, social skills, and general thought patterns.

What Is Alzheimer's In Dogs?

Alzheimer's is the disease caused by dementia. Many doctors dispute whether dogs get Alzheimer's, while others feel it is an advanced state of dementia in dogs. Some doctors define the condition by the many signs which are also common in humans. But no matter how it is defined, as dogs are living longer, canine cognitive dysfunction syndrome, (CCDS), is somewhat the equivalent of Alzheimer's in people.

DEMENTIA & ALZHEIMTER'S - What Is It?

*What Are The Terminologies Used To Identify Dementia In Dogs?

You will notice different doctors use different words to describe cognitive disease in dogs. To understand the many names and descriptions, I asked veterinarians about the terms used: cognitive decline, cognitive dysfunction, canine cognitive dysfunction syndrome, dementia, Alzheimer's in dogs, and other terms. Their answers should give you, the reader, a better understanding of how this disease is perceived.

A source I found while doing my research was the work of Dr. Edward Bassingthwaighte, a Holistic Veterinarian, who created a system of healing bodywork for animals. Here is some of what I learned from him, "As dog's age their brains tend to 'wear out' which can cause dog dementia."

When I asked about dog dementia and its relation to Alzheimer's, Dr. Rebecca Fraser, who has an Integrative House Call practice, told me, "The official term is CCDS, canine cognitive dysfunction syndrome. She said, "To clarify, I don't think veterinary medicine fully understands all the causes, such as, amyloids, substances that form in the brain, and neuronal atrophy, loss of neuron connections or other causes that have been noted in the literature. The naming of the condition is appropriate since it affects dogs in a spectrum of symptoms and severities, but doggy dementia can be used as a term pet parents understand."

I next questioned Dr. Julia Brugliera, whose practice is a both Holistic and Traditional. She stated, "Instead of calling the disease, dog dementia and Alzheimer's, with canines we call it 'Cognitive dysfunction syndrome'. Sometimes this can be similar to a 'sundowners' type syndrome where we see some confusion or restlessness in the early evening hours and difficulty settling down for the night."

Dr. Valarie Tynes, a Veterinary Behaviorist, explained, "Cognitive dysfunction syndrome, also called, CDS, is a neurodegenerative disorder of 'senior' dogs characterized by a gradual, progressive cognitive decline."

SHAMROCK'S STORY

The information seems to state that this disease in dogs is remarkably similar to dementia and Alzheimer's in humans, but Dr. Pema Mallu, who is an Integrative, Holistic Veterinarian, disagreed. "Dogs don't get Alzheimer's; they get cognitive disorder or dementia."

This statement seemed to be very controversial as some veterinarian's state this emphatically and others don't agree. Because I want to present all sides, I asked Dr. Mallu if it were possible that the reason was because dogs don't live long enough for the symptoms to become Alzheimer's? And without waiting for a reply I added, "But that of course is changing all the time as is the life span for dogs."

Dr. Mallu clarified, "It is what I have seen and read in the veterinary literature."

As you can see, this is a topic that not everyone interprets the same; then how much more difficult is it for you, the pet parent?

With all the information I gathered I believe whatever it is called, doggy dementia, dementia, cognitive decline, cognitive disorder, cognitive dysfunction, (CD), canine cognitive dysfunction, (CCD), cognitive dysfunction syndrome, (CDS), canine cognitive dysfunction syndrome, (CCDS), or any other terminology this is a very serious brain disorder that definitely affects dogs and can be compared to dementia and Alzheimer's in humans!"

Now that we have all the terms identified, next we need a better understanding of the stages of this disease.

*(Note: Because I have interviewed doctors from all over the world there may be spellings, or phrases, which are different than those accepted in a particular country).

How Does Doggy Dementia Develop?

Dr. Bassingthwaighte clarified the development of dementia. "Part of the reason is that nerve cells reduce as dog's age. This causes neurotoxins to accumulate and when combined with high levels of

DEMENTIA & ALZHEIMTER'S - What Is It?

free radicals," unstable molecules that damage cells, "it can lead to cognitive decline."

According to Dr. Tynes "Cognitive dysfunction syndrome is a result of an irreversible brain disorder that is similar to Alzheimer's Disease in humans." She continued, "In this condition, brain volume shrinks, b-amyloid plaques," which is plaque that binds to brain cell, "accumulate in brain tissues and, there is a decrease in the functioning of certain neurotransmitters. Other problems associated with aging, such as an increase in toxic free radicals, decreased oxygen levels to the brain and changes in how the brain metabolizes glucose, all lead to pathology that results in decreased memory, cognitive function and motor function as well as sleep-wake cycle changes."

Also, regarding plaque accumulation in the brain, Dr. Lisa Melling who looks at dogs from both a Homeopathic and Holistic position stated, "Over the years whether in people or dogs, we have learned so much and know that poor habits such as diet, vaccinations, and treatments, for example heartworm, flea and tick in dogs, exercise, etcetera, add to the causes of plaque in the brain."

My interview with Dr. Ava Frick, who trained in the Traditional Veterinary style, but later transitioned to Holistic approaches, went further and began to delve into how the disease manifests itself in the brain tissues. She told me, "It involves the autonomic nervous system and the fight or flight, or calmness balancing of the hypothalamus, parathyroid, thyroid and adrenal glands." Dr. Frick also offered, "When there are deficiencies in the dog's body, such as from exposure to environmental contaminants, food that is not healthy or balanced for the dog, and excess toxicity from heavy metals, these all play a major role in the messages that are sent to the brain.

"All these issues overload the body and add to the mental stress and anxiety in the dog's mind. With this additional anxiety there is an imbalance between the sympathetic, fight or flight reactions, and the parasympathetic, calmness, balance, therefore the adrenals are overworking, and other organs are overtaxed."

SHAMROCK'S STORY

Dr. Elisa Katz, who started practicing in Conventional Medicine and is now specializing in Homeopathy and Canine Rehabilitation and Manipulation, suggested the possibility of electromagnetic fields also being a contributive factor to canine cognitive issues.

Dr. Brugliera said, "Typically the disease starts with behavioral changes. The pet becomes more withdrawn or confused. Sometimes these pets will have difficulty sleeping at night or can even get lost in familiar surroundings."

I wanted to understand if Dr. Wendy Jensen, a Homeopathist looked at cognitive issues in dogs from a different perspective. She said the best way to treat animals is to look at everything, not just signs; get a full history and then go back to when things started. She suggested, "Even an ear infection or analyzing what drugs were given can provide important information about the pet's conditions. Homeopathy prescribes through dealing with the whole pet, not just the current signs or symptoms; it is a process."

How Common Is Doggy Dementia?

Is this disease common in dogs? How do you know if your dog has it?

I was privileged to be able to interview Dr. Alice Villalobos, even though she is now retired. Her long history in the veterinary community had won her awards and acclaim and because she had trained in veterinary oncology and end of life care, I felt her information would be extremely important. She told me that after over 48 years of practicing, she had seen many dogs, ranging in age from seven years old and up that had some signs of this canine cognitive dysfunction.

Dr. Bassingthwaighte agreed, "Canine cognitive decline is more common than most dog parents realize! Approximately fifty percent of dogs over age eleven have shown at least one sign as they age. For example, by fifteen and sixteen years of age, that number increases to sixty-eight percent of dogs that may show at least one sign of CCD."

DEMENTIA & ALZHEIMTER'S - What Is It?

Dr. Tynes pointed out, "Both the prevalence and the severity of CDS increases with age in dogs. In one study of one hundred and eighty dogs, ten percent of the eleven to twelve-year-old dogs had two or more signs of CDS, while thirty-six percent of the fifteen to sixteen-year-old dogs had two or more signs. In another study of four hundred and seventy-nine dogs, forty-one percent of the dogs over fourteen were affected. In a more recent study that involved prospective screening, prevalence ranged from thirteen to sixteen percent in dogs eight to eleven years of age. Virtually every dog over the age of thirteen showed some signs of CDS."

Dr. Bassingthwaighte also advised, "As dogs age they become more likely to develop this disease. Other factors also include the size of the dog. Larger breeds tend to show signs earlier, some as early as five or seven years old. But that is not the only predisposition. Neutered dogs tend to have a higher risk for the disease."

Dr. Gerald Buchoff uses many different therapies in his veterinary practice. Whether Holistic, Homeopathic or Traditional Chinese Medicine, he believes that 60 % of dogs over 10 years old will have some form of dementia, and that there are treatments that can reverse the progression.

Dr. Brugliera, sees the signs of CDS typically in dogs between 13 and 15 years of age. Occasionally, she sees a dog that is 11 or 12 and starting to show some signs of aging but that is rarer. Recently she has seen dogs that have been 16 or 17 that are still having a great quality of life but are beginning to have some signs of cognitive decline, especially in the evening hours.

Dr. Mary Gardner's niche may be end of life care, but her information about this disease further explained why pet parents need to take notice. "Abnormal aging behaviors may be related to CCD. One study found that CCD affected twenty-eight percent of dogs eleven to twelve years old, and sixty-eight percent of dogs fifteen to sixteen years old, making the condition surprisingly common."

SHAMROCK'S STORY

And when I questioned whether the disease is more prevalent in one breed or another, Dr. Brugliera felt that all dog breeds can be predisposed to having these cognitive issues.

But Dr. Debbie Gross Torraca, was more specific regarding breeds and this disease. In her capacity as an Orthopedic Specialist in Canine Rehabilitation and Physical Therapy, she has worked with many breeds and is a firm believer that certain breeds and genetics make dogs wired to be more anxious.

I told her Shamrock was a Springer Spaniel, and she replied, they are on the top ten list of high anxiety dogs.

I was amazed by that information and relayed that Shamrock was the calmest and most patient dog of all the nine dogs I ever had. Therefore, with the understanding that she wasn't hyper, how could I have been prepared for her to develop dementia?

In my discussion with Dr. Douglas Knueven, an Integrative, Holistic veterinarian, he pointed out that no one has really tracked one cause for CCDS. But he said the research indicates it is probably a genetic predisposition. Therefore, the whole idea is to keep your pet as healthy as possible to avoid disease, especially when the dog may be predisposed to certain diseases.

When talking about how we can be proactive with our pets it is important to also understand your dog's genetics. Dr. Fraser clarified, "It is not so much breed, but weight and age. Size or obesity will predispose any breed to diseases of tissue inflammation. Dogs of an appropriate weight tend to live longer but other factors also play a role. Most disease is environmental and there is much that we can control, and, in some cases, these play an even bigger role than genetics."

When Dr. Fraser sees a pet, the stages of the disease will play a part as to how well she can slow or stop the progression. "With many chronic diseases, it took so many years to develop, and Chinese meds take half the time to reverse. So, if a dog is thirteen, it might take four or five years to turn around the effects. Therefore, the best advice is to start early to prevent problems, rather than trying to deal with them when they are full blown diseases."

DEMENTIA & ALZHEIMTER'S - What Is It?

But dementia and Alzheimer's are still thought to be "old" age diseases, so the next question is, "How old is my dog?"

Is Age A Factor? Understanding Your Dog's Age!

To understand age and disease better, we need to look at the fact that, "Dogs as young as 5 can get canine cognitive disease," therefore we need to know how old your dog is.

How Are A Dog's Years Calculated?

The understanding that "one year of life equals seven in people years" has changed. The new science indicates the first year of life ages the dog the most. In fact, during that first year, most sizes, except extra-large, (over 100 pounds) age approximately 15 years, double of what was previously thought.

By 6 Human Years Age Progression	Medium Dogs 42 Years Old	Large Dogs 45 Years Old	X-Large Dogs 49 Years Old

So, you can see the rate of aging increases for dogs based on their size, and as they age the differences also change.

By 10 Human Years Age Progression	Small Dogs 56 Years Old	Medium Dogs 60 Years Old	Large Dogs 66 Years Old	X-Large Dogs 79 Years Old
By 15 Human Years Age Progression	Small Dogs 76 Years Old	Medium Dogs 83 Years Old	Large Dogs 93 Years Old	X-Large Dogs 114 Years Old

The second year adds approximately, 9 years Each subsequent year adds approximately 4 years					
Year #	1	2	3	4	5	Age At 5 Years Old
Age Progression	15	+9	+5	+5	+5	+ 36 Years Old

But size does make a difference. Yes, the extra large 100 +lb. dogs are considered 45 years instead of 36.

This changes for different size dogs after the sixth year. The medium and larger sized dogs increase at an average rate of 4 to 6 years per human year, instead of only 4 years.

And there is another kicker, different dog breeds age differently!

SHAMROCK'S STORY

When I researched breeds, Shamrock's breed, Cocker and Springer Spaniel, become senior at 8 to 10 years (depending on the mix) and have a lifespan of 12 to 13 years of age.

These calculations become even more important when we understand that dogs "5" years and older can develop dementia and Alzheimer's.

And if "senior years" begin between 5 and 7 years old, which diseases, like dementia and Alzheimer's do you need to be most AWARE of for your dog?

For me, doing this research provided an understanding that since Shamrock exceeded those numbers, even with the dementia and Alzheimer's, there is a great deal of hope for our dogs!

Even with this new age calculation, I also believe love and care, awareness and preventive measures may give your dog a better chance at a wonderful life filled with many good days and years!

DEMENTIA & ALZHEIMTER'S - What Is It?

Causes Of Doggy Dementia

Since we now understand that doggy dementia or canine cognitive dysfunction syndrome, can occur in any dog at any point from five years old and up, depending on the size, breed, and other influencing factors, I wanted to examine those aspects and see what causes this disease to manifest itself in our dogs.

How Can We Understand Dementia In Dogs?

Dr. Bassingthwaighte told me, "It is also important to understand that this disease is progressive and when a dog has at least one sign, most will develop more signs within a year. The biggest problem is confirming this disease is the cause of the dog's symptoms. Dementia does not come on suddenly, so the signs are so easy to miss and are assumed to be just the dog slowing down due to normal aging."

Dr. Buchoff expressed, "The best medicine is to be a proactive pet parent. That can make all the difference in your pet's quality of life and development with the disease." He also feels that depending on the pet and the stage of the disease, there are many treatments available that are not just stop gaps but can reverse the progression.

Over the course of my research, I have learned the importance of early detection. Unfortunately, many dogs are not seen for evaluation of dementia, until the end of the journey, rather than at early outset.

Because of the delay in diagnosis and treatment, the options become limited. At that point, some veterinarians may try traditional drugs first and see if the dog responds, and then go from there. Time becomes a "big" factor!

Diagnosing
What do the veterinarians I interviewed say about this disease; it's causes, signs and symptoms and how it can be diagnosed.

Understanding What Causes Dementia & Alzheimer's In Dogs
If we can better understand what are believed to be the causes of dementia in dogs and the signs and symptoms to be aware of, maybe we can stop the progression sooner.

Because Dr. Lisa Bartner is a Veterinary Neurologist, I asked her to explain the cause of this disease. She said, "In medicine generally, it is hard to prove cause and effect. There are no perfect correlations proving a cause, and it is more than likely there are multiple factors that result in CCD development. However, environmental, and genetic elements could be to blame, at least in part."

Dr. Gardner explained the disease this way, "CCD is a neurobehavioral disorder that interferes with a dog's cognitive function, including the ability to gather information about their surroundings and decide how to respond appropriately. Studies have demonstrated a number of changes to affected dogs' brains, including brain shrinkage, protein deposits, and oxidative damage, however, whether these changes are due to CCD or normal aging is not known, as they are also observed in the brains of normal older dogs."

At 15 years old the Virginia Tech neurologists believed that Shamrock may have had cognitive decline, so I asked Dr. Gardner, about normal aging versus this disease.

"Dementia is a condition commonly associated with aging in pets that is shown by decreased cognitive function. However, some medical conditions can lead to dementia in pets, including: brain tumors, encephalitis, some tick-borne illnesses, liver disease and cognitive dysfunction."

DEMENTIA & ALZHEIMTER'S - What Is It?

Dr. Gardner further advised, "If it is determined that your dog's symptoms are cognitive decline then understanding the disease will be a great help to the pet parent."

I asked Dr. Torraca to further clarify breed as a cause. "Knowing your dog's breed genetics can help you be aware of triggers that might indicate CCDS." Even though Shamrock wasn't excitable, her breed predisposed her to be anxious!

"Therefore, it is always best not to put your dog in a situation that will cause them anxiety. But some situations can't be helped. For instance, many dogs are traumatized in the car, or by thunderstorms."

I told Dr. Torraca that both Shamrock and her sister Clover were found huddled together under a garbage dump after Hurricane Katrina. Understandably, after that experience neither one of them ever dealt well with thunder, wind, or torrential rain. Surprisingly, Shamrock was calmer than Clover, who would escape under the covers for protection, but Shamrock would just shake. Being held or comforted never worked. But that was the only time in her life when she "showed" anxiety.

As far as the car, both dogs loved their drives and wanted to go in the car all the time. But looking back now, when we started to realize the signs in Shamrock, she did start shaking in the car.

So that definitely proved Dr. Torraca's statement; with the symptoms of dementia Shamrock's breed driven anxiety did surface. But, because she was never an anxious dog, I was unprepared, and never connected the two!

Dr. Kevin Landau practices Traditional Chinese Medicine and he told me about breeds that might be more predisposed to the disease, but he said that he was not sure of which breeds are more statistically likely to get this disease. He did agree that Cockers and Springer Spaniels like my Shamrock, are more susceptible. However, to my surprise he added, "It was not so much with King Charles Spaniels; as they don't usually live long enough, they tend to be victims of cancers, long before dementia has a chance to set in."

SHAMROCK'S STORY

Dr. Clay Bernard is a Holistic veterinarian trained in the ways of Traditional Chinese Medicine. He explained to me, "When approaching any pet condition from a Traditional Chinese Veterinary Medicine, TCVM, perspective, it's all about that pet and what underlying patterns of imbalance are presenting based on a detailed history and examination. In the case of canine dementia, or any chronic disease, certain systems of the body have become out of balance over time which leads to the various physical manifestations noticed by a pet parent and veterinarian. Canine dementia is considered a 'Shen Disturbance' which falls under the Heart System in TCVM. The Shen is considered the mind or spirit, and any consistent abnormal behavioral change falls into this category."

Once Dr. Bernard has those patterns established, he can better decide if there are deficiencies that need to be looked at such as, "Yin, or Qi Deficiency." Yin and Qi are concepts in Chinese medicine.

DEMENTIA & ALZHEIMTER'S - What Is It?

Signs & Symptoms

Dr. Bartner and I discussed that when Shamrock was around 13 years old, she had stopped wagging her tail, barking at strangers, and no longer sat in her favorite spot at a window where she had a good view of everything outside. Anyone I told just suggested, "She is old, and these changes do start to occur." Also, her sister Clover, who she went through Hurricane Katrina with, had died when they were both 10 and it was surmised that Shamrock was showing signs of loss and loneliness, that we may not have previously noticed. Now I will admit that may have been true, but in retrospect, I now know those were the first signs of this disease for her.

Dr. Bartner responded, "Early signs are also hard to confirm. Even an MRI at that point might have been normal. Having a neurological exam, or an MRI may not be definitive and pet parents need to weigh the advantages against the disadvantages. For example, dogs need to be anesthetized for this procedure, so that needs to be weighed against what the MRI may reveal, and, if anything does show, then what can be done with those results."

Since she is a neurologist, I discussed the second visit Shamrock had at Virginia Tech for a full neurological exam, and tests. The visit proved inconclusive as they found no "definitive" reason for her symptoms. The doctors felt that having an MRI done would be a next step, but, they cautioned, it might not produce any significant answers. They suggested she might be suffering from arthritis, which made sense, since she was a Springer Spaniel. If that were the case, she could be having pain that might mimic neurological issues. Their examination did not confirm any signs of pain, but they said dogs can hide their pain quite well. They prescribed pain medication, but their final statement was it might also be, "signs of aging, depression or, "cognitive decline!"

Dr. Bartner responded, "CCD is a diagnosis made based on symptoms, and pain can be caused by many other problems. Symptoms can overlap with other diseases including tumors. Even strokes can look similar."

Dr. Lisa Radosta, a Veterinary Behaviorist stated, "Canine cognitive dysfunction causes changes in the brain created by plaque, but many dogs seen have normal neurologic examinations. Also, up to eighty-three percent of dogs presented to veterinary behaviorists, and note, these are not 'old' dogs, and dogs referred by their veterinarian, have systemic illness, discomfort or pain. That is a strikingly large number. However, if that is the case with younger dogs, consider how many older dogs are more likely to have systemic disease, pain or discomfort?"

I admitted to Dr. Landau, that as a pet parent I was so confused. He said when he sees dogs that may be showing signs and symptoms of doggy dementia, he tries to question the pet parents about what they are noticing in the dog's behavior, like not wagging their tail. "Changes are important such as the way the dog moves and if there are signs of stiffness. These tend to be some of the earlier signs." Also, he sees some lower back issues with mobility stiffness.

I told him that these were some of the first signs we saw in Shamrock. But, because she was a Springer Spaniel everyone felt these symptoms were normal for her, so of course we didn't associate them with dementia. Also, she was only 13 years old when the limping started, and at that time, no one told us there could be any relationship to other issues. All they did was prescribe gabapentin for her pain and stiffness and advised a regimen of physical therapy.

When I discussed with Dr. Landau the dog massage therapy and "Doga," that I did with her every day, which seemed to really help, I wondered if, looking back, it was like putting a Band-Aid on a much bigger sore.

DEMENTIA & ALZHEIMTER'S - What Is It?

All Dr. Landau could tell me was, "Sometimes dementia starts as this non-specific 'old age', stiffness complaint."

Shamrock's limping and stiffness at 13 years of age, was almost three years before we ever heard her condition associated with "dementia" or "cognitive decline"....

Signs To Be Aware Of

Dr. Rachel Mar, an Integrative veterinarian, told me, signs which she wants pet parents to be aware of that can indicate cognitive dysfunction in dogs include behavioral changes, quality of life and changes to a pet's normal habits; all of which should, at the very least, signal a call to the veterinarian. She expressed to me how important it is not to just throw off symptoms with the thinking that this is "normal geriatric behavior. Getting old is a condition not necessarily a disease. For many veterinarians, any dog that lives past 10 years of age is considered old!" Dr. Mar wants pet parents to remember that when they look at a dog's life, that dog can live as long as they can....

Her helpful advice is to not ignore the little signs. Many times, we have a tendency to dismiss things we see as being insignificant changes.

I told her I realize now that I did that with Shamrock! Things I can now see were early signs included: when she stopped barking at strangers or didn't sit at the window waiting for us to come home. At the time, I thought she missed her sister Clover, but, looking back, I now realize these signs were so much more.

Dr. Mar suggested, "If we pay more attention to signs, we may be able to start preventing any problems before they get to the point beyond recovery."

We continued to discuss how veterinarians only see pets for short periods of time, so pet parents must be in tune with their pet and relate what has been abnormal in their routines. By mentioning these changes to the veterinarian, the doctor can better assess the dog's condition. Don't feel paranoid about anything out of the ordinary, and be sure to relate these changes, no matter how small or seemingly unimportant. At the very least it can lead your veterinarian to ask more questions and can give a fuller picture of what is going on with your pet.

Dr. Knueven acknowledged that signs of cognitive dysfunction can be so subtle and can progress so slowly that the pet parent doesn't recognize what is happening. "It is so easy to see other issues that are causing symptoms and to refuse to see disease. So, being aware of signs will help the parent not ignore or confuse what can be cognitive issues."

Understanding Specific Signs

To inform pet parents about the disease I asked Dr. W. Jean Dodds, who specializes in hematology, immunology research and diagnostic veterinary pathology, what are the canine cognitive dysfunction signs for pet parents to be aware of?

Here is an extensive list that she provided: "Incontinence, Confusion/disorientation in familiar surroundings, Increased sleeping/insomnia, Loss of interest in people and events, Forgetfulness of housetraining habits, Failure to recognize familiar people and animals, wandering aimlessly/pacing, Loss of appetite/forgetting to eat, Staring into space, Decreased activity level, Lack of response to name/commands and Failure to pay attention."

I relayed to Dr. Dodds that even before Shamrock was diagnosed, she was having some mild occurrence of several of these symptoms, but we didn't know enough to pay attention at that time. We just kept connecting the dots back to her sister Clover who had died suddenly, and we just felt that was the reason for her occasional changes in behavior. That may have had an effect, but as time went on many of these other signs showed up. One of the hardest to understand was when she stopped licking our faces.

Dr. Buchoff told me about other signs he sees that may indicate cognitive issues. They are a loss of hearing, walking, and stopping suddenly, walking into walls or corners and the dog not knowing how to back out. They can also be very non-responsive, such as not greeting pet parents at the door.

DEMENTIA & ALZHEIMTER'S - What Is It?

Dr. Mallu gave me more clarification, "This disease is exhibited by symptoms such as pacing and circling and a symptom we call 'sundowner syndrome' which is the dog sleeping all day and being awake at sundown or awake all night and pacing while we sleep."

Dr. Bernard said that when he sees a dog with symptoms of dementia or Alzheimer's, he first looks for patterns, such as, how the pet is behaving, eating, sleeping, or acting. He looks for changes that occur such as day/night issues.

These day/night issues led me back to the internet and an article by Dr. Theresa DePorter, a Veterinary Behaviorist. She had written about what happens to dogs suffering from CCDS at night. She talked about how sleep is essential and anytime it is disturbed, especially in older dogs, it should not be ignored, and that dogs that have cognitive dysfunction, can reverse day and night.

Examining the patterns of when they sleep and when they wake may help to establish a good routine. She went on to state that it is important to allow your dog time to have the final "bathroom out" before bed, so they don't have to wake up for elimination. She also stressed that some dogs enjoy spending quality time before bed with their pet family while others just want to go straight to sleep after their last "out!" Either way, keeping regular sleep routine schedules is especially important.

I learned that there may also be other things that can be done to help your dog get better sleep. For instance, if your dog has pain from joint or arthritis issues an orthopedic bed may help. Older dogs may feel the cold more and that can affect their joints, and their sleep. Adding warmth to their bed, could provide some relief. Also adding a gentle massage before bed and low lighting with soothing music can be sleep enticing. But waking at night may occur no matter how much you have prepared, especially for senior dogs, who can have a harder time holding during the night and may wake up from an urge to go.

After reading this information I contacted Dr. DePorter to ask if she would put together a more in-depth reasoning for the nighttime waking. Here is her article:

SHAMROCK'S STORY

Article:
Nighttime Waking
By Dr. T DePorter

"When we get a puppy, we hope that puppy will be with us for a lifetime. Dogs are living longer, expert medical care is readily available, and the human-animal bond is strong. Sixty-six percent of pet parents say they view their beloved dog as a member of their family and want them to have the best quality of life.

But as with people, old age is inevitable and sometimes so is age related cognitive decline. It is easiest to understand what happens to our pets when we can relate those experiences to people. There are many correlations between human Alzheimer disease and canine cognitive dysfunction syndrome.

According to the Alzheimer Association: "Alzheimer's Disease is the sixth leading cause of death in the United States. More than 5 million Americans are living with the disease."

There are many reasons why CDS is misunderstood in dogs; probably under-reported and under-diagnosed. Sadly, when the dog exhibits problem behaviors, which may be mistaken for behavioral problems, which means not only is the primary problem of CDS not addressed, but the pet may be put through unnecessary and misguided tests and training programs. Medical conditions may also mimic or confound the diagnosis. One of the problems is there is not a definitive test for CDS, and the clinician must rely on the pet parent to recognize and describe behavior changes.

In the laboratory, memory function may be evaluated but the average pet parent is not well equipped to note when their dog's memory began failing. Common symptoms such as nighttime waking or confusion may also be under reported or under recognized until the impairment is extreme.

Nighttime Waking – Special Considerations

Nighttime Waking is a primary concern for pet parents. The stress of many consecutive nights of sleep deprivation and a feeling of hopelessness may have many pet parents

DEMENTIA & ALZHEIMTER'S - What Is It?

believing there is no solution and leaning toward euthanasia. Promptly reducing anxiety and reestablishing normal sleep-wake cycles may be sufficient to ease the crisis of sleep deprivation. Melatonin may be useful as part of a bedtime routine ritual and may be best given 30 minutes before bedtime. Optimally melatonin should not be re-dosed at other times of the day when used to establish nighttime sleeping patterns.

Some medications, such as diphenhydramine, phenobarbital, or trazodone may offer sedation effects if given at or near bedtime. The senior dog may be more susceptible to the sedative effects of these medications. In senior pets, especially if liver function might be compromised, clonazepam, lorazepam, or oxazepam, (drugs which lower brain activity), might be preferable to alprazolam (Valium), or diazepam, (Xanax), which are used to treat depression.

The best way to begin is to determine if the dog is having difficulty settling down at night or if the dog wakes up in the middle of the night since these patterns will suggest alternative responses. For the dog that has difficulty settling down at night but then sleeps well, situational use of anxiolytics, (medication used to treat anxiety), may promote sleep.

The dog that goes to sleep and then wakes up in the middle of the night may be experiencing pain, elimination urges, confusion or even seizures. Consider a trial of gabapentin, an adjunctive therapy for pain management. Gabapentin may also have mood stabilizing effects and anticonvulsant properties which may be useful.

In addition, provide a comfortable sleeping area with a *calming diffuser, for support of emotional wellbeing. Some elderly dogs' benefit from a heated bed which may provide comfort for neuromuscular disorders.

Sometimes when your dog wakes, a little reassurance helps a confused pet settle back down. Some pet parents aren't sure what to do and so they ignore their pet during the night. This may result in more confusion and anxiety in your dog that is already experiencing cognitive distress.

SHAMROCK'S STORY

Certainly, punishment or reprimand for behaviors caused by confusion is contraindicated.

A daytime routine that includes fresh air, sunshine and exercise may help reset the daytime/nighttime cycle. Excessive or extreme increases in exercise should be avoided. Mentally stimulating interactions are best. Shared activities which celebrate the special bond and relationship with a senior pet are preferable to imposition of strict obedience regimes.

The senior pet shares a unique bond and relationship with their family. Identification and management of problem behaviors due to age-related cognitive decline or CDS ensure these issues are addressed with the compassion our old dogs deserve.

It is also important to have an annual screening with your veterinarian for both early identification and education regarding these symptoms."

*(Note: Calming Diffuser-See Recommendations-pg 250).
**(Note: All medication suggestions should be discussed with your veterinarian prior to usage).
Article provided with permission from Dr. DePorter

After reading this article I searched the Alzheimer's Association website for information about this disease in humans and found the following: By 2050 the number of people with Alzheimer's is expected to rise to approximately 13 million, and between 2000 and 2019, deaths from Alzheimer's have increased 145%.

What does this say about the possibilities of this disease for our dogs!

How To Tell If Your Dog Might Have Dementia?

Dr. Bassingthwaighte told me, "Some of the things you can look for are, staring into space or getting lost in familiar places, getting stuck in corners or under tables, barking at nothing, and pacing endlessly.

"Sometimes dogs present a completely different personality, totally opposite of the dog you have always known. Some even develop strange habits that they never had before, such as floor licking.

DEMENTIA & ALZHEIMTER'S - What Is It?

"There is also 'sundowners' syndrome' which is one of the most prevalent of the signs. Your great sleeper suddenly has turned nights and days upside down or sleeps very little, and then becomes restless, sometimes even collapsing into much needed sleep."

I told him "Exactly the way you have described, 'sundowners' is what I went through with Shamrock. Sometimes she would just "collapse" on the floor and be fast asleep. Other times just lying on the floor with her couldn't calm her enough to get her to sleep, even for a few minutes."

Dr. Bassingthwaighte pointed out, "But the one sign pet parents become most aware of is when their perfectly housetrained dog starts going in the house. In this case either holding is an issue, or the dog no longer knows how to signal the need to go out.

"But the important thing for pet parents to know is that even though this disease is progressive and degenerative, you as the parent, can make choices to slow down the progression and hopefully with time and a course of action, clear up the signs. The best way is to be alert, know the signs, and don't ignore what you see... the dog's health and quality of life may well be benefitted by an early diagnosis."

Dr. Radosta made it clear that, "Age is not a disease." Then she clarified, "If pet parents feel there is something wrong with their dog, such as CCDS, they need to communicate with their veterinarian and understand there may be a need to do certain testing to rule out any systemic disease first, before suggesting how to proceed. "

At The First Notice of Signs - Visit Your Veterinarian

Some doctors have told me that they unfortunately see many dog dementia patients towards the end of the journey, rather than at the onset. At that point they will try traditional medications first and see the dog's responses, if any, and then go from there.

I have also been told that from a holistic point of view, it is especially important that the dog have an evaluation as each pet is different and must be tested individually, and not all dogs respond the same, so this cannot be a cookie cutter diagnosis.

Dr. Villalobos clarified, "These signs and symptoms range from restlessness, to confusion, pets having accidents, irritability and generally not sleeping as well." All these changes lead the pet parents to her door. And that is her best advice, "Do not wait to make that appointment! Do it as soon as possible to find out what is happening to your beloved pet." She also stated that there are other illnesses that can mimic CCD which is why it is imperative to see your veterinarian as soon as symptoms arise.

But one thing is clear; guessing or even assuming what is happening to your dog can lead you down the wrong path. It is so important to see your veterinarian to confirm the diagnosis. Many times, it is not black or white and other issues may be involved.

DEMENTIA & ALZHEIMTER'S - What Is It?

Diagnosis

It is fine for us as pet parents to be aware of signs and to want to help our babies, but, as I have learned, this is an extremely complicated disease and just doing research on the internet is not as conclusive as we might like. When you begin to notice signs, it is essential to visit your veterinarian, and talk about what you have seen. Then you can better understand the signs and make a plan for moving forward.

In my interview with Dr. Gary Landsberg, a Veterinary Behaviorist, and author, we discussed how cognitive decline and dysfunction can occur in dogs based on aging of the brain. To make a definitive diagnosis he uses recognition of signs of cognitive dysfunction to advise pet parents what to look for and then discusses with them prevention and treatment.

The first step in diagnosis is to identify the signs. Is the pet showing signs of disorientation or confusion, changes in its social interactions with people or pets; new or increasing signs of anxiety; waking at night, house soiling or alterations in activity such as aimless pacing?

When Dr. Landsberg sees these signs in dogs, he must determine the cause; are they related to canine cognitive dysfunction syndrome (CCDS) or a result of health issues or due to behavioral causes such as changes in the household or scheduling. So, he will consider all the signs, together with the results of his physical examination and laboratory findings including blood and urine tests.

He told me, "To diagnose cognitive dysfunction, the veterinarian will first need to rule out any medical causes including whether the signs are due to pain or declining vision or hearing. In fact, many of the signs of pain in pets are the same as signs of cognitive dysfunction."

For example, with Shamrock she stopped wagging her tail. At that that time, we didn't associate her lack of tail wagging with mental decline, as she was only 13 years old. By 15 years old, the veterinarians and the neurologist were looking for other conditions; arthritis, or brain tumors, but could find nothing to confirm either diagnosis, nor could they find any signs of pain or discomfort.

Dr. Landsberg suggested if a pet is not wagging its tail, pain is a primary possibility. But, if medical and behavioral causes are ruled out, then this would confirm a diagnosis of CCDS. He said, "One study showed that in dogs over eight years of age, forty-two percent of dogs with no signs of cognitive dysfunction did have signs six months later and twenty-four percent of the dogs with mild signs progressed to moderate dysfunction in six months.

"Cognitive dysfunction has a relatively slow degression, where we see a small to moderate progression in signs over time, although they may wax and wane. Studies have found that over ten percent of dogs aged eight to eleven and over sixty-five percent of dogs aged fifteen and over may be affected with CCDS." Dr. Landsberg further stated that his job is to make sure what he is seeing is CCDS and not due to other medical or behavioral causes.

When a pet presents with signs of canine cognitive dysfunction, Dr. Mar approaches the physical as well as the neurological. Her evaluation can help rule out possibilities like a tumor and whether it is appropriate to recommend an MRI as a diagnostic option. To treat the signs in a more conservative manner, she may work on remedies to reduce the pacing, pet screaming and other episodes the pet might be having.

With a better understanding of the signs of CCDS, I wanted to comprehend the difference in dogs aging normally, and those with cognitive issues. I told Dr. Gardner I expected some sign of "slowing down" from aging, but with the enormous differences I was seeing in Shamrock, I felt these were not normal aging signs.

She responded, "When your veterinarian sees your pet for the possibility of CCD that is where it can get tricky. Since CCD is a

DEMENTIA & ALZHEIMTER'S - What Is It?

behavior disorder, your veterinarian cannot use any specific test to make a diagnosis. Many veterinarians use a questionnaire to identify pet behaviors consistent with CCD and assign each patient a score based on the number of CCD behaviors they exhibit. Diagnosis may also include ruling out other medical conditions that could be responsible for your dog's behavior changes. For example, vision or hearing loss could explain incoordination, failure to respond when addressed, and decreased interactions. Arthritis pain may prevent your dog from comfortably walking outside to empty their bladder or bowels and lead to house soiling."

When he sees these signs manifesting in the pet, Dr. Buchoff will try to break down the causes. He said, "It is important to check blood, looking at the thyroid gland and other organs, blood sugar and electrolytes and to check for circulatory issues. If any of these vital functions are abnormal, the effects are generally not good."

Dr. Landsberg also reminded me that it is important to understand that both CCDS and medical health problems become increasingly more common with advancing age. Therefore, while the signs he sees may be CCDS related, medical conditions could also be causing or adding to the signs. He clarified, "In the case of an elderly dog with arthritis, the dog might present primarily with behavioral signs, however, if the dog also has CCDS, you may see additional signs emerge and progress with time."

Dr. Tynes told me when she sees a dog with possible signs of dementia, she will perform a physical examination and any tests that can help her make a proper diagnosis. She said, "I need to differentiate between normal and, or unwanted pet behavior and behavior that is signaling a medical condition."

Dr. Elizabeth McKinstry who practices Traditional Chinese Medicine and Veterinary Medical Manipulation, also told me that she uses many techniques when pets present with signs of dementia. The first thing is to treat the pet according to the patterns that she sees. Her testing includes hair analysis; looking for heavy metals and leaky gut, which are present with these types of symptoms.

SHAMROCK'S STORY

Dr. Frick also spoke about hair analysis. "A good way to confirm mind body overtaxing and stress is to have a hair tissue analysis test performed. Hair analysis gives a reflection of not just current issues, but a synopsis of the past 90 days."

I was unaware of this type of testing and told Dr. Frick, that all Shamrock's blood and urine tests were good, so why would we do a tissue analysis test?

She explained that when all the blood and urine tests are negative (meaning in the normal range), it is more likely that they are not necessarily looking at things associated with dementia. And that blood typically indicates abnormal values when there is cellular destruction not revealing all the function tasks for which the organs are responsible. The difference with testing hair versus blood is that hair is greater than 1000 times more concentrated. The hair analysis is done to get to the cause, not the disease, by looking at cell mineral level availability and cellular physiology.

Fur analysis is also a method of heavy metal testing. Dr. Frick pointed out, "It is like a mineral blueprint of that dog's biochemistry. This testing can provide pertinent information about metabolic rate, energy levels, sugar and carbohydrate tolerance, stages of stress, the immune system and glandular activity. Once these tests have been performed, then the veterinarian can see how to proceed and make more appropriate nutrient recommendations."

Dr. Katz helped me to further understand fur testing. "Fur mineral analysis can measure systemic mineral content over several months as opposed to blood which measures just one moment in time. Hair is like a time capsule and can see minerals stored in fur to see what diseases are in pets and which toxins such as aluminum and low levels of calcium and magnesium which worsen anxiety and hyperactivity. Also, high sodium from adrenal glands is an indication of inflammation."

In my discussions I learned that Holistic veterinarians have many different diagnostic tools. Another such tool is "muscle testing." This test can find the weaknesses in the body and the stresses on the different organs. With cognitive problems it may be the liver, not the brain that needs support. These tests can also help determine if there are viruses, parasites, or heavy metals in the

DEMENTIA & ALZHEIMTER'S - What Is It?

body; these are things that might not readily be seen on regular blood tests.

Dr. Fraser added more information regarding testing procedures, "Certain pets may also need diagnostic testing to determine other underlying causes. One such cause can be a urinary tract infection. Females are more prone to these problems, because they squat, and their urethrae is shorter, but such infections can affect male dogs too! Blood pressure and thyroid issues are also key to rule out brain tumors which can present identically to CCDS. However, diagnosis of a tumor requires anesthesia and an MRI, which might cause other issues, so we are often treating a patient not knowing exactly what the underlying cause is."

She also said, "A good analysis may also include a Chinese medicine evaluation specifically designed to look for cognitive issues. Most times this can be a disturbance linked to the liver energy which can affect the heart energy where the Shen is housed. Shen is how we describe behavior. It can also lead to phlegm in the brain, or a brain tumor, but since every pet patient and circumstance is different, we need to treat the patient rather than the symptoms."

Dr. Radosta recommended a full workup; a baseline including a full panel of blood work, thyroid testing and urinalysis. She emphasized; it is also important to check the dog's stress levels, including cortisol, the "fight-or-flight" hormone.

Dr. Dodds conveyed to me, "If a dog with CCDS is well fed and well supplemented then their environment and allergies have to be looked at. Examples are what detergents are being used to wash their bedding, or other chemicals used in the house. Another big factor can be mold. Small amounts of mold may not be harmful to the pet parent but even minute amounts can cause harmful effects in pets."

What Else Can The Signs Indicate?

Dr. Tynes pointed out, "There needs to be a distinction between the signs and the symptoms of cognitive decline and many other health conditions, whose signs may be similar. For example, conditions such as osteoarthritis are common in aging dogs, and clinical signs of nighttime anxiety are also common. These signs may be a result of anxiety associated with cognitive decline or anxiety secondary to pain. And it can be hard to differentiate the two. Chronic pain is known to cause anxiety. Dogs that pace at night and can't sleep may do this because they are in pain or because of cognitive decline, or a complex combination of both."

I told her that some of the veterinarians that saw Shamrock said she did not show any signs of pain. But Dr. Tynes does not rule out that there may still have been pain. "Most animals are excellent at hiding signs of pain. Typical diagnostic tests don't necessarily always reveal signs of pain in dogs."

Dr. Gardner advised, "Before the veterinarian makes a conclusive diagnosis of CCD, the next thing to do is to first rule out everything else. It's important to note that there can be multiple things going on and other diseases may be presenting the same or similar signs."

Dr. Radosta sees dogs for excessive panting and performs a full range of tests. In many cases, the results indicate the cause of the panting is arthritis pain.

DEMENTIA & ALZHEIMTER'S - What Is It?

Visual Guide To Identifying Signs – Seeing Is Believing

The saying, "A picture is worth one thousand words," is very true and this guide can bring all these signs into better prospective.

Dr. Dodds has provided by permission, this illustrative guide that represents some of the possible signs used to identify canine cognitive dysfunction.

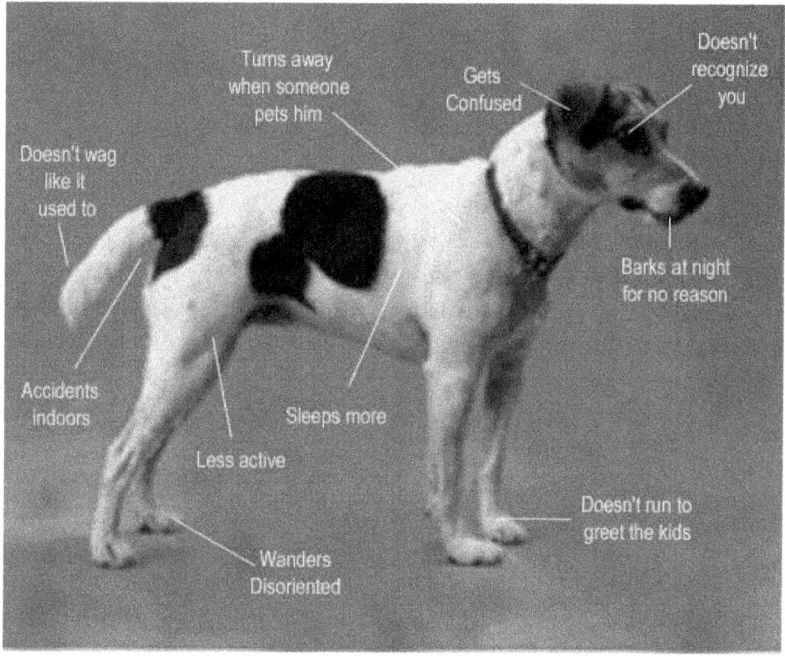

Dr. Gardner emphasized, "Unfortunately, many parents of senior dogs chalk these signs up to normal aging, and fail to mention them to their veterinarian, or seek treatment."

I asked how does a pet parent know when these signs might be CCD?

She gave me a good suggestion, "When you notice at least two signs of cognitive decline, then it's time to check with your veterinarian. Dogs with CCD can experience a variety of behavior changes. To better identify these symptoms, the acronym DISHAA was coined."

SHAMROCK'S STORY

DISHA (A) (L)

To get a better handle on your dog's signs and symptoms DISHA, also called DISHAA or DISHAAL is a guide that is very helpful for pet parents. DISHA Stands for **Disorientation, Interactions, Sleep-wake cycle alterations, House-soiling, Activity level changes.** Sometimes included, adding the next **"A" for Anxiety level changes** and also **"L" for Learning and Memory.**

Dr. Gardner provided an "extensive" understanding of what each sign indicates:

"Disorientation — Dogs with CCD often become disoriented in their normal environment. Affected dogs may:

Pace and wander aimlessly
No longer recognize familiar people or animals
Become stuck behind furniture or an open door
Wander through areas they do not typically use
Seem lost in their own backyard
Lose their sense of time

Interactions — CCD can cause your dog to interact differently with people and animals. Affected dogs may:

Lose interest in playing or interacting with family members
Stop seeking attention
Become grumpy and withdrawn
Become more dependent or clingy

Sleep-wake cycle alterations — This CCD component is often referred to as "sundowners" dementia and affects a dog's normal sleep patterns. Affected dogs may:

Sleep more during the day
Restlessly pace at night

DEMENTIA & ALZHEIMTER'S - What Is It?

Vocalize at night

House-soiling — CCD can interfere with your dog's ability to understand that eliminating inside your
> home is unacceptable or cause them to forget where they normally go. Affected dogs may:

Urinate and defecate in your home
Have frequent accidents without understanding they are inappropriately eliminating

Activity level changes — Your dog may become less active and have a decreased response to
> people and their environment. Affected dogs may:

No longer react when you come home or enter a room
Have no interest in exploring during daily walks
Stop grooming themselves, and appear unkempt
Have a decreased appetite

Anxiety level changes — Anxiety is common in dogs with CCD, and your dog may easily become restless or agitated. Affected dogs may:

Pace and wander
Vocalize
Drool excessively
Become anxious when left alone."

This information was provided by permission from Dr. Gardner,

DISHA - Further Explained

The understanding of signs and symptoms is so important and can be so easily missed or confused with other factors, including just plain old, old age, therefore I wanted to provide pet parents with as much information as possible. Here is some additional information about DISHA:

Dr. Bartner suggested use of the DISHA scale may help pet parents better understand and monitor for those symptoms, but it must also be said that the dog's history of how symptoms developed is very important. She clarified, "Strokes have a fast onset, while tumors usually have a slower onset, but dogs can still show similar signs with each, and with CCD. The DISHA scale prepares the pet parent to think along the right lines and have a better train of thought."

SHAMROCK'S STORY

She continued, "DISHA also is very helpful in noticing a trend in the abnormal behaviors. This observation can reveal valuable information and pet parents can bring this proof of a trend to their veterinarian.". This will also provide much more information than one or two exams might. But Dr. Bartner stresses, "Like cancer in the body, the sooner CCD is recognized the sooner it can be treated."

Dr. Radosta also felt that it is important for pet parents to understand and determine if their dog might have CCDS by using the DISHA Screening Tool for evaluation.

Dr. Tynes believes animals need to be considered for pain and uses DISHAA to make a more accurate diagnosis

The DISHAA Evaluation Tool provided on the following pages, assigns a number to each sign within each category and a total score to determine your dog's cognitive acuity.

*(Note: the DISHA(A) (L) evaluation tool**:** This assessment was created by: Dr. Gary Landsberg, DVM, DACVB, DECAWBM, to aid in the recognition and diagnosis of canine cognitive dysfunction syndrome and the form was designed by Purina).
Reprinted by courtesy and permission from Dr. Landsberg and the Purina Institute.

DEMENTIA & ALZHEIMTER'S - What Is It?

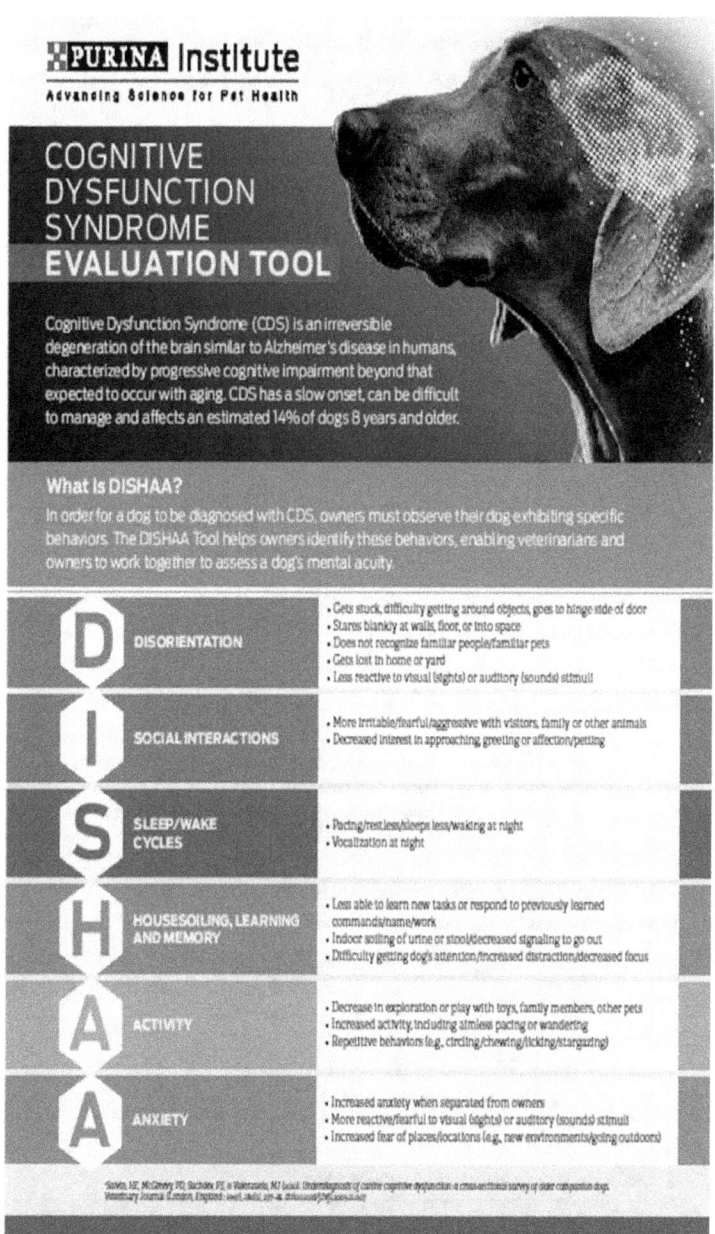

SHAMROCK'S STORY

PURINA Institute
Advancing Science for Pet Health

COGNITIVE DYSFUNCTION SYNDROME
ASSESSMENT TOOL

Cognitive Dysfunction Syndrome (CDS) is an irreversible degeneration of the brain similar to Alzheimer's disease in humans, characterized by progressive cognitive impairment beyond that expected to occur with aging. CDS has a slow onset, can be difficult to manage and affects an estimated 14% of dogs 8 years and older.

D — DISORIENTATION
I — SOCIAL INTERACTIONS
S — SLEEP/WAKE CYCLES
H — HOUSESOILING, LEARNING AND MEMORY
A — ACTIVITY
A — ANXIETY

What is DISHAA?

DISHAA is a tool to help you and your veterinarian assess the mental acuity of your dog, and for your veterinarian to potentially diagnose Cognitive Dysfunction Syndrome (CDS).

Date: _____

Owner's name: _____   Pet's name: _____

Age: _____   Gender: ☐ Male ☐ Female   Neutered/Spayed: ☐ No ☐ Yes

Breed: _____   Weight: _____

BCS (Body Condition Score 1-9): _____   Current Diet: _____

Medications and Dosage Frequency: _____

Please complete this canine senior pet cognitive assessment. If you've noticed changes in multiple behavioral categories, be sure to talk to your veterinarian today about the health of your pet's aging brain.

BEHAVIORAL SIGNS

Identify signs that have arisen or progressed since 8 years of age and older.
Score as 0=none, 1=mild, 2=moderate, 3=severe

	Score
DISORIENTATION	
Gets stuck, difficulty getting around objects, goes to hinge side of door	
Stares blankly at walls, floor, or into space	
Does not recognize familiar people/familiar pets	
Gets lost in home or yard	
Less reactive to visual (sights) or auditory (sounds) stimuli	

Please complete assessment on other side.

DEMENTIA & ALZHEIMTER'S - What Is It?

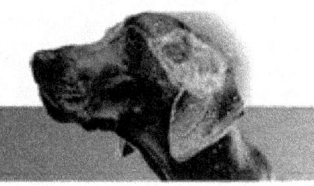

COGNITIVE DYSFUNCTION SYNDROME
ASSESSMENT TOOL
CONTINUED

BEHAVIORAL SIGNS

Identify signs that have arisen or progressed since 8 years of age and older.

Score as 0=none, 1=mild, 2=moderate, 3=severe

	Score
SOCIAL INTERACTIONS	
More irritable/fearful/aggressive with visitors, family or other animals	
Decreased interest in approaching, greeting or affection/petting	
SLEEP/WAKE CYCLES	
Pacing/restless/sleeps less/waking at night	
Vocalization at night	
HOUSESOILING, LEARNING AND MEMORY	
Less able to learn new tasks or respond to previously learned commands/name/work	
Indoor soiling of urine ___ or stool ___ /decreased signaling to go out	
Difficulty getting dog's attention/increased distraction/decreased focus	
ACTIVITY	
Decrease in exploration or play with toys, family members, other pets	
Increased activity including aimless pacing or wandering	
Repetitive behaviors, e.g., circling ___ chewing ___ licking ___ stargazing ___	
ANXIETY	
Increased anxiety when separated from owners	
More reactive/fearful to visual (sights) or auditory (sounds) stimuli	
Increased fear of places/locations (e.g., new environments/going outdoors)	
TOTAL (BE SURE TO CARRY OVER THE SCORES FROM FRONT SIDE OF SHEET)	

Once this form is completed, your veterinarian will determine the cause of these signs through a physical examination and recommended diagnostic tests. However, even if your senior pet is experiencing multiple health issues associated with aging, there may be some degree of CDS.

A score of 4-15 is consistent with mild, 16-33 is moderate, and >33 is severe CDS.

SHAMROCK'S STORY

DISHA is such an incredible tool, and its use can help pet parents watch for early signs and chart their dog's progression. Even if your dog has a very low score, the first step would be a discussion with your veterinarian, followed by an analysis of systems you can put in place in your home to help protect your dog.

When I took the test for Shamrock considering her beginning symptoms, her evaluation was less than mild, but by the time she showed more signs of CCDS, her evaluation was approaching moderate; showing a clear indication that her signs were increasingly worse.

One of the common cognitive signs is many dogs have soiling in the house. With Shamrock there was no soiling, but that was probably because we determined when she needed to go based on hourly observances and that by taking her out on this schedule, she was okay and didn't forget where to go. But when she got outside, she might just stand there, and not want to come back in, sometimes for hours. I would stand there with her, never sure if she still needed to go... or what else I should do for her.

The key is still where it all starts! "EARLY DETECTION" and "ACTION!" Being aware that this disease can attack your dog's brain... no matter what breed, or what age! Understanding what it can do to your beloved dog, should hopefully spur on every pet parent to know the signs and what can be done.

If I had known about DISHAA at that point, I might have better understood Shamrock's, small signs and the Virginia Tech doctor's suggestion of this disease being a probable cause. Maybe I could have accepted the situation quicker and been more aware of how the disease might progress. But looking back, I believe I definitely would have taken notice that her behavior signs were consistent with cognitive decline.

I can't go back, but I hope that my experience can help pet parents see the need for using DISHA at the first sign of cognitive issues

DEMENTIA & ALZHEIMER'S PREVENTION

Knowing the steps to prevent this disease

might mean never having to deal with it!

SHAMROCK'S STORY

Prevention - Flea &Tick, Heartworm, Spay & Neuter, Vaccines,

The best way to deal with a disease is to not get it in the first place. Is it possible to prevent dogs from getting canine cognitive issues that can rob them of their quality of life?

General Prevention

I knew from my research that veterinarians were divided as to whether dementia could be prevented, and if the word Alzheimer's would ever be associated with dogs; but the jury is still out on that question!

The answers I did get are varied, informative, and sometimes even confusing, but thankfully in many cases extremely hopeful for pet parents and their beloved dogs.

I asked veterinarians, "If you were to see a puppy and a senior dog, both with the concept of preventing, or when necessary, dealing with the effects of canine cognitive dysfunction syndrome what would your advice be?

Here's what I was told:

Even though Dr. Bassingthwaighte is in Australia which puts us on opposite time zones I knew his information on the topic of this disease would be important, so I sent him a list of questions. I especially wanted to know his thoughts about pet parents dealing with "Doggy Dementia."

He sent back a voice recording which is the basis of our communication, and said, "Doggy dementia has a genetic

DEMENTIA & ALZHEIMER'S – Prevention

component, and some dogs are more likely to develop the disease than others. However, if the pet parent does the right things with their puppy, they can significantly reduce the likelihood of developing doggy dementia and possibly limit the severity if their dog does develop the disease."

This statement gave me hope about the possibilities of prevention.

I further discussed this issue with Dr. Mar who told me, "Prevention is the best form of medicine. Therefore, it is important to ensure that at your puppy's initial veterinarian visit, you have the information you need to raise a healthy dog, especially if it is of a certain specific breed. Leaving your veterinarian after your puppy's first check-up should lead you to feeling like a more educated pet parent. For example, certain breeds are prone to certain diseases so your veterinarian can advise you how these diseases may occur, the risk factors, and signs to watch out for."

Dr. Landau stated, "Prevention begins with looking at how we treat our animals from the time they are born regarding, vaccines, heartworm, flea and tick and other treatments, including the diets we feed them." He believes that examining these issues may very well show they are contributing to what we see in later years. He continued, "We also need to be more aware of the need for individualized healthcare for management of infectious disease, prevention, vaccinations, and that we should not necessarily have a 'one size fits all' medicine."

"Prevention is the best answer." Dr Jensen said when she sees a pet like Shamrock that already is older and has so many signs and symptoms it may sometimes be too late to make a substantial difference. But when she sees a dog from the time it is young, she can help the pet parents make good decisions that will help the pet through its entire life; and give the pet the best quality of life. "Our pets are part of our families and that is what pet parents need to consider when deciding how to take the best care of their "baby!"

When I asked Dr. Melling whether she believed this disease could be prevented in most dogs, she told me, "There is not one easy answer to this question, because every patient is different. We can avoid toxins that may occur from over-vaccination, monthly use of topical or internal pesticides, and processed, low quality pet foods. In some dogs, CDS is the result of a lifetime of toxins – these patients are the most difficult to treat. Prevention is easier."

She continued, "I recommend keeping toxins in our pets to a minimum. This can be done by feeding a fresh food diet, keeping vaccines, and the heavy metals that often accompany them, to a minimum, avoiding chemical pesticides, and using homeopathy whenever possible to treat illness and injuries instead of drugs. Finally, fresh air, low stress environments, and regular exercise are crucial to keeping stress hormones low in our pets."

Dr. Tynes clarified, "Management of cognitive decline in dogs is aimed at reducing the risk factors and slowing the progression of the disease." She suggested many ways to do this, "Nutritional supplements, functional foods, and medications aimed at reducing the effects of oxidative stress and inflammation, correcting nutritional deficiencies and metabolic changes associated with cognitive decline and improving neuronal health all can play a valuable role in management of this condition."

In terms of treating dogs with CCDS, and the question of can this disease be prevented, Dr. Bassingthwaighte concluded, yes and no!

And from what I have heard and seen, that unfortunately turns out to be the answer in many cases. Everything depends on the care provided from a puppy to and adult dog, meaning what prevention measures were started early enough and what treatments were given to halt the progression of the disease.

My interview with Dr. Pedro Luis Rivera, who practices Integrative Veterinary Medicine began with the question of whether dog dementia can be prevented, slowed or even stopped. He told me it is a degenerative process in the body, but that yes, we can nudge what we do to slow, and even minimize its effects.

It was so reassuring to hear Dr. Rivera say that we can slow and minimize the effects of the disease, so my next question of course was "How?"

DEMENTIA & ALZHEIMER'S – Prevention

He advised that we must start when dogs are young. "As our puppies are growing, we need to maintain their attention span and keep the brain's firing." But he also cautioned, that as they are still in the process of growth development it is important to be careful. "Slow and gradual training will help their brains develop properly, and caution should be used to avoid excessive stress. Chronic stress can lead to dog's brains not firing correctly and developing areas of the brain which are not being accurately stimulated. Therefore, don't push your puppy to the limit, remember slow and gradual are the most effective methods for development of healthy brains.

"When you are training your puppy, you are stimulating the total brain, not just one area, which helps the puppies brain develop to its fullest potential. Helping your puppy develop emotionally, socially, and physically are the keys to good brain development. As puppies are maturing their bodies are benefitted by hormonal changes." Dr. Rivera suggested, "When there is a choice for spaying and neutering, being a conscientious pet parent is preferable. If you have the choice to delay, it is important to wait at least until after the first heat."

Dr. Katie Kangas, who also has an Integrative Veterinary Care practice, said, "Holistic veterinarians have different guidelines to create a healthier life and more graceful aging. The dog is looked at as a whole being, their life experiences, surroundings, both physical and emotional, all with the understanding that any disease is not caused by one thing, but can be created and exacerbated by many things, including excess vaccines, toxins and processed foods."

Dr. Sasan Haghighat, who practices Traditional Chinese Medicine and rehabilitation treats cognitive dysfunction in pets by looking at many factors; the whole patient, rather than just the signs, including their surroundings and even their guardian. He told me, "The emotional state of a pet is as important as the physical and therefore it is essential to give guidance to the pet parent for the best emotional environment. It is also essential to provide a calm, clean environment, free of toxins and pesticides."

Spay & Neuter, Flea & Tick, Heartworm, Vaccinations-
General Information

SHAMROCK'S STORY

Dr. Marcie Fallek has transitioned over the years from Conventional medicine to Holistic and Homeopathy and she told me, "Years of over vaccination and poisoning by flea and tick preventatives, chemicals and environmental toxins can contribute to cognitive decline. Limiting or eliminating these toxins can buy more good years for your pet."

Dr. Katz also believes that if there was more information and education regarding the issues surrounding the use of flea and tick products, vaccines, and diet, we might see less pets with cognitive issues.

Dr. Kenneth Fischer studied various forms of veterinary medicine from Conventional to Holistic and tries to balance the use of his knowledge of both when treating dogs. He stated, "I feel that the use of vaccines and preventatives such as heartworm, and flea and tick control products should be minimized. I believe that veterinarians often automatically recommend these products without consideration of the downside effects they may have. These effects may be mild or severe, and may include vomiting, diarrhea, lethargy, skin irritations, neurologic signs including seizures, and in rare, but extreme cases, death. I feel that an animal guardian and his or her veterinarian need to have the conversation about what the 'real risks' are in that pet's situation, lifestyle, climate, etcetera, versus the 'cookie cutter' party line, 'one size fits all' approach. If an animal is in more of a state of optimal health, then they may be at less risk for the diseases that these preventatives are used for. Natural therapies include oral supplements that may help a pet be less attractive to biting insects. There are also chips or tags that may be placed on a collar that emit a frequency that deters biting insects as well. But I do not endorse specific products unless I am talking to an established client."

Discussing treating animals with vaccines, heartworm, flea and tick products, Dr. McKinstry felt these can all make it harder on the immune system to fight diseases and that these can be treatable with natural substances that won't compromise the immune system.

DEMENTIA & ALZHEIMER'S – Prevention

Vaccines, heartworm, flea and tick treatments are a very important discussion to have with your veterinarian. The purpose of a vaccination is so the dog's immune system will respond by producing antibodies which can fight off future infections. Dr. Dodds suggested, "…titers, a blood test that measures antibodies, done a year after the first series of vaccinations and before the next." These titers will test for the presence of antibodies for some canine diseases and will help indicate if a dog needs additional vaccinations." But she added, "With rabies of course, we have to follow the state laws."

Dr. Haghighat told me, "Even as puppies, it is important for pets to get the vaccines that are needed, but after that to make use of titers to measure what vaccines, if any, are to be continued. With heartworm it is important to do blood testing. To repel fleas and ticks. you can use herbs and topical natural treatments."

Continuing this topic, Dr. Mar told me, "Heartworm, and flea and tick treatments are also issues that should be discussed. Where you live should determine what you really need."

I responded by telling her that with Shamrock, because our flea and tick problems were not bad, we used diatomaceous earth in the yard and other natural deterrents, like sprinkling coffee grinds and products with lavender, which also helped with mosquito infestation. One time she did get fleas after we had a rabbit invasion, and we prepared Dawn dish detergent and olive oil in a mixture and used a Q-tip to apply the solution to any fleas we saw in her coat. They would die immediately. We used a flea comb repeatedly and bathed her in that solution with oats, which killed any remaining fleas that were on her. We spread diatomaceous earth on all carpets, let it settle and then thoroughly steam cleaned the carpets and her bedding.

Regarding ticks Shamrock did get a few in her lifetime, but whenever we walked her outside our property, we would check her before she came back in the house and recheck her for a few days thereafter. If a tick was found it was removed immediately and the bite site was treated with hydrogen peroxide, Vaseline, or, if it looked infected, Bacitracin.

SHAMROCK'S STORY

As I am not a doctor, I cannot say that any of these treatments would necessarily work for other dogs, and feel it is best for pet parents to do their own research and always consult their veterinarians.

Spay & Neuter

Regarding puppies and the issue of spay and neuter Dr. Mar told me, "The best way is to wait until they are about a year old or have at least gone through one or two heat cycles if female. With male's, neutering should be between one or two years. This timing is to ensure they have fully developed. Of course, there are always individual situations in which this timing may not be ideal for your puppy. In these cases, definitely discuss this with your veterinarian to ensure what timing is best."

Dr. Bassingthwaighte, told me, "Dogs should not have these procedures until they have reached physical maturity, at least two or three years old, but never before six months. Young desexing has really awful health ramifications."

Dr. Fraser noted spay and neuter is another very crucial point in helping our dogs get a better start in life. When we spay and neuter dogs at very young ages; usually within the first weeks or month of their lives, we take away most sex hormones. She further explained, "The body's normal system of development works with thyroid, sex hormones and the whole endocrine system which is important for muscular and skeletal growth. When spaying or neutering is done before these systems develop the lack of appropriate hormones can cause growth plates not close on time." These "growth plates" are areas of cartilage near the end of your puppy's leg which allow your dog's bones to grow. These plates start to close at around nine to eleven months. Therefore, at the very least, all spay, and neutering should be delayed until the growth plates close.

"Also, based on a study at UC Davis, some breeds are more predisposed to certain diseases, and some breeds should never be spayed or neutered. Our society and many veterinarians have been taught to spay and neuter by six months of age, but it's detrimental for the pet's good development. Holistic medicine is more open to this understanding."

DEMENTIA & ALZHEIMER'S – Prevention

Most shelters across the United States spay and neuter all dogs before adoption, regardless of age. Dr. Fraser works with holistic shelters, which battle their states with medical reasons not to spay and neuter for at least one year.

She wants pet parents to understand, the issue as she relates it to ovary sparing; leaving the ovaries intact, and vasectomies; male sterilization for birth control in humans. Dr. Fraser tries to convey the point, "Keeping these organs as long as possible is better for good hormone production and long-term health."

Vaccinations

Dr. Landau feels a good place to start prevention is with questioning why we give vaccines from eight weeks on. He advised, "We can come up with ways around these vaccines such as with titer testing and the understanding that most animals don't need vaccines as often, after they have been vaccinated as puppies. "Many animals depending on where they live, their environment etcetera, may not need vaccines or chemical treatments to prevent fleas and ticks."

I told him I felt there was a lot of over vaccination and mentioned that after asking our veterinarian about certain vaccines, and in consideration of Shamrock's age, we agreed they could be stopped. But I was sorry to add, that after speaking with other pet parents, I heard that many don't like to question their veterinarian when told their pet needs a particular vaccine, drug or treatment.

Dr. Bassingthwaighte specified that, "Minimal vaccination, to give adequate prevention," is his philosophy. "This is a complex issue because you need to give puppies a chance to develop protections from maternal hormones. That is why there are usually three vaccines at different time periods - eight, twelve and sixteen weeks. At eight weeks, sixty percent or more of dogs vaccinated will mount an immune response. By twelve weeks over ninety percent will have developed a response, but at least sixty percent of these dogs will be given the second shot, which will not give them any added protective value and possibly can cause them to have a reaction.

"By sixteen weeks the remaining ten percent of dogs and, or the five percent or less that didn't respond to the first two vaccines with development of antibodies, may need the third shot, but again sixty percent plus didn't need the second and certainly do not need the third shot.

"The problem is that you can't titer test and get accurate results until after sixteen weeks, until after you know there are no maternal antibodies. The reason is the titer can't differentiate between the maternal antibodies and those created in response to the vaccines.

"However," Dr. Bassingthwaighte continued, "there are a few options. Some pet parents will just have the eight-week vaccine and wait and take the risk. Some will do the first two vaccinations, or others just wait until after twelve weeks and do the titer. There are risks in all the choices.

"Alternatives to vaccination include homeopathic disease protections, but currently, there is not enough evidence to support this assertion.

"There is also a way to give your puppy low level exposure to some puppy diseases. A veterinarian in the United States would take crated puppies to where there were racoons with distemper and expose the puppy to the ground for a few minutes. These dogs tested with antibodies. A pet parent can emulate this experiment by taking their puppy to a busy dog park and put them on the ground for five minutes, repeat this procedure for a few weeks and then have a titer test done to see the results. Again, this is only as long as the dog is over sixteen weeks."

Also, because there are other issues with puppy exposure and socialization, this would be another topic to discuss with your veterinarian before proceeding.

Dr. Mar is more conservative concerning puppy vaccines, and she advised, "Giving vaccines depends on the dog's environment and what is absolutely necessary. Where you live should also help determine which vaccines are needed, but with an understanding of each pet and what they might be exposed to.

"If a pet has a certain disease and the state requires a vaccine that the veterinarian feels is detrimental, then they can write a letter stating the pet should be exempt. Also, instead of giving a vaccine the veterinarian can do titers, and then decide if the vaccine is needed.

"But when giving vaccines is necessary, the vaccines should be separated in order not to overload their systems. Once a dog has

DEMENTIA & ALZHEIMER'S – Prevention

reached geriatric years, most vaccines are no longer needed unless the pet is with outside dogs, or in an environment where they are exposed to a particular disease that would be more immediate in development versus their expected life span."

Dr. Jensen felt vaccines should be avoided whenever possible. "A good discussion with your veterinarian before the vaccine would be to ask, what is it for? Why does the dog really need it? But also, is there any other way, such as, titers, natural treatments, or even waiting until the disease presents itself."

Dr. Katz mentioned that one cause of dementia may be vaccinations. "Heavy metals, used as adjuvants, substances added to the vaccines to boost the immune system response, have been shown to be neurotoxins and may contribute to the cognitive degenerative conditions as well as many other health conditions."

When discussing vaccines and their effect on the immune system, Dr. Knueven, who has written books on these topics, shared his advice, "Vaccines are indeed double-edged swords. They are a useful tool for preventing some terrible diseases that can kill our pets, but at the same time, they can adversely affect the immune system and the overall health of the animal.

"As 'good' as vaccines are, every pet does not need to be vaccinated for every disease, every year. All pets do need to be vaccinated for rabies. This is a legal issue due to this 'zoonotic,' disease, meaning one that has the potential to spread from animals to people. Besides, the vaccine keeps millions of pets safe too."

He continued, "When you take your dog to the veterinarian for a 'distemper' vaccine, you are most likely getting more than you bargained for. It is extremely rare for any veterinarian to give only distemper in a vaccine. The vast majority of distemper vaccines come with between four and seven different disease entities in one shot.

"The basic canine distemper vaccine includes distemper, parvovirus, adenovirus, and parainfluenza. This 'combo' shot may also include two strains of leptospirosis and, or coronavirus. From the conventional point of view this 'supersizing' of the vaccine is considered a good thing. However, holistic veterinarians have concerns about the effects such vaccines have on the dog's immune system.

"I believe that every pet needs its basic distemper vaccine. This needs to be boostered several times in puppies to ensure immunity. After a year of age, the distemper vaccine in dogs has been proven to last from four to seven years. That is correct and has now been scientifically proven that yearly vaccination for distemper is unnecessary."

Therefore Dr. Knueven's recommendation is that four years after adult vaccination, dogs get yearly titers done. Since a titer demonstrates whether or not the immune system can respond to the disease, as long as the titer result is adequate, there is no need for the vaccine.

"As for the other vaccines that are available for pets, they should be given on an as needed basis. For instance, there are certain regions of the country where leptospirosis, commonly called "lepto," a contagious bacterial infection that can affect both humans and animals is prevalent, therefore dogs at risk of exposure should be vaccinated. This vaccine is an exception to the rule as far as length of immunity. If your dog needs it, the vaccine should be administered yearly. Similarly, the Lyme disease vaccine is helpful for those dogs that are at risk and needs to be given annually.

"The kennel cough vaccine is of very limited help in preventing upper respiratory infections in dogs kept in close quarters. Unfortunately, most kennels and groomers require that dogs be kept up to date on this vaccine. There is also a coronavirus vaccine which has been characterized as 'a vaccine looking for a disease'. Even the American Animal Hospital Association states that this vaccine is not recommended for dogs."

Dr. Knueven concluded, "Having worked for five years at an animal shelter, I have seen first-hand the benefit of proper vaccination. As a holistic veterinarian, I have witnessed the devastating effects of over-vaccination. For our pets' optimal health, a balance must be struck."

DEMENTIA & ALZHEIMER'S – Prevention

Speech:
(excerpted from) webinar speech
San Mateo Dog Training Club
July 28, 2020
Vaccine Issues
W. Jean Dodds. Dvm

"For over 50 years we have been over vaccinating our pets. There is no such thing as an 'up to date' or 'due' vaccination. Veterinarians can now offer, separated vaccine component's, rather than give them all together, since the published data show more adverse reactions when multiple vaccines are administered together.

Key Points on Vaccine Issues

Modern vaccine technology has afforded effective protection of companion animals against serious infectious diseases. but this advancement brings increased risk of adverse reactions (vaccinosis). Some are serious, chronically debilitating and even fatal.

Must balance this benefit: risk equation; "Be wise and immunize but immunize wisely!" Dr. Ron Schultz)

The Benefits of Vaccination

More lives saved; more animal production safeguarded than any other medical advance. Millions of people, pets and livestock vaccinated annually

•Reactions relatively rare ---about 3-5 events per 100 vaccines given

Only the presence of antibody can prevent infection. •An animal with a positive blood serum antibody test is protected from infection. Vaccines create Memory Cell Immunity. In this process the immune system mounts a faster and more effective response when exposed to the same antigen.

When to Vaccinate Puppies? Which Vaccines are Needed? What About Socialization?
Puppies Maternal Immunity & Protection
Vaccine Dosage
Age
Optimal age for response

SHAMROCK'S STORY

For Puppies   12 weeks + (Same for all breeds and sizes)

Earliest age for safety - 6 weeks for Puppies

Should receive MLV or recombinant "Core" vaccines (canine distemper and parvovirus) preferably either at 9-10 and 14-16 weeks of age (minimum protocol), or, at 9, 12 and 16-18 weeks The actual effective age varies. And as to whether the vaccine will be blocking effects of maternal immunity

Rabies vaccines are all adjuvanted killed products and are given as required by law, preferably always given separately from other vaccines, and as late as legally allowed –e.g., 20-24 weeks of age. Thimerosal (mercury) - free rabies vaccines are preferred and safer

Last puppy vaccine at 16-18 weeks for protection

Titers- As a marker of immune status

Vaccine Titer (Serum Antibody) Testing

Assesses the immunologic status of animals against common, clinically important infectious diseases

Determines if vaccine boosters are required or advisable

Once animal's titer stabilizes it should remain constant for many years

Protection is indicated by a positive titer result

Any measurable antibody level shows protection

Titers sustained unless animal has medical problem such as cancer or receives high/prolonged doses of immunosuppressive drugs

Viral vaccines prompt an immune response that lasts much longer than that elicited by classic antigen

Clinicians often do not distinguish between these two kinds of responses

Available Vaccine Titers for Dogs

Distemper Virus
Parvovirus
Adenovirus 2 (hepatitis)
Bordetella
Leptospirosis
Lyme disease

DEMENTIA & ALZHEIMER'S – Prevention

Corona Virus [not recommended]
Rabies Virus (RFFIT: non export)
Boosters
Periodicity of Booster Vaccinations
No evidence that annual boosters are necessary
Need to lengthen intervals -(every 3-7 years or more for healthy adults)
Geriatric animals vaccinated only with caution
Monitor serum antibody titers instead
Protection is indicated by a positive titer result
Any measurable antibody level shows protection
Therefore, giving boosters to immunized animals is unwise, as it will introduce unnecessary antigen, adjuvant and preservatives

Vaccinating that animal would not cause a significant increase in antibody titer, but hypersensitivity to vaccine components (e.g., fetal bovine serum) may develop

Furthermore, the animal doesn't need to be revaccinated and should not be revaccinated since the vaccine could cause an adverse reaction (hypersensitivity disorder)

Reasoning to Support Titers:
Possible Adverse Vaccine Events = Vaccinosis
Affects those genetically predisposed
Can be acute, sub-acute, and delayed for 30-45 days
Data regarding Dementia and Alzheimer's)
New data links reactions to integrity and function of gut microbiome

Heavy metal exposure from vaccines is an emerging concern for humans, pets and livestock. Aluminum and mercury found in brains of autistics, and from vaccine adjuvants that cross the blood –brain barrier after injection, then persist life-long.

Not all vaccines protect against disease completely. Those that do include: distemper virus, adenovirus, and parvovirus in the dog,

Examples of vaccines that only provide temporary protection are for leptospirosis, Bordetella, canine influenza, rabies virus

While these vaccines may not protect the animal from infection, it should keep the infection from progressing to severe clinical disease

Alternatives to Current Vaccine Practices

Measure serum antibody titers

Avoid unnecessary vaccines or over-vaccinating

Caution vaccinating sick or febrile animals

Tailor specific minimal vaccine protocol for dog breeds or families at risk for adverse reactions

Start vaccination series later (9-10 weeks, dog

Alert caregiver to watch puppy behavior and health after boosters

Avoid revaccination of those with prior adverse events

Summary on Vaccine Policy

In 2003 the American Animal Hospital Association (AAHA) stated that 'Current knowledge supports the statement that, 'No vaccine is always safe, no vaccine is always protective, and no vaccine is always indicated.'

Also, the late Professor Michael J. Day, Professor of Veterinary Pathology at the University of Bristol, and chairman of the WSAVA (World Small Animal Veterinary Association) Vaccination Guidelines Group and the WSAVA One Health Committee and Vice President of the WSAVA Foundation and a member of the AFSCAN Project Board, stated, 'Vaccination should be just one part of a holistic preventive healthcare program for pets that is most simply delivered within the framework of an annual health check consultation.'

Vaccination is an act of veterinary science that should be considered as individualized medicine, tailored for the needs of the individual pet, and delivered as one part of a preventive medicine program in an annual health check visit."

Reprinted by permission from Dr. Dodds

Flea & Tick Treatments

Dr. Jensen felt extensive discussion with your veterinarian applies to flea and tick collars and medications. "There are so many natural remedies that can be used such as: diatomaceous earth, and

DEMENTIA & ALZHEIMER'S – Prevention

aromatherapy products that repel fleas and ticks. There are also other ways to keep fleas and ticks from your yard, but sometimes the best prevention is monitoring, checking the pets after they have been out, using a flea and tick comb to search for problems and if ticks are found, removing them immediately and treating for any fleas discovered."

Dr. Mar said that when fleas and ticks are an issue, there are oral medications which she feels are more effective than collars, but with the understanding that putting any chemicals into the pet's body has to be weighed, protection versus risks.

Flea and tick treatments are another very important discussion and Dr. Bassingthwaighte, said to avoid these treatments, as they can cause seizures in dogs. He mentioned not using NexGard, Provecta or Seresto; as, "The results can be very bad!" *(Note: This statement was made prior to this book's publication and because data changes, as with all recommendations, before using any flea and tick product, please check with your veterinarian first regarding these and other treatments).

Dr. Dodds wanted pet parents to be aware of issues concerning flea and tick treatments. "Beware of using flea and tick medications and collars as there is concern for seizures, unprovoked aggression, and other side effects such as affecting blood cells, bowel, kidneys, and liver. Advantage II for fleas, Advantix II for fleas and ticks and Frontline are currently considered safer to use." *(Note: This statement is prior to publication and data changes. As with all recommendations, please check with your veterinarian first regarding these and other treatments).

As I learned from my experiences, Dr. Dodds believes, "Treatment for lawns and homes with substances like diatomaceous earth for flea and tick problems is more natural and not harmful to your pet."

SHAMROCK'S STORY

Flea & Tick Prevention
Report:
W Jean Dodds. Dvm
(Excerpted From) Report Fleas & Ticks On Pets
Fall, 2020"
Isoxazoline Parasiticides

"Flea and Ticks can be issues for your dog depending on your environment.

Here are Alternative Natural Supplements and Approaches

Keep environment cleared of places fleas and ticks can hibernate

Supplement with Food grade brewer's yeast and garlic

If your dog gets an infestation:

Use flea comb

Bathe often with natural herbal repellant shampoos (e.g., peppermint, neem, soaps)

Essential Oils (e.g., Kin + kind, Wondercide, Vetri-Repel)

Use flea and tick wipes

Rid fleas in the home

Use human grade Diatomaceous Earth (DE) on pet, rugs, carpets, in food. Sweep/vacuum up excess

Wash everything especially pet beds, blankets and carriers. 15-20 min in a hot dryer can kill adult fleas, larvae and eggs

Vacuum house regularly. Pay attention to dark corners and shadows

Steam carpets, floors and furniture if possible

Try to use natural flea control such as Wondercide, Flea busters and Diatomaceous Earth (DE) spread around floors and carpets

Rid fleas in the yard

Mow lawn and trim overgrown hedges and bushes

Remove dead leaves and twigs from flower beds and under bushes.

Add Flea repelling plants (e.g., Lemongrass, rosemary, sage)

Natural alternatives are preferred whenever possible."

Reprinted by permission from Dr. Dodds

DEMENTIA & ALZHEIMER'S – Prevention

Heartworm

Many veterinarians I spoke with agreed, there are times when dealing with CCDS that some preventative medicines, like heartworm may be suggested. Even though there can be many risks associated with these treatments, veterinarians agree the best way to approach this subject is with an open dialogue. The pet parent needs to understand when these treatments are necessary and if they in fact need to be given, then what can be done to better support the immune system, so their pets can better manage the stress of these treatments.

As with many treatments I learned there are also more natural ways to do things, so by discussing these options, pet parents can understand that these treatments should not always be used as the first line of defense. There are options that can make a significant difference between using prescription medicines or using nutrition to help the body in a preparative and holistically supportive way to make the pet stronger; to be its own first line of defense.

Dr. Dodds reminds us, "When giving a heartworm treatment it is important to know that even though the recommendation is every thirty days, which is for ease of reminder, however, heartworm can be given every six weeks instead of every thirty days, and still be effective." But she added, "Be sure that you give it not later than every forty-five days!"

Her advice was, "Also remember that heartworm is caused from an infected mosquito and takes time to develop, so age and how high a risk area you live in is important to consider. Also, if your pet does contract heartworm, one pill kills exposure."

Heartworm medication causes concerns for Dr. Jensen. She said, "There are only certain areas of the country where pets would be likely to get heartworm, which is contracted from mosquito bites. The other issue is that the lifecycle of a heartworm is about five to seven years, so if a dog is already in advanced years, they would probably outlive any chances of dying from the disease. So again, there are many questions to ask before starting heartworm treatments."

But Dr. Mar stressed, "In certain areas where mosquitoes are a problem, heartworm prevention is a highly recommended treatment. These again, are all topics that should be discussed with your veterinarian."

Flea & Tick, Heartworm, & Vaccinations
Summing Up These Issues - Some Final Thoughts
I asked Dr. Melling, "Understanding that you treat patients and not diseases, then does all the new information we have regarding CDS change your recommendations for new puppy parents?"

She replied, "Holistic practitioners look at the whole pet, not just one part of the pet. New puppy consults in my practice are at least sixty minutes long so we can address the issues for the pet, and I can create individualized recommendations. These would be based on their lifestyle, including nutrition, titer testing to avoid over-vaccination, and homeopathy and chiropractic to keep the vital force, their immune system, healthy."

Dr. Tynes commented on what can be done to help our pets as they age. "Many times, dogs do not need to continue vaccinations after a certain age and it is better to do blood tests which can measure their organ function and immune status, so that early recognition of problems can allow for more effective management of conditions associated with aging."

Dr. Mar strongly suggested, "If pet parents choose not to vaccinate or use other treatments, they should educate themselves and always discuss these issues with their veterinarian and question the pros and cons, costs and benefits, depending on their individual pet."

In light of all the information, I felt as a pet parent, it is so important to ask questions. But many pet parents I spoke with said they usually give their dogs the medication their veterinarian provides, without question. Some parents also added, since that is

DEMENTIA & ALZHEIMER'S – Prevention

the veterinarian, they chose to care for their dog, they should follow their advice.

Dr. Landau suggested, "I hope pet parents will understand that they should ask questions and see what options there are, and definitely ask about alternatives to heartworm and flea and tick treatments, if those treatments are warranted." As a final thought, he concluded, "We should vaccinate only when necessary and keep our pets on medicines only when absolutely necessary. As pet parents we should ask questions about what each treatment is for and if it is prescribed for prevention, then be sure to know what the risks are, but always try and see if there are more natural alternatives."

SHAMROCK'S STORY

Diet & Supplements- Your Dog Is What You Feed!

Diet and Supplementation are issues medical doctors have disputed for years. Which diet is best, what foods are healthiest, etc., etc., so why should the discussion be any different in the veterinary world?

I believe that the right food is essential for good health. We are a country that has fallen into the fast-food climate of eating and in doing so, we do not always make the best choices. There are so many studies I have read about the benefits of healthy eating, but when it comes to our pets, even if we eat healthier diets ourselves, sometimes we feed our dogs based on television advertising, supermarket placement or even coupons and price.

I had always fed Shamrock the formulation that addressed her needs and had the best first four ingredients. This food was made by a reputable company with a long reputation of quality dog food. I also supplemented her diet with multi-nutritional supplements and other age supporting minerals recommended and both the food and supplements were discussed with her veterinarian.

Around 15 years of age, I switched gears. Instead of her dog treats as snacks, I began sharing healthy foods we ate, like apples, peanut butter, and green beans. I also supplemented her dog food. I researched the best foods for her ailments and again, after talking with her veterinarian, made these changes. I can't tell you whether this helped but I can say that she had at that point exceeded how long the doctors believed she would live, and her quality of life was good.

DEMENTIA & ALZHEIMER'S – Prevention

In the following discussions, you will read many different and sometimes conflicting views. If you feel diet and supplementation can be helpful for your dog, consider all the options and then, since each dog's needs are different, discuss the information with your veterinarian.

Here is what I have learned about diet and supplementation.

Important Food Information
I began my talk with Dr. Kangas to better understand the effects food can have on the body. She helped me to realize the relationship of food to illness.

"The microbiome is defined as the ecosystem of microorganisms in the body, which we depend on for immune system function and to protect us against germs, for example, pathogenic or harmful microbes. The microbiome also has an important role in processing ingested food into energy, and conversion or utilization of nutriments, vitamins and minerals that are important for life. The gut microbes are also responsible for directly and, or indirectly manufacturing important neurotransmitters used by the brain and the nervous system.

"Therefore, it is important to understand how the microbiome affects brain health and the role the gut plays. The current understanding is that the gut is number one in the gut-brain connection, while the brain is number two. There is a close cohesion between the systems and their interdependent functions. Understanding the microbiome in a sick dog will usually indicate the detrimental effects after having fed poor quality, processed food for years."

Dr. Evelyn Kass is known as a "Pet Nutrition Doctor," and practices Integrative Medicine. She stated, "Food is the most important issue in dog health," and that her mission is to explain what real healthy food is. She believes that like people, we feed our pets the wrong foods. "Most dog foods are too high in carbohydrates, and dry dog food can contain fifty percent or more carbohydrates. Dogs don't need carbs at all! Dogs also don't need sugar because simple carb's turn into sugar! These types of foods cause inflammations of the gut, eventually leading to diseases of the body and brain. The excess sugar in the blood gets oxidized causing

SHAMROCK'S STORY

Advanced Glycation End products. These, 'AGE's,' are compounds formed in the body when fat and protein combine with sugar which contribute to aging and form plaque in the brain. In fact, there is research suggesting that at least some forms of Alzheimer's in people are like a type 3 diabetes! For these reasons dog food should contain less than fifteen percent carbohydrates and these should be complex carbohydrates that are slower to absorb and cause less rise in blood sugar."

To restore good health, Dr. Katz explained, "We need to create good gut bacteria!" The problem is that most veterinarians get little or no real nutritional education. What is known comes from pet food companies and their representatives detailing their products. They try to make their food interesting enough so the veterinarian will recommend it for the pet.

"The other issue is the lack of nutritional education for the pet parents. What the pet parent sees on television in ads and the coupons that are distributed may generally be what entices them to buy these foods. Unfortunately, many pet parents don't even look at the first three ingredients to see what the pet food is made from. Even when they seem to feel the food is good quality, without nutritional guidance, they have no idea if it is good for their pet." Dr. Katz added, "In many cases by the time I see the pet, they have come in as a last resort and the parents are willing to do anything to change their pet's eating habits."

In an article he wrote entitled, "Why Eat Raw," and excerpted here in part, Dr. Knueven, explained food in a way we might better understand, to help when deciding what to feed our dogs.

Article:
Why Eat Raw
By Dr. Knueven

"Just imagine for a moment that you are sitting in your medical doctor's office after your yearly exam, and the doctor pulls out a 40-pound bag of kibble and plops it in front of you. Your eyes are immediately drawn to the beautiful images of vibrant people eating handfuls of dry nuggets. And then you see the label, People Chow.

DEMENTIA & ALZHEIMER'S – Prevention

Then your doctor tells you that you can go home and get rid of your refrigerator and stove, and when you go to the grocery store you can bypass the fruits, vegetables, and meats, and head straight to the People Chow aisle. He informs you that this new "complete and balanced" product is the only food you should eat for every meal, day in and day out, for the rest of your life.

Hopefully, you would refuse such medical advice. Eating only processed food does not make sense. How could this food company be so arrogant to think they could create balanced nutrition in a bag? Besides, if you were not killed by malnutrition, you would likely die of boredom. So, how is it that we have bought into this idea for our pets? No wonder our dogs eat garbage when they get the chance!"
Article excerpted with permission from Dr. Knueven

What Should You Know About Kibble? What Is Kibble?

Kibble is defined as coarsely ground meal or grain made into small, dry pellets for use as pet food.

How Is Kibble Made?

Looking for an explanation I found Dr. Chris Zink and her work.

Dr. Zink, who specializes in Canine Sports Medicine, provided information from her work, "Regarding what is best for dogs to eat," which has been excerpted with her permission; from her book, *Discovering Your Dog. New information on how to give your canine pal a longer, healthier life.*

She wrote, "How Kibble is Made? All kibbles are made in essentially the same way. Wet and dry pet food ingredients, some of which already have gone through heating and other processing, are mixed to form a dough. High pressure and heat are applied to cook the dough which is then forced through tubes. Pieces of the extruded tube-shaped dough are cut off to make pellets. The pellets are then passed through a heated dryer to remove any remaining moisture and the food is sprayed with animal fats to improve flavor, vitamins to attempt to replace those damaged during the heating process, artificial colors to improve visual appeal, and preservatives. That's how it's done. Kill off some of the nutrients, then spray them back on.

"It turns out that the superheating process during the production of kibble changes the quality of some nutrients in a way that no spray can replace. When certain amino acids within a protein are heated in the presence of sugars, a series of chemical rearrangements occurs, called the Maillard reaction. The final products of this reaction are called advanced glycation end-products or AGEs."

In conclusion Dr. Zink stated, "Increased levels of AGEs in dogs have been seen in diabetes, cataracts, osteoarthritis, canine cognitive dysfunction syndrome, vascular dysfunction, and atherosclerosis."

What Food Should You Feed Your Puppy?

There is so much information about what to feed your dog to help them live a better life that I wanted to speak to a Board-Certified Veterinary Nutritionist and get a sense of what might help from puppy to senior regarding CCDS. Dr. Lindsey Bullen began by saying, "It is very challenging for pet parents to do what is best, understanding that prevention may not always be possible, sometimes bad luck, genetics and environment can all be factors, but at puppy age, we just don't know.

"As long as your dog is on a complete and balanced diet for puppy growth, that is key. The food should be manufactured by a reputable company with a nutritional department and multiple nutritionists on staff that are board certified, and who specialize in diet formulation.

"The more nutritionists, the more the company is invested in nutrition. The more people in a department the more likely the diet will be a good one."

My next question was what can a pet parent do when choosing the best food to feed their puppy?

Dr. Bullen responded, "From puppy stage it is best to ask your veterinarian. You can also call the company and ask questions, especially regarding the food being tested and their staff of nutritionists."

But she made an important point, "The pet food or grocery store clerks are not the ones to ask as they are lacking the necessary training to make an educated recommendation."

DEMENTIA & ALZHEIMER'S – Prevention

I replied, "Looking down the aisles at all the foods can be daunting." So, I began by asking the same question that goes through my mind in the store. "Is the most expensive really the best?"

And her reply was, "Expensive doesn't equal better. Dogs need a complete and balanced diet."

Dr. Rivera told me that nutrition is important at every stage of growth, as every stage is different and has different needs. He suggested, "Feed a diet that is age appropriate which includes healthy fats for good brain function and a healthy nervous system. He also advised, "Even as puppies grow into full adulthood, agility is very important. At that point making sure your dog is developing their muscles and joints will give them a better quality of life. As dog's age they especially need that muscular structure developed over years to help with what their older body is not replenishing. A healthy muscular and well-oiled joint system supports older dogs being able to maintain a good level of athleticism."

The concept of diet is to feed the puppy for their growing needs with the understanding that the food should provide a healthy all-around pet as the dog ages.

Food As Prevention

I asked Dr. Frick what she might recommend to help our pets prevent and or deal with issues of disease.

She told me, "Start feeding REAL food!" She then added, "REAL food means anything that is less cooked or processed or purchased at a grocery store." Agreeing that not everyone has the time or the money to ensure home cooking, raw or dehydrated food, Dr. Frick told me, "BAKED KIBBLE, is a good option, or our pet parents can become good label readers. That means checking the first five ingredients, those representing protein in dog food, to be sure they are whole foods from a good source."

Dr. Frick further offered, "In the early nineteen hundred's and before, livestock veterinarians looked to farm conditions, the soil, water, any possible contaminants like mold or spoilage throughout the raising of livestock and growing crops. When the soil and the feed were good, the livestock, their income and livelihood for the family, was healthy and the dogs living there were doing well too. When farms had problems, it was important to understand the underlying reason. The questions asked were, 'Are there nutrients missing from the soil?' and 'Are there toxic levels of minerals or vitamins?'

"In the nineteen fifties food production for dogs developed into a mechanical industrial revolution, 'Make it easy for people to feed pets.' Where veterinary colleges had previously focused on herd health based on nutritional considerations and corrections, with time and the invention of chemical drugs, the focus on nutrition, fell by the wayside. Then food companies became the driving force, directing doctors as to which foods were best to feed, but no one considered the co-efficient of the body degradation processed foods would introduce to our pets.

"Veterinarians were not being taught that these processed foods were harder for the body to digest and therefore did not understand the makeup of these foods. In turn, they moved farther away from the needs for dog food's nutrient necessities. Just as with humans, the more processed foods you eat, the less healthy you will be.

"Another factor lacking in the teaching of veterinarians about nutrition is that 'feeding for the breed' is an important consideration. The closer the dog is to their true breed, the more they should eat like the area of the world from which their breed originated." For example, dog breeds from Asia would eat differently than breeds from Europe or Australia etc. Dr. Frick continued, "To feed for your breed it is best to research your dog's heritage and get information about the foods available in that area and then try and develop an appropriate food guide for your dog.

"Dr. Frick's list of some examples:

Welsh Corgi: Welsh Highlands - Cabbage, potato, oats carrots, beef, rabbit, fish

Beagle: England - Beets, potato, lamb, rabbit, poultry

Chihuahua: Mexico - Mango, avocado, poultry, rice

Malamute: Alaska - Saltwater and freshwater fish, poultry, lamb, rice

Lhasa Apso: Himalayas - Lamb, goat, poultry, fish, rice

Basset Hound: France -Venison, rabbit, poultry, lamb, beets

DEMENTIA & ALZHEIMER'S – Prevention

Greyhound: Egypt - Poultry, lamb, dried fruits (dates, figs), nuts (almonds), barley, rice

Labrador Retriever: England – Fish, poultry, lamb, dairy, green vegetables"

She also said, "Essential minerals that are lacking from a good diet produce dogs that are ninety-four percent calcium and magnesium deficient. These minerals calm muscles and nerves. All organs need to be in sync to deal with the over loading and the added mental stress."

Dr. Knueven expressed, "Diet is the key to good health. Dogs should eat as close to what evolution has programmed them to eat. Wolves are not eating starchy potatoes or grains! It is totally unnatural for dogs to consume grains. Pets benefit from an evolution-based diet rather than the starch-rich, highly processed convenience pet foods most pet caregivers currently feed. Animals simply cannot be healthy if their bodies are not provided the raw materials and nutritional signals that are needed.

"My definition of natural nutrition is a diet consisting of ingredients that a particular species has evolutionarily adapted to eat. This diet would provide the macronutrients, proteins, fats, and carbs, micronutrient vitamins and Phyto-nutrients balance, which is ideal for their health. Such a diet is, by definition, a balanced, raw food diet. No dog evolved eating kibble or canned food."

Dr. Knueven then referred me to an article he wrote that fully explained his dietary advice. "It seems to me that, conventionally, we are going at pet nutrition from a totally wrong direction. We start with ingredients that carnivores were never meant to eat, then we strip out all the nutrients with our processing, and finally we sprinkle in some synthetic vitamins and supplements to try to balance obvious deficiencies. A more intelligent approach would be to start with a look at what canines have evolved eating over the past five million years. Evolution is a slow process and pets have certainly not adapted to processed foods over the past 70 years that they have been available.

"The closest wild relative of our pet dogs is the wolf. In fact, as different as some dogs appear when compared to the wolf, they are the same species. In the wild, wolves have a varied diet that depends on seasonal availability. They prey on the weak members of big game herds such as elk and moose. They also eat small game, earthworms, grasshoppers, fruits, berries, and other vegetation. When the first wolves became domesticated dogs about one-hundred-thousand years ago, this new species became more reliant on human food scraps. This diet consisted of unused portions of butchered animals as well as "table" scraps."

Dr. Fraser pointed out, "Food, and the energy it provides is the building block of health. When used in a therapeutic manner, proper diet can reverse disease, decrease inflammation, and truly serve to help the body heal and achieve homeostasis, the body's ability to maintain stability creating the best environment for good health."

But she has many methods to help pets. "One of the most important systems in the body is the microbiome of the gut. It plays a huge role in the immune system, behavior, mental health, allergies, GI disease, weight, etcetera. Stress, medications, and environment can all damage the microbiome." Through therapy, she can adjust the microbiomes in the gut, by replacing a sick pet's microbiome with a healthy one. This can be done with enemas or oral administration. "It is a very powerful tool in achieving homeostasis in the body which causes issues from the gut to the brain, so proper balancing of the gut is important for well-being."

And whether Dr. Fraser is utilizing therapeutic ketogenic diets and, or Chinese herbs, she pointed out, "It is important to remember each patient is different, so there is a need for trial and error. Therefore, the sooner dogs get off highly processed food and change to a diet of whole food, anti-inflammatory, low carb, good fat, protein and minerals, the better chance of preventing, and, or minimizing the many issues that face older dogs."

Dr. Kangas made it clear, "Many veterinarians don't know about true nutritional benefits!" She told me, "In Medical school veterinarians are not taught a great deal about nutrition, and the minimal nutrition training provided is generally biased, coming from veterinary experts affiliated with the big commercial food companies. Veterinarians are also not trained on using natural substances to assist with supporting health or healing or in use for disease management. Veterinary training focuses on the use of prescription drugs and the ways to use them to help address

DEMENTIA & ALZHEIMER'S – Prevention

problems caused by disease. Unfortunately, big pharma has a huge influence on both medical doctors and veterinarians, as does the commercial dog food industry. When it comes to food, most veterinarians just suggest heavily processed commercial food for their patients."

I had read an article on the internet in which Dr. Patrick Mahaney, a Concierge Style veterinarian, spoke about CCD and diet. I spoke with him to learn more about his advice regarding this disease.

Dr. Mahaney discussed the importance of diet. "Diets rich in anti-oxidants and vitamins can help prevent tissue damage that can lead to CCD. Whether for a puppy or an older dog, this is one of the most important considerations." He told me how important it was also to avoid processed food. "Many of these foods seem to appear healthy, but in fact they are so processed that the good nutrients of the ingredients become lower in quality."

Diet, Supplementation & Disease

Dr. Brugliera told me, "Diet and supplementation have been at the top of many veterinarians list as extremely important for good long-term results when preventing and or treating CCDS.

I asked her what she recommends, "A lightly cooked diet is usually the best for most older dogs. There are also a few raw diets that can be lightly cooked for elderly dogs."

Dr. Buchoff also believes food is the first line defense; attacking the disease from the point of pet nutrition through a good diet.

Discussing Shamrock's health before the cognitive issues, I mentioned to Dr. Dodds she was diagnosed with hypothyroidism and was on Synthroid, to help restore proper thyroid levels

Dr. Dodds told me, "Diet impacts thyroid function," and thyroid hormones play a role in brain development and function.

I never knew that in addition to the Synthroid Shamrock was taking, certain foods/supplements would help support her thyroid and in turn help her brain and cognitive issues.

SHAMROCK'S STORY

Speech:
(Excerpted From) Webinar Speech
Mid-Kentucky Kennel Club
July 22, 2018
Behavior & Cognition
W. Jean Dodds. Dvm

"These Foods/Supplements are important for thyroid function:

Soy – dietary goitrogens, but anti-thyroid effect protected by iodine

Iodine – vital to thyroid function; excess and deficiency can occur

Zinc – critical to immune function, and health of skin

Selenium – protects against oxidative damage, boosts immunity

Vitamin E – neutralizes free radicals; protects against cancer, aging

Vitamin B-6 (pyridoxine) – keeps CNS healthy function

Vitamin D – balances cellular and humoral immunity, regulates insulin and

Glucose"

The speech continued:

"With CCDS, Brain Health, Memory and Cognition are so important, and food plays a role in the factors to control aging and memory.

Functional foods that improve cognitive activity in aging dogs include vitamins E and C, and resveratrol, acting as antioxidants, along with a mixture of colorful fruits and vegetables to provide anthocyanins and reduce cellular oxidative stress and reduce free radical damage. Alpha-lipoic acid + L-carnitine, mitochondrial cofactors. Omega-3 fatty acids help improve brain health and function and slow loss of cognitive function with aging.

Requirement for essential nutrients increases not only during periods of rapid growth or reproduction but also in geriatrics, because immune function and bio-availability of nutrients generally wanes with aging."

DEMENTIA & ALZHEIMER'S – Prevention

For control of aging and memory, Dr. Dodds made these recommendations.

The Mediterranean type of diet - fish, nuts, for dogs: not macadamia, walnut or hickory nuts, Brazil nuts and cashews are high in fat, pistachios, pecans, almonds can be moldy, aflatoxins, some dogs are peanut reactive, whole gluten-free grains, olive oil, fresh produce.

Also be sure to avoid Trans Fats and Saturated Fats, eat less dairy, red meat and fried foods.

Eating a heart-healthy diet is also good for the brain. Eat plenty of omega-3 Fatty Acids, causes twenty-six percent less brain lesions. Also eat smaller meals throughout the day helps digestion. Eating fruits, vegetables, and berries, of various colors and green tea, enhances memory and alertness, it is anti-inflammatory and can be put on body and sores, and in foods.

There are 10 foods essential for Brain Health and Memory:

"Leafy greens (folate, vit. B 9) - kale, spinach, collard and mustard greens,

Cruciferous vegetables (folate, carotenoids) - broccoli, cauliflower, bok choy, Brussel sprouts

Beans/ legumes (choline)

Whole grains (gluten-free = quinoa, millet, rice, soy, corn, flax, TEFF, tapioca)

Berries/cherries (anthocyanins, antioxidants, vits. C & E)

Omega 3 fatty acids (antioxidant, anti-inflammatory)

Yellow Squash, asparagus, tomatoes, carrots, beets (folate, vit. A, iron)

Nuts (omega fatty acids, vits. E & B6, folate, magnesium)

<u>**CAUTION: macadamia, walnuts are unsafe for pets**</u>

Seeds (zinc, choline, vit. E)

Spices (antioxidant, anti-inflammatory)

And then there are other Superfoods such as:

Eggs - high in quality protein and choline for brain and memory

SHAMROCK'S STORY

Kiwis - antioxidant-rich, vit. A, C & E, potassium, high in fiber

Quinoa - high in protein and fiber, iron, zinc, vit. E, selenium

Salmon - high omega-3 and iron, low calorie and low saturated fat

Sweet Potatoes - high in vit. A & C, calcium, potassium"

Exercise is also important, in modest amounts with tasks to learn and perform."

Dr. Dodds last comment to the Kennel Club was her motto, "Let food be thy medicine and medicine be thy food." Hippocrates
Speech reprinted with permission from Dr. Dodds

Dr. Dodds also told me, "Behavioral changes are also brought on by diet." Diet can have major effects, but she wants pet parents to know not to give too much chicken, or deer, even if those sources are in chews, or fats." And when the pet refuses to eat as Shamrock occasionally did, she suggested adding harmonic herbs, which give an aroma to the food that will help interest them in eating, such as basil, oregano, sage and thyme. She gave me another great tip, "Also, foods like frozen green beans can be among their favorites and encourage eating."

Dr. Kass was very upfront with me about dog dementia. "I am not sure there is a true treatment for dementia, though there are many supplements and nutrients that can help. This is an inflammatory condition in the brain which is best prevented whether in dogs or people." She continued, "Brain health is an important issue to address in pets and people, but like most diseases, it starts in the gut, and I believe that food is key!" Her motto, is, "Let Food Be Thy Medicine," from Hippocrates, an ancient Greek physician who is traditionally referred to as the "Father of Medicine."

Dr. Kangas recommends having a vitamin panel done for all her patients, as several key nutrients are usually deficient in the majority

DEMENTIA & ALZHEIMER'S – Prevention

of pets. "I love recommending vitamin B12 for pets with a chronic disease issue or chronic inflammation and definitely for aging pets."

She explained, "As we age, we do not absorb as much of this nutrient, across the gut wall, from our food. And supplementing this is always safe and generally very beneficial. Vitamin B12, cobalamin, is excellent for supporting cellular energy, energy production and the mitochondria of the cells, as well as muscle and nerve tissue integrity and brain health. I see many geriatric pets and chronically ill pets who respond beautifully to this, either in oral form or injectable form."

Dr. Kangas then turned her advice to another important supplement, vitamin D, "Deficiency of this vitamin is also a very common and a significant issue for pets. They do not have the capacity to absorb vitamin D from sunlight and rely completely on diet and food to supply this important nutrient. Low vitamin D is a link to all chronic inflammatory patterns and infections. This issue can be corrected with either foods, if it is a mild deficiency, or with a vitamin D3 supplement at appropriate dose based on the testing and body weight."

From my research I learned the big point to take notice of is that almost every veterinarian agreed that when they see a pet in the early stages of cognitive decline, they can adjust their diet with a variety of foods targeted with minerals to help the brain before any further damage is done. Foods like sardines, were considered an excellent choice.

I also discovered that once the veterinarian was able to determine where the deficiencies were coming from, a very simple technique for figuring out what to feed your dog might come from the expression, "When the brain is not working, eat brain food!" Good brain foods are brain organ meat. If the liver isn't working, eat liver, if the kidneys aren't working eat kidney hearts, etc. As you can see, these are all good organ meats, and each can be paired with what ails your pet. The best way to get these good foods is fresh, frozen, freeze dried or in supplement form. But the research also stresses that each dog has different needs, or can be sensitive to different foods, therefore, before you make any changes these should be discussed with your veterinarian.

SHAMROCK'S STORY

With the next stage of the disease, dogs need foods that will enable nutrients to get across the barriers. Deficiencies can be best addressed with colorful foods and supplements like omega-3s, MCT oils, wild cut salmon oil and more. I next delved into how food can be used, after the disease is present.

The Power Of Food-Food After Diagnosis

Dr. Haghighat advised, "Once there is a change in the emotional and physical atmosphere, the need is to help the pet's physical condition by making good diet adjustments of micronutrients. These treatments include a clean diet, with whole foods, non-GMO, pesticide-free food that provides the necessary nutrients for the body to heal and recover. Therefore, it is best to feed, lots of green vegetables, antioxidants, correct amount of fat omega-3, turmeric activated with black pepper, coconut oil, fish oils, Hawthorne berry, ginkgo biloba, blueberries, unprocessed foods containing no pesticides and in conclusion to give a diet that is low carb and the right amount of fat."

Dr. Kass told me she uses food and nutritional support as medicine for her patients and teaches pet parents how to create a healthy lifestyle for their furry family members through educational workshops and individual consulting.

After healing herself from the damage caused by two autoimmune diseases using only diet and herbs, she realized the power of food to heal. "Using the principals she learned from her own struggle, she then healed her older cat of pancreatitis and inflammatory bowel disease." By changing Phoebe's diet and adding some nutritional supplements, she noticed in addition to healing her gut issues, that the excess weight and skin sensitivity that had been part of Phoebe's life since she was less than a year old, disappeared. She knew then that she had to use this approach on her patients. They responded in the most amazing ways!

Dr. Kass gave me additional information about diet, nutrition, and supplements, and one of her statements really rang true for me, "Feeding your pet is not 'one size fits all'." If your pet is sick, it is extremely important to have a nutritional study to assess the right foods for your pet to eat. She added, "Dogs are carnivores and therefore require fifty to seventy-five percent meat content in their

DEMENTIA & ALZHEIMER'S – Prevention

diet. But, how much for each dog, and which meat is important? Organ meats are wonderful additions for dogs: livers, heart, kidney. "They are high in nutrients, like folate and vitamin B12 and are a great source of protein and minerals like iron, selenium and zinc.

"Dogs also love fruits, vegetables, seeds and nuts which are good healthy foods for them. The best way to tell if the prepared food you are buying is healthy is to look at the first two ingredients which should be meat. Also remember the least processed a food is, the better. Fresh has more nutrients than processed." Dr. Kass also stated, "Freeze dried is a great way to get the convenience of dry with the benefits of whole food, but it is more costly. Be sure to add water before feeding.

"Even salmon which should be healthy can have issues as Atlantic Salmon or Farm Raised, is not as healthy as 'Wild Caught', so stick with Pacific Salmon.

"When in doubt you should always consult a nutritionist or ask your veterinarian for good recommendations.

"When dogs are ill it is best if you cook all their foods to be sure you are not adding stress to their digestive system.

"Raw diets are great for many pets, but Dr. Kass stressed, "Raw can be dangerous if the dog is sick or compromised. But you don't want to overcook food either. Overcooking, especially meats can cause dangerous carcinogens to be formed in the food.

"Home prepared whole food diets can have amazing health benefits, but they must be balanced if fed long term, so you will likely need some help with this."

Dr. Torraca expressed, "A good diet that is balanced with less carbs and more protein, is very important, and the less the food is processed, the better."

I told her when Shamrock was starting to show more signs of cognitive decline, I shared our food like salmon and chicken and added fresh veggies such as broccoli and green beans to create a good balance with her dog food. I also added small amounts of sweet potato and pumpkin, which she loved. These changes which added home cooked foods seemed to make a difference. She was eating again and seemed more herself.

I also told Dr. Torraca, "I used a teaspoon of salmon oil with her food and sprinkled turmeric and a drop of extra virgin olive oil. The salmon oil and turmeric were very pungent and gave her some sniffing sensations that engaged her senses and sparked her desire to eat, while being nutritionally good for her

"One of her go-to foods; the food she loved most, even when she didn't want to eat was peanut butter. We played a kind of sniff game and sometimes added pieces of diced apple which she liked to chew.

Dr. Torraca expressed and important concern, "Just be sure the peanut butter doesn't have xylitol." Xylitol is extremely toxic to dogs, even in small amounts."

Sometimes even Shamrock's favorite foods were not enough to get her to eat.

Dr. Torraca also commented, "Dogs get bored easily with food, so sometimes if they are not eating, try changing up their food."

During my research I learned that Chinese Medicine looks at dog food as an integral method to help heal their body. For example, if the tongue is red, and the dog is panting a lot; this might lead to looking for a yin deficiency and then the right foods, such as eggs, would enable the body to cool down.

Turkey is a good protein, but it has tryptophan and can sedate, so to balance the effects of turkey adding a good carb such as millet, barley or brown rice would be beneficial.

Another eye opener was how much to feed. For many dogs going through cognitive issues, less is more. They don't always want to eat and sometimes feeding less at a meal, but trying to feed more often, is a better way to ensure they don't lose weight but still receive the vitamins and nutrients needed.

When Shamrock put up a fuss about eating, even her favorite foods, and she wasn't able to settle down enough to want to eat, I pre-made lots of snacks with good protein sources and vegetables. I then divided the food into small portions and gave them to her throughout the day. Instead of her normal dog treats, apples and peanut butter, steamed broccoli, even hard-boiled eggs, became her new treat food.

What Food To Feed For Dementia & Alzheimer's?

I next delved into obtaining more specific diet information regarding dementia and Alzheimer's. I found this was not a "cut and dry," situation...there was definitely some conflicting thoughts.

DEMENTIA & ALZHEIMER'S – Prevention

Not all doctors I spoke with agreed regarding the best diets for cognitive issues, so you do need to discuss diet for your pet with your veterinarian. Even though they may not necessarily agree on diet choices, the one thing I believe all the veterinarians agreed about was that diet can make a great deal of difference when dealing with dementia and Alzheimer's.

Dr. Landau said, when he sees degenerative neural progression that leads to dementia and Alzheimer's the goal is to slow down the progression. Amyloids, which build up in the nervous system and form plaques in the brain, are often responsible for neurodegenerative conditions like dog dementia. At that stage he can make dietary recommendations, add supplements, and herbs that are more targeted to reduce this inflammation, and help slow the progression of dog dementia.

Dr. Landsberg suggested a key step is to adopt the right nutritional support, which has been demonstrated to improve signs and slow the decline of cognitive dysfunction, learning and memory. He recommended, "Quality diets with good nutritional balance, and therapeutic diets that might be supplemented with MCT oils, fatty acids, antioxidants, vitamins and minerals to improve energy metabolism and mitochondria function in the brain, reduce inflammation and protect and support neuronal health." He also stated, "Nutritional supplements may help improve the dog's condition."

I asked him about the shared problem of this disease with humans and the prospects of using human products.
He advised, "There are several supplements, therapeutic diets and medications that might be effective for treating the clinical signs and slowing the progression of cognitive dysfunction, some of which are developed from, or have the same ingredients as medications and supplements used in humans."
He went on to explain that there are also times when he would prescribe medicines and natural supplements to help manage the signs. "If the pet is not sleeping, or has bouts of anxiety, then drugs, natural supplements, and pheromones to calm, reduce anxiety, and

promote sleep may be used to deal with the specific clinical signs in dogs.

I wanted to understand more about the role diet could play in changing the course of pets with dementia.

Dr. Bullen recommended a diet with antioxidants that also has tons of enrichment.

I had spoken with neurologists that treat Alzheimer patients and a Keto diet seems to make a world of difference.

Dr. Knueven commented, "There is evidence that a ketogenic diet can help dogs with signs of CCDS. These diets are low in carbohydrates, with added MCT oil, omega-3 fatty acids, and are balanced with omega-6, which can also help with seizures, as omega-6's are pro inflammatory."

Dr. Bullen's comments regarding this diet for dogs with CCDS, stated, "A Keto diet, high-fat, adequate-protein, low-carbohydrate may or may not be appropriate for each individual dog. This diet gets calories from protein and fats and reduces carbohydrates, thereby tricking the body into a caloric deficiency. The diet forces the body to burn fats rather than carbohydrates. Ketones are formed when there is not enough sugar or glucose to supply the body's fuel needs...but ketones designed by the body, shouldn't be fuel for metabolism.

"Going farther from what is normal for the body can potentially put the body at risk. Fat is not a bad energy source and provides essential fatty acids. MCT oils, medium chain triglycerides, like coconut oil, can be beneficial."

Dr. Bullen also added, "Nutrients, protein fat and carbohydrates are necessary for a balanced diet. Carbohydrates aren't a bad thing. They help the body produce energy, which when you dog eats carbs, turns to glucose, which is needed as a source of energy. A pet's ability and need to utilize carbohydrates varies on the pet's individual needs"

I heard a lot about adding specific foods for dogs with CCDS and next asked about her recommendations, and some of the foods I gave Shamrock, such as salmon oil, small amounts of green beans, broccoli, and apples.

DEMENTIA & ALZHEIMER'S – Prevention

She replied that, "Salmon oil is very high in anti-inflammatory and essential fatty acids like the omega-3s, EPA and DHA. These are good at reducing inflammation."

As far as adding human foods, she said, "She is never sure how the pet will respond." Dr. Bullen's best advice is to start slow and watch for any reactions. "Additionally, human foods should not account for more than ten percent of the pet's total caloric intake, or it could unbalance their diet.

"For treats, she emphasized, "Don't give table scraps or human food instead use complete and balanced kibble. Just be sure your dog still eats their regular amount of food."

"The sooner you act, the better the results will be," was the advice I received from Dr. Bassingthwaighte. "Diet is a key to preventing and even delaying dementia, but also to slowing signs once they appear. Feeding a healthy, complete, whole food diet is that key. Adding appropriate supplements is another, high-quality omega-3s, and antioxidants of which blueberries are a superior source for good brain health. Another suggestion is green tea steeped, then served cold.

"Diet and the role food plays is always an important topic when talking about doggy dementia." He advocated for fresh whole food, preferably raw, but he did add, "Home cooked is fine! Seventy-five percent meat, twenty-five percent veggies and little or no grains or carbohydrates. Avoid potatoes and give only small amounts of sweet potatoes and pumpkin, unless the dog has a particular need for these foods." He emphasized, "I encourage pet parents never to give processed kibble food, unless there is no other option.

"Something else to be aware of is that dogs may also exhibit signs because of pain. Turmeric can help a great deal because it reduces inflammation."

Dr. Kangas pointed out, "Another factor of nutrition that is misunderstood is that dietary fats can be healthy. Good dietary fats are very beneficial and many health professionals now understand that fact, especially from research regarding Alzheimer's, dementia, and other brain diseases.

"The low-fat craze of the nineteen-eighties and nineteen-nineties led to low-fat diets that have created more health problems.

SHAMROCK'S STORY

Belief systems have been set for many people including doctors and veterinarians, that dietary fats cause health problems such as heart disease, clogged arteries, obesity, pancreatitis, etcetera. Veterinarians often prescribe or recommend low-fat diets for canine patients with any type of G.I. upset."

Although these bland/low-fat diets are considered more easily digestible, Dr. Kangas added, "This should be a short-term treatment solution and not a long-term plan. Low-fat diets that are continued indefinitely can be very damaging to health, including reduced brain function."

She continued, "There is certainly a distinction between healthy dietary fats and poor-quality such as refined and hydrogenated oils, etcetera." When considering food for your dog, Dr. Kangas wanted pet parents to better understand, "There is also the concern that the fats in heavily processed foods, for example, foods heated at high temperatures, are rancid. Indeed, fats become toxic when heavily processed through heating. Heavily processed commercial foods can cause gut issues and imbalances for many reasons."

Dr. Gardiner gave me some other tips for helping to improve dog's cognitive function. "Choose a diet or supplement with omega-3 fatty acids and antioxidants to support brain function. Use a puzzle feeder or treat puzzle, which is any object that you can fill with food or treats to make the dog search and find the surprise inside. These can be toys, mats or other objects that not only are used for feeding but engage the dog's mind."

For some pet parents it may still be easiest to rely on commercially processed foods for their dog with cognitive issues,

Dr. DePorter explained, "A senior diet, Canine b/d, Hills Pet Nutrition, has been shown to improve the signs and slow the progress of cognitive decline. It is supplemented with a combination of fatty acids, antioxidants (vitamins C and E, b-carotene, selenium, flavonoids, and carotenoids), as well as DL-a-lipoic diet and L-carnitine, which are intended to enhance mitochondrial function. In a laboratory study, the combined effect of the enriched diet plus the enriched environment provided the greatest improvement.

DEMENTIA & ALZHEIMER'S – Prevention

"Another commercially available diet, Vibrant Maturity 7+ Formula Dog Food," (Nestle´ Purina Pet Care), "is a diet that includes enhanced botanical oils containing medium-chain triglycerides," (MCT), "to provide ketone bodies as an alternate source of energy for aging neurons, dual defense antioxidant blend of Vitamins E and A along with minerals zinc and selenium. Vibrant Maturity has also been shown to significantly improve cognitive function in senior dogs by providing an efficient fuel source for the senior dogs' brain."

Dr. Bullen told me that a good choice for dogs with cognitive issues is Purina Neurocare, (requires a veterinarian's prescription). This food is formulated to help support cognitive health and immune function in dogs. It is crafted in collaboration with nutritionists, researchers and veterinarians and uses chicken as the very first ingredient along with a unique blend of vitamins and nutrients.

Dr. Mar talked with me about prescription pet food/diets that are now being formulated to help prevent brain aging in geriatric dogs and recommended by veterinarians. "Purina currently has a diet formulated to promote brain health and healthy aging, called 'Bright Mind'." *(Note: There are currently many different varieties of Bright Mind, so this needs to be discussed with your veterinarian).

Food Choices- Raw, Freeze Dried Processed, Homemade

These are controversial issues that veterinarians' debate regarding the pros and cons of raw, freeze dried, processed and even home cooked foods, but one thing they do seem to agree with is the statement that a good balanced diet is essential for your dog's health!

Dr. Fallek felt that diet can also play a large part in promoting long term health. "Nature intended for dogs to eat raw food. Ten thousand years of domestication has not changed their DNA! Animals cannot thrive on kibble or canned food."

But Dr. Bullen felt there was a need for caution with feeding raw. "Raw may not be the best as there can be a risk of bacteria," so she said she prefers not to recommend raw, and added, "Freeze-Dried is not better it is basically the same as raw."

But there were other doctors that felt the benefits of raw or freeze dried would make them good diet choices.

Diet is a big issue. Dr. Jensen prefers dogs be fed a diet of raw and fresh foods. She told me, "Quality freeze dried foods are now readily available in grocery and pet stores." She wants pet parents to consider their own diet, "Do you eat the same food every day? Do you care about the ingredients or processing of the food you eat? So, start with those premises when thinking about how you feed your dog."

In his article, "Why Eat Raw," Dr. Knueven, stated, "The ideal diet for most pets consists of raw meat, bones, organ meat, and shredded fruit and vegetables. Raw ingredients provide nutrients that get cooked out of processed foods. This type of natural diet also leaves out excessive carbohydrates, preservatives, and artificial colors.
"The importance of proper nutrition for dogs cannot be overstated. It is impossible to have a healthy organism without providing the raw materials that Mother Nature intended. I have seen numerous animals overcome troubling conditions simply by making dietary changes. Not every disease can be cured with nutrition, but all conditions can be aided with this natural approach. Healthy nutrition is the foundation for every pet's well-being. The best way to ensure that a pet is getting optimal nutrition is to mimic its ancestral diet as closely as possible. That's why I recommend balanced raw diets for pets."

Dr. Fischer provided the following information. "The one thing that I would say is that dogs should be fed 'biologically appropriately', throughout their lives, which, in my opinion most are not. To me, this means that for one thing, dogs would be best served, literally and figuratively, by a diet that is minimally processed, versus the ultra-processed diets that most dogs are fed. The ingredients in most foods are of low quality. They are processed at extremely high temperatures and under a tremendous amount of pressure that

DEMENTIA & ALZHEIMER'S – Prevention

results in a material that we call food but is a mere shadow of what would best provide for a pet's optimal nutrition. Minimally processed foods would include foods that people eat, what is often referred to as 'people food'. I prefer to refer to it as 'real food', with a few exceptions for certain foods that are considered toxic to pets.

"Another type of food I suggest is called, 'base mix' foods. These are foods that provide a base to which pet parents can add meat, vegetables and water to form a kind of stew.

"Better quality commercial foods include what I call 'fridge foods,' whole, fresh foods that are found in the refrigerator section of the store, and raw foods. Raw foods may either be frozen raw or freeze-dried raw. When the foods are made from fresh, wholesome ingredients, and they are minimally processed, they can do so much more to nourish a pet than the ultra-processed foods that most dogs eat."

When Dr. Katz sees a pet patient with signs of dementia, she has many forms of diagnosis and treatment at her disposal. She suggested. "Diet is one of the first things to look at when faced with these symptoms. Dry processed dog foods are made by extrusion. That process uses heat and very high pressure to create a kibble. But what is also produced at these high temperatures and under high pressure; are excessive chemicals in the food. Acrylamides and hyper cyclicals Heterocyclic amines are created, and these chemicals are known carcinogens. The more processing the less the food is recognized by the body and the harder the digestion. This creates and fosters bad intestinal bacteria; this bad bacterium can also be created from the over-use of antibiotics."

She also talked about diet by stating, "Processed diets and the chemicals put into the pet's body most likely are also big contributors to cognitive issues in dogs. Pesticides and herbicides are likely to be contributing factors, as well."

Dr. Buchoff advocates for a natural, organic, raw diet, and told me, "Eating food in its natural, unadulterated state is best for health and wellness." He explained, "Dogs are natural carnivores and benefit from food that is as close to what their diet would be in nature. Your domestic pet shares ninety-nine percent of the same DNA as their wild counterparts. When animals, including your pet eat whole, raw food which is high in digestible protein and the natural nutrients, their health is optimized, paving the way for longevity and wellness."

I wondered about the differences between, raw, frozen pet food and freeze-dried or dehydrated food.

Dr. Buchoff continued, "The main difference is raw is minimally processed, retains its high moisture content, and does not require any application of heat that can put vital nutrients, beneficial bacteria, and enzymes at risk.

"The high heat processing used for dry kibble and canned foods depletes the nutritional value of your pet's food. Many of these products also contain grains and other starches, flavor enhancers, preservatives and other unhealthy ingredients to prolong shelf life and to mimic nature's own vitamins and minerals."

Dr. Buchoff added, that under the principles of Traditional Chinese Medicine (TCM), the body has both "yin," (cooling, quiet, passive), energy and "yang," (heat, inflammatory, aggressive), energy. Any imbalance in the yin/yang force is an indication of non-optimal health. "Too much yang energy may be present in pets with food allergies and intolerances, who seek cool places, pant heavily, and are very restless, while too much yin energy may be indicated in pets with poor appetites, weakness, fatigue, and incontinence, for example. Feeding cooling or neutral formulas to a pet with too much yang energy is recommended, as is feeding warming formulas to pets with yin abundance."

Dr. Fraser stated, "Diet is key! When the dog's diet is not appropriate, it leads to imbalance and inflammation in the body." She advocates for a complete and balanced whole food diet, raw, home cooked, or a minimally processed commercial diet, to ensure the optimal health of her patients.

When it comes to a choice, Dr. Mahaney recommends human grade food versus feed grade. "Human grade foods have a higher quality and a lower potential for toxins. That means foods that are all-natural, made from premium ingredients, which are free of by-products, preservatives, and fillers, which look like food, and are therefore minimally processed. For dogs that already have CCD,

DEMENTIA & ALZHEIMER'S – Prevention

foods that are rich in nutrients are best, and cooked is preferrable to raw for easier digestion."

Susan Thixton is a Pet Food Advocate and Pet Foodie and an author. "Pet Foodie," is an informal term for pet food consumers that provide their pet with health promoting delicious foods, rather than simply providing a pet food that meets basic nutritional needs. She said, "Most commercial pet foods depend on supplements to provide your pet with the required nutrition. However, any veterinarian or nutritionist will tell you natural, real foods are always a better source of nutrition than supplements. As example, in a single tablespoon of roasted chicken, your pet will be provided with eighteen amino acids, sixteen vitamins, ten minerals, protein and healthy fat. Steamed broccoli provides your pet with vitamin A, niacin, riboflavin, vitamin C, vitamin K and is a great fiber source. And the best part, all this nutrition is in its most recognizable form for your pet's body to utilize...it's food, not supplements.

"Meatloaf and green beans for your dinner tonight? Share your meal with your pet. Pull some of the ground beef before you add seasoning. For raw simply feed to your pet. For cooked, make a small meatloaf of ground beef, green beans, and tomato paste. Bake until lightly done, cool and serve! Your dog can share some of almost any meal you prepare. Share your roasted chicken, your cooled baked sweet potato, or even a few bites of your steak! A Pet Foodie makes sure that their pets have some real food every single day! Pet Foodie pets get a variety of real food added to their daily diet and benefit from the nutrition it provides!!!"

Ms. Thixton' s advice for pet parents, "I want you to become a Pet Foodie slowly. Examples of the best way to do this are, Ten-Pound Dog - begin with approximately one teaspoon of meat or fish, two teaspoons of vegetables, lightly cooked and, or one teaspoon fruit added to the regular diet daily. Increase weekly until one-third of the diet is a variety of real food.

"For a Thirty-Pound Dog, begin with approximately one tablespoon of meat or fish, two tablespoons of lightly cooked vegetables and, or one tablespoon fruit added to the regular diet daily. Increase weekly until one-third of the diet is a variety of real food.

SHAMROCK'S STORY

"For a Sixty-Pound Plus Dog, begin with approximately two tablespoons of meat or fish, four tablespoons of lightly cooked vegetables, and, or two tablespoons fruit added to the regular diet daily. Increase weekly until one-third of the diet is a variety of real food.

"Very, Very Important! Before you transition your pet to a Pet Foodie pet, inform your veterinarian. Some pets might have diet restrictions that need to be addressed. Don't give more than one-third of the diet as real food unless you follow recipes or add supplements to balance the diet.

"You can share your food or prepare just for your pet. Some Pet Foodies share their own meals with their pet. An example of sharing would be a couple of bites of scrambled egg with breakfast and, a couple of bites of steak and broccoli with dinner. And some Pet Foodies prepare meals in advance for their dog.

"Here is a sample recipe for 'Pet Foodie Food' for dogs. Start with one cup cubed chicken, dark and, or, light meat, one cup steamed broccoli cut into bite size pieces, one cup black beans boiled until soft, one-half cup apple cubes, lightly steamed peeling removed. Combine all the ingredients. Store in BPA free container. Be sure to serve within three days of preparation or freeze any portion not served within three days."

Ms. Thixton added, "PLEASE NOTE, pet parents should not randomly give their pet solely home prepared foods without following a recipe for a balanced diet, a diet that provides all of the required nutrients in the proper amounts. Be sure to speak with your veterinarian first, before making dietary changes!"

Apples have been recommended by many of the veterinarians, and as a pet parent that loved to give apples to Shamrock, I wanted to explain that I never gave her the seeds in the core. I had read that apple seeds contain a substance called amygdalin that can release cyanide when it interacts with digestive enzymes. Because of this statement, I discussed giving Shamrock apples with her veterinarian and did not feed her the seeds. Because I do not want to give any medical advice, I can only tell you what I did and definitely suggest you speak with your veterinarian.

*(Note: See below under Commercial Dog Food, subtopic, "Foods to Avoid." Look for the * in that list regarding this issue).

DEMENTIA & ALZHEIMER'S – Prevention

Commercial Dog Food -Pro's & Con's
Veterinarians Weigh In

Dr. Bullen laid out a wonderful way to ensure that you are getting food from a good, reliable company. "Step one, the company should have a designated department for nutrition. Step two, when you call their nutrition department speak to experts from said department, not random employees. Step three, be sure there are designated teams who handle quality control.

"Also, when a company owns their own manufacturing facility, they tend to have more say in their product development and therefore can maintain a better-quality control. They often will more readily test ingredients, being sure there are no contaminants, and making sure that during manufacturing nothing accidentally gets into the food. They also test for pathogens and molds and will send samples out to independent labs to do internal testing to make sure everything is accurate. They may also perform tests to determine diet digestibility and feeding trials to understand how the ingredients stay together best for pets to thrive.

"The best companies are one's that are transparent." If they say essential nutritional information is proprietary, Dr. Bullen is often less likely to recommend their food. Another way to tell if a company is reliable is to visit their web site and check to see if there is any misleading or partial information. She suggested asking questions such as, "Are they doing and sharing research? Do they have peer reviewed information, and is it backed by public disclosed information?" Dr. Bullen also said, "If a food makes a unique or wild claim, the company needs to show the supporting data." But she wants pet parents to know that even if their diet is great, but their employees' bad mouth other foods or their marketing has misleading information; she suggests caution.

I really appreciated the advice about commercial dog food producers, but my concern was the food itself. Next, I asked, "What about all the dog food that is recalled each year?"

Dr. Bullen pointed out that there are times when these are simply human error. But she emphasized, "When a company does a voluntary recall, it is because the company realizes that something slipped through, and they are trying to make it right and involve the

FDA to facilitate. Companies that hold to these highest standards are Purina, Royal Canin and Hills."

Taking all this information into account, everyone has their preferences. There are lots of factors that go into the decision of which dog food to choose: cost, ease of purchase, preparation and or feeding, but also which food is really the best for your dog. As you can see when you, as the pet parent, are trying to decide what food to feed your dog at their stage of growth or for prevention or during disease, this is a discussion you should have with your veterinarian.

But this discussion about food to feed is not complete without a list of what food to avoid!

Foods To Avoid-Avoid-Avoid!
In addition to what to feed your dog, Dr. Dodds provided this list of avoid!

"Avoiding Glutens: Protect brain function in geriatrics and those with gluten intolerance by avoiding wheat, barley, rye, oats unless labeled gluten-free, kamut, spelt, farro, and couscous, which are linked with impairment of brain function, including learning disabilities, attention-deficit-hyperactivity disorder, and memory problems. Gluten sensitivity may manifest exclusively as a neurological disease.

"Avoiding carbs with high Glycemic Index! Impaired glucose metabolism caused by sugary foods can promote brain starvation, leading to memory problems, like canine cognitive dysfunction. These foods can also lead to hunger-related behavioral problems. Simple carbohydrates digest and absorb quickly, hence the rapid rise and fall in blood sugar concentrations, so pets feel hungry again quickly."

Then There Is Never, Never, Never FOOD Land
Never Give These Foods To Your Dog!
I could not conclude a chapter about diet without a list of foods NEVER to feed your dog! These two lists agree on most foods, and each adds other foods. Please NEVER give any of these to your dog!

DEMENTIA & ALZHEIMER'S – Prevention

Dr. Kass provided a list of foods that are so important to know about! "But no matter what we feed our pets we must 'NEVER' give them people foods that are poisonous to their bodies"

These foods have been put in alphabetical order for ease of identifying foods not to feed!

"The list contains:

alcohol	*apple seeds (contain cyanide)
chocolate	cooked bones
corn cobs	fat trimmings
fruit pits -(large)	grapes
macadamia nuts	onions
raisins"	

And Ms. Thixton the pet foodie said, "Good to feed, would include just about any food, **excluding the following:**

"Alcohol	Caffeinated beverages
Candy	Chocolate
Cooked bones	Fat trimmings
*Fruit seeds and pits	Gum
Garlic raw	Grapes
Macadamia Nuts	Onions
Raisins	Salty/Sugary foods
Yeast dough."	

*(Note: refers to apple seeds previously mentioned to avoid)

My research also revealed that as much as dogs love peanut butter and it makes a great treat and an even better help for getting dogs to take pills this **WARNING** is for an additive!

Please always read labels and "NEVER" give your dog a product that contains the additive, "**Xylitol!**" This additive can cause toxicity within 10 to 15 minutes of a pet eating a product containing xylitol or may be delayed for several hours. Because it can cause low blood sugar in dogs they can throw up or even have a seizure, or just seem weak and pass out. Liver damage can occur within a few hours or in a few days. If your pet ingests this product don't hesitate to get them to a veterinarian immediately!

To be safe, ALWAYS read labels.

This sugar substitute can be hidden in many products. I found it in a new toothpaste I tried, and in mints. Xylitol can also be in gum and some chocolate baking goods, vitamins and even in cosmetics.

SHAMROCK'S STORY

I cannot stress enough how important it is to know what's in products before we give them to our dog's...that also might be anything they could accidently get into!

Supplements -
List Of Supplements:
In order to better understand supplements here is a list of some that are mentioned.

Antioxidants – protect cells from free radical damage and oxidation like vitamin A, C, and E, also found in broccoli and other leafy green vegetables

Antinol – a joint supplement

Astaxanthin - a carotenoid found in fish like salmon

B Vitamins – can support the immune system, boost energy, promote cell health, help with brain function, concentration, nerve function and appetite

Bacopa - a plant used in traditional Indian Ayurvedic medicine. Currently used for Alzheimer's, promotes mental clarity and focus and helps memory

CBD oil - cannabidiol, found in cannabis plants *(Note: See CBD Oil -pg 183).

CoQ10 -ubiquinol- produces cellar energy for your heart and other organs

Ginkgo Biloba – has powerful antioxidant qualities

Green Lipped Mussels - have omega-3 fatty acids

Keto Diet – diet built around high-fat, adequate-protein, low-carbohydrates

Lion's mane mushroom- may enhance brain function, help with anxiety and depression

Melatonin – a hormone the brain produces which helps with sleep,

MUFA's – Monounsaturated Fatty Acids- plant based found in food

Omega Fatty Acids, - omega-3 and 6 are unsaturated fats the body does not make that are good fats helpful for brain health and fighting inflammation and treating chronic disease. Only omega-9 is less essential as the body does make this

DEMENTIA & ALZHEIMER'S – Prevention

PUFA's – Poly Unsaturated Fatty Acids - unsaturated fat that is found in the diet in both plant-based foods and animal sources.

Selenium- a mineral that helps with thyroid and immune functions

Turmeric /golden paste extract- blend of turmeric powder, ground black pepper and healthy fats, like coconut oil, olive oil

So how do we improve cognitive function?

Speech
to the KENNEL CLUB
Dr. W. Jean Dodds

"There are nutrients that can be included in the diet.

Anthocyanins (pigmented foods): Give berries their rich pigment; antioxidants; also benefit cognitive health of senior dogs, and is most potent is Aronia, the chokeberry; and is a greater antioxidant than all other berries and has anti-cancer; anti-bacterial, anti-viral and even anti-diabetic; and anti-inflammatory properties.

DHA and EPA omega-3 fatty acids: Fight obesity, decrease inflammation, combat arthritis and cancer, and promote overall health. They benefit neurotransmission and cognition, plus brain health and structure, since the brain contains up to 60% fat, and are used together to benefit mood. EPA from marine sources such as fish oil decrease the cytokines of depression. Individuals reactive to white fish (including sardines and herring) or salmon oils can use krill oil, anchovy oil, and plant oils (olive, moringa, sunflower, safflower, hemp).

Medium-Chain Triglycerides (MCTs): like coconut oil, break down and absorb rapidly, unlike fats. They're a quick source of non-carbohydrate energy, and readily cross the blood-brain barrier supplying 20% of brain energy requirements. MCT's are also important for ketone production, which help the body use omega-3 fatty acids more efficiently and helps age-related cognitive decline by providing alternative source of brain energy.

SHAMROCK'S STORY

Phosphatidylserine (PS): Commercial animal products combine PS as with gingko biloba, vit. E, pyridoxine (vit. B6) and grape-skin extract, which improve canine cognitive function, decrease sleeping problems, apathy, and disorientation, Increases playful behavior and response to commands.

Phosphatidylcholine: Phospholipid choline is critical for cell membrane structure and function. It increases production of acetylcholine which helps reverse signs of cognitive and other neurological disorders of aging pets.

SAMe (S-adenosyl methionine,): improves neuron membrane fluidity, increases serotonin and dopamine metabolites, reduces effects of depression in people, and may help Alzheimer's patients,

Silibinin (milk thistle extract): prevents impairment of both short-term memory and recognition memory. This nutrient works as an antioxidant which protects the brain from oxidative damage."

Speech reprinted with permission from Dr. Dodds

When your dog is diagnosed with dementia there are many supplements and prescription medicines that may help. Many of the veterinarians I spoke with were solidly in agreement about supplementation and in some cases even choosing the same supplements to help with this disease.

Here is some of their advice.

Dr. Bernard suggested, "The key is always prevention, so the earlier you can identify and start balancing patterns of deficiencies in the body, the better. In addition to foods, adding herbal formulas will help to strengthen the nerves and can alleviate many of the clinical signs.

"The same goes for the use of antioxidants like vitamin E, selenium, CoQ10, also known as, ubiquinol, and astaxanthin in senior patients. It's best to start using these before, or as soon as early signs of dementia are noted."

Dr. DePorter stated, "Prevention may truly be the best medicine. Dietary supplements may provide an efficient way to include

DEMENTIA & ALZHEIMER'S – Prevention

antioxidants in a pet's diet. These supplements may be especially beneficial if initiated before the onset of clinical signs of cognitive impairment but there are no long-term clinical trials to support this extrapolation. And a combination antioxidant therapy may be more effective than single component supplementation."

She also talked about SAMe [S-Adenosyl-L-methionine], which is found in all living cells and is formed from methionine and ATP. SAMe may help to maintain cell membrane fluidity, receptor function, and the turnover of monoamine transmitters, as well as increase the production of glutathione. In a placebo-controlled trial in dogs, greater improvement in activity and awareness was reported in the SAMe group after 8 weeks.

Dr. Mahaney told me, "It is also important to supplement your dog's food with antioxidants, and anti-inflammatory fish oils, such as, omega fatty acids, 3 and 9, which are anti-inflammatory. Although the body needs omega-6 fatty acids to form healthy tissues, he recommends just letting pets get omega-6 from their meals, as supplementation with omega-6 could promote inflammation." He also suggested, "SAMe and vitamin E can also be helpful, as can herbs such as turmeric and ginger."

I mentioned to Dr. Mahaney that I gave Shamrock a teaspoon of Salmon Oil twice a day, which is full of omega fatty acid, and she loved it! Not only was it rich in anti-inflammatory oils, but because of the smell she got a lot of "fun sniffing!"

He agreed that the good supplement and the "smell" stimulation, made for a good combination.

Dr. Katz recommended using supplements that are complex antioxidants, "As aging is caused by oxidative damage."

Dr. Bullen also mentioned certain antioxidant and mitochondrial supporting supplements to try such as: alpha lipoic acid, L-Carnitine, and SAM-e with milk thistle.

Dr. Kass advised, "Supplements are very important. Fish oil is a great source of omega-3 fatty acids which are important for brain health. And it is important that any diet be balanced with proper vitamins and minerals to keep nerves and brain functioning optimally.

"Some herbs can be helpful too. Ginkgo biloba and Bacopa are two that have been studied and shown to have benefits for brain health.

"Oxidative stress is a major component of inflammation in the brain and elsewhere in the body." Dr. Kass said instead of taking antioxidant supplements there are products that she strongly recommended *(Note: See Recommendations-pg.250). "These products work to lower oxidative stress. by upregulating the natural antioxidant pathways in the body, which can work at the cellular level effectively slowing or reversing aging."

Dr. Rivera advised, "You can also speak with your veterinarian about vitamins such as B-12 and vitamin E, which are indicated to help nerve regeneration. But as with adding anything, they can provide the proper dosing and tell you if there are any contraindications."

Dr. Landau may suggest changing the dog's diet to minimally processed foods and foods that can adjust the Yin and Yang. Then he would add in specific supplementation to help the nervous system function better as well. Supplementing with fish oil to slow degeneration and inflammation to the nervous system can also help.

Dr. Katz told me, "There are also Chinese herbs and formulas that may help with restlessness at night by adjusting for a Yin deficiency."

Dr. Mallu clarified, "In terms of Chinese medicine this is a deficiency of Yin, the peaceful cooling water nighttime energy. This yin deficiency thus causes the animal to pace at night and sleep during the day. and I assess my patients in terms of Chinese medicine and see if we need to nourish their kidney Yin with Chinese herbs.

"We also look at their diet and feed neutral meats, pork, duck, beef while avoiding warm meats, chicken venison and lamb."

DEMENTIA & ALZHEIMER'S – Prevention

Dr. Mar said, "Herbal preparations can be given based on Chinese diagnosis, which will help balance the pet's deficiency needs."

Sometimes herbs and supplements can address early dementia, but more often, Dr. Fallek has found homeopathy to be the key to success.

Diet, Supplements, Prescription Food & Medicines

What is prescription or Veterinary dog food? From my research I learned that these foods are formulated to meet specific health needs. The companies that sell them require veterinary approval, which is done by prescription. They can be purchased through your veterinarian, or at online sites. Places where you can purchase these products before checkout will state that veterinarian approval is required for purchase. They will ask for your pet and veterinarian's information and will only complete the order when they receive verification from your veterinarian.

The need for the prescription can delay purchase, but another concern for consumers may be that these foods are very expensive. Since these are specifically formulated for health issues it is extremely important that you discuss all aspects of these foods with your veterinarian before you begin your purchase.

Dr. Radosta said, "If the dog's testing is normal, but the pet still shows signs of CCDS, the veterinarian can prescribe a diet such as Purina Neuro Care."

She continued, "For dogs that are not sleeping, the pet parent can add a supplement called, SAMe," (This supplement is for CCDS clinical signs, but not specifically for dogs who aren't sleeping), "but does support mental and cognitive health in dogs. SAMe can also help increase serotonin, which regulates appetite, digestion, sleep, and memory.

"There are other factors to take into consideration. If a dog has been anxious all their life, that anxiety will get worse as they age. There are prescription medications such as diazepam that can help slow the progression.

SHAMROCK'S STORY

"If none of these treatments work, the next step might be selegiline, which is an antidepressant. This drug can have side effects and cannot be stopped abruptly." But Dr. Radosta also stresses, as with any prescription medications, they sometimes need to be adjusted or changed to get the best results. "Even after the dog has been on the medication for a while, these drugs may need to be tweaked and adjusted according to the dog's signs and symptom changes."

Dr. DePorter talked with me about selegiline, also known as Anipryl, and Selgian. "This oral prescription medication is used to treat cognitive dysfunction in dogs." CDS is a progressive disorder and regression is inevitable. Dogs who improve while taking selegiline should continue receiving this medication; lifelong. *(Note: Selegiline should not be used concurrently with other monoamine oxidase, (MAO) inhibitors, including amitraz, (Mitaban® Preventic®. Extreme care should be exercised with selective medications such as antidepressants, narcotics, dextromethorphan, buspirone, trazodone, or tramadol).

Dr. Tynes spoke a great deal about diet and supplements. Her advice, "It is better to spend, money on good diets, appropriate diagnostics, medications and, or supplements."

She also emphasized, "But even with supplementation, the evidence shows the sooner they are started the better they will work. There are supplements that have been studied and shown to help, such as, fish oil omega-3, SAM-e, and MCT oils. Many of these are also recommended for humans with dementia."

She further explained that omega-3 long-chain, polyunsaturated fatty acids (PUFAs) are considered fundamental to brain function, with eicosatetraenoic acid (EPA) and docosahexaenoic acid (DHA) considered most important. PUFAs play a vital role in maintaining cell membrane structure, and cell-to-cell communication. "Studies in humans providing DHA and EPA together in the form of fish oils have shown that they can improve cognition in healthy adults and slow cognitive decline in those with mild impairment. For aging dogs, PUFAs are frequently combined with other supplements or in diets for brain health, and based on evidence, they are likely to be helpful.

DEMENTIA & ALZHEIMER'S – Prevention

"Studies in humans also have shown that physical and mental activity and diets containing fruits, vegetables, seeds, legumes, nuts and fish oils, combined with a diet that includes both omega-3 fatty acids and B vitamins, can help to slow cognitive decline. Studies in laboratory beagles have shown a beneficial effect of nutrition on improving signs and slowing progression of CDS in dogs. In one study, dogs fed high-quality commercial diets appropriate to their age, size, or health, were two point eight times less likely to develop CDS than dogs fed low-quality commercial food or table-scraps.

"SAMe is another supplement that may be helpful in ageing dogs. Studies in humans have shown that decreased levels of SAMe are associated with the presence of Alzheimer disease and supplementation with SAMe leads to higher levels in the brain."

When I asked Dr. Tynes about the human progress seen with the Keto diet in treating dementia, she said, "The Keto diet may help because the diet includes foods that increase ketones in the brain, which should also help in dogs, but there is not a lot of dog research on the subject, so she recommends supplementing with diets high in MCT oils and antioxidants."

She believes proper diet is critical for optimal health and maintaining good cognitive functions. "There is a growing body of evidence supporting the role of certain nutritional supplements and dietary ingredients in cognitive and behavioral health. Although much of the research is in laboratory animals and humans, extrapolation of the data, combined with the studies in dogs makes this mode of therapy promising.

"Because the data demonstrates that cognitive dysfunction is most successfully managed when identified early in the course of the problem, clinicians should be proactive in screening patients for these conditions.

"Elderly dogs should be seen twice yearly by their veterinarian and screened using the DISHAA scale so that signs of CDS can be recognized earlier than later. Clinicians should become familiar with each supplement's ingredients and their mode of action as well as the patient history and any current medications and supplements being given before recommending additional medications or supplements.

"Special diets and nutritional supplementation should always be used in conjunction with a complete program of environmental management, enrichment, and behavior modification in order to increase the likelihood of the best outcome."

Dr. Tynes added, "Avoid new dog food fads. Dogs are omnivores and their dietary needs are similar to humans." She trusts companies such as Hills, Royal Canine, and Purina because they invest in the research that helps us to better understand and manage conditions such as CDS. They all make diets that are thoroughly tested and found to be appropriate for animals of certain ages and in some cases with certain medical conditions. One of the best indicators of the food's nutritional value for your pet is to look at the first four ingredients. If they are natural and food you would eat, and you can understand and pronounce the rest of the ingredients, that is a pretty good dog food.

She prefers following established research, but if the tried-and-true process does not work after sufficient time, she feels there is no reason not to try other things. Home cooked diets are fine as long as you have a veterinarian or veterinary nutritionist assist you with the recipe. "With any intervention, you must always compare risks to benefits. Raw diets have been shown to carry pathogens that can be problematic for the dog and make people very ill." Dr. Tynes said, if she saw a home-made cooked diet from a veterinarian who is also board certified in nutrition, then she would feel okay."

Regarding diet, Dr. Villalobos stated, "Supplementing with fatty acids may be beneficial for better brain and neurological function."

My research indicated that when pets are ill and don't want to eat there is an even greater need for good supplements to balance what they are not getting from food. One such supplement used with dogs that are cognitively challenged, as with dementia, is lion's mane mushroom. I never tried this supplement, however, from discussions with some veterinarians, they felt the results were good. Other's felt the jury was still out or had no knowledge of this supplement. Again, if you investigate and think this might be a good choice for your dog, please first discuss this with your veterinarian.

Dr. Bernard had said that he has not seen any official data on the use of "Lion's mane mushroom," for dogs with degenerative neurological conditions, but that he has come across it in some

DEMENTIA & ALZHEIMER'S – Prevention

human studies and has mentioned it to several of his pet parents to try. He said, "I can't say how much it helps, but I'm optimistic based on human studies that it can only help."

Dr. Holly Landes, who practices Traditional Chinese Veterinary Medicine, told me, "Supplements can be expensive, but, I have not had any luck with pharmaceuticals, personally."

Dr. Bartner said, "Diets containing high concentrations of MCT have shown some promise in dogs."

Dr. Bassingthwaighte explained, "For older dogs seven to eight years of age, this is a good time to start an active holistic treatment plan and add other supplements like green-lipped mussels, Antinol, turmeric golden paste extract, or CBD oil."

He added, "There are also many other supplements that can help including, SAMe, ginkgo biloba, melatonin, which helps with sleep, and vitamins B, C, and E. A discussion with your veterinarian as to which is best, and the proper doses for your dog, is recommended. Also, you can seek a holistic veterinarian or a skilled naturopath for more advice."

There has been a revolution of famous people promoting their own pet foods and I wanted to know about "CELEBRITY" and "Boutique" diets for dogs. And what about when they target "buzz words" that indicate they can help with disease with added supplements?

Dr. Bullen suggested these are, "Just fads! The food could be fine, but the marketing is driving the information and that is not how dog food should be chosen."

Dr. Cindy Baker, practices Traditional Chinese Medicine and uses many of its modalities. She provided some diverse information about supplements. "Older dogs have complex diseases that contribute to cognitive decline. No two patients are alike. One pet may be on seven or eight supplements and medications, while another just needs support for memory.

SHAMROCK'S STORY

"There are also complex supplements that include more than one nutrient."

Dr. Baker continued, "That takes me to my soap box on supplements. Quality, safety, dosage, and efficacy are key. Many people read reviews or the manufacturer's own 'research'. Third party research and testing will inform us if the supplement has the ingredients listed, since supplements and nutraceuticals are not regulated by the Food and Drug Administration.

"Safety should be based on true research and use. Doses for animals are often extrapolated by human studies but may not be accurate. Efficacy is proven once a product faces double blind studies and long-term use.

"One example is omega-3 fatty acids which have profoundly positive effects on the brain, heart, joints, and kidneys. The doses in many fish oil products are much too low to impact these organs in the dog. Sometimes, dogs cannot even tolerate the correct doses unless it's part of the diet, as in baked in the food. Homemade diets may not have enough antioxidant support to help the body use the omega-3's properly, so the diet must be considered in adding these.

"First, check the serving size. Many times, you will need 2-3 capsules per serving. The concentration of the ingredients is given 'per serving,' so you need to know how many capsules, teaspoons, milliliters written as 'ml', this is indicating.

"Secondly, check the ingredient list for the actual amount of EPA, known as eicosatetraenoic acid, and DHA, the abbreviation for docosahexaenoic acid. For inflammation in our pets, these are the two important types. Your veterinarian can suggest the desired amounts of EPA and DHA depending on the area of the body that we are treating, and the size of your pet.

"The way to calculate the amount of omega-3 is, add together the EPA and DHA components. This is the actual useful omega-3 in the capsule or liquid that is significant. If milligrams, written as 'mg', are not listed, and only percentages are given, you can call the company to get the actual amounts if you want to use the product.

"Many over the counter products will have, for example 'one-thousand milligrams Fish Oil' on the label. When you check the ingredients, however, you may find only one hundred-twenty EPA and sixty milligrams DHA. This means if your dog should have one

DEMENTIA & ALZHEIMER'S – Prevention

thousand milligrams, you need five capsules to make up one-thousand milligrams of the useful components.

"Most of the time, we want to give the smallest volume of liquid or capsules with the greatest concentration of the product need.

"Thirdly, check for 'Good Manufacturing Practice labels.' These indicate the product complies with safety and ingredient standards, as well as manufacturing protocols. For pet supplements, look for 'NASC' on the label. This is the 'National Animal Supplement Council'. This indicates the manufacturer submits to intermittent testing of ingredients to ensure the label reflects the true ingredients indicated, with no contaminant, as well as other standards."

Again Dr. Baker stressed, "I would also add that appropriate doses should be discussed with the pet's doctor as these evolve."

I am also listing supplements that I used for Shamrock. This is not a recommendation but just a list of supplements, but I cannot confirm or deny their help for her condition

These supplements were okayed by Shamrock's veterinarian.
Only Natural Pet® Senior Brain Wellness Soft Dog Chews
Vedco NutriVed Chewable Vitamins for Dogs 180 Tablets
Turmeric -Sprinkled on her food
Salmon oil
GABA
Brewer's Yeast

If you believe any of these may help your dog, please research the supplement and because each dog has unique needs, do not start any supplement without first discussing the supplement and appropriate dosage with your veterinarian.

Early Prevention Steps To Take

I know there is no guarantee that anything we do will prevent our sweet babies from getting dementia, but many of these veterinarians believe strongly that when taking the right steps, we can give our precious puppies and even senior dogs a better chance against this dreaded disease. The consensus is that "Early Prevention," may be the best way to battle this disease!

I asked Dr. Haghighat what can be done with dogs that may have beginning signs of cognitive decline?

SHAMROCK'S STORY

He responded, "It depends on the animal and how far the disease has progressed. If the pet is not at an acute stage of the disease, then the pet's health can be restored, even at an older age, but again, everything depends on the progression. So, it becomes very important to see the veterinarian as soon as any signs indicate a cognitive issue, or unexplained pet changes."

When I spoke with Dr. Mahaney, I asked him about early prevention from the point of view of a veterinarian that sees a dog in their own environment. He suggested that a house call may help the veterinarian better evaluate the dog before, during and after any signs of cognitive issues. He stated, "The importance of starting puppies off on a good road, diet, exercise, and good behavioral traits can all be beneficial whether as a means of possibly preventing or delaying the onset of CCD."

Dr. Gardner told me cognitive dysfunction can start anywhere from seven years old and progress from there. There are several medical, dietary, and herbal therapeutic options available which can be discussed with veterinarians to help pet parents find the best options for them and their dog. With that being said, the sooner pets are started on these options, the better.

Dr. Landes said, "I also think it helps to start early with prevention, however, there is no way to predict which patients will be affected by CD, at least that I know of, that can be used in general practice, so often clinical signs are present before treatment is started."

Dr. Bartner explained, "The success of most treatments lies in early recognition, which can be very challenging. There may be signs of the disease, but in most cases, it is very difficult to recognize what might be cognitive and behavioral as opposed to what might have other physical causes. The bigger problem
 is that often signs are so slow in developing, and most people don't recognize them. It is human nature to rationalize an abnormal behavior and place it into a logical packet, but in doing so, pet parents may miss many more subtle or worsening signs. Many times, by seeing their dog every day, they may not distinguish that

DEMENTIA & ALZHEIMER'S – Prevention

the gradual signs they are seeing are 'abnormal.' Much like not realizing your child has grown taller until a visitor points it out. These subtle and gradual changes are the key to early detection. But we know from our own experiences, that in hindsight or retrospect, we usually see things more clearly."

And that was certainly the issue for me with Shamrock!

What's Happening To Me, Mommy?

SHAMROCK'S STORY

CANINE COGNITIVE DYSFUNCTION

From Disbelief to Realization

My baby has dementia...

Now What?

SHAMROCK'S STORY

Why Does My World Keep Changing?

16 Years Old

The next few months were very trying. Shamrock's symptoms would get better, and she seemed like herself again, then, just as quickly, she would get worse. The only guide I had was from what I saw based on my uncle's progression with dementia, from age 90 to 96 when he died of complications from Alzheimer's.

I made sure to remain acutely aware of changes in Shamrock. Many of her original behavioral symptoms were now becoming more acute and now physical symptoms were becoming more evident.

Sometimes she would bang into walls that she always knew were there or go outside and not know why she was there. I would catch her staring into space for long periods of time. She would maneuver herself into small places and then not be able to get out. Suddenly, she had no concept of how to back up.

Eating and sleeping became difficult tasks, I now had to sit on the floor and hand-feed her while I played games such as hide and seek, that were an attempt to keep her interested.

CANINE COGNITIVE DYSFUNCTION

She'd sleep in spurts, so I would lie down with her and gently stroke her forehead and between her eyes. This would sometimes calm her enough to go to sleep.

One of the hardest issues for me was not being able to comfort her. Shamrock didn't want to be held for any length of time, except for our hugs during "Doga" and daily massage...those were still the best times of the day!

There were days when she was so exhausted, she slept for prolonged periods of time. I used that time to search the internet for any information about these new symptoms. There was just too much to sort through, so I absorbed what I could and let my instincts and previous experiences as a pet parent, guide the way.

I had always eaten healthy foods, and I knew that diet was a big part of good health. I also knew that certain foods were good for the brain and were comfort food. I talked with her veterinarian and then started Shamrock on supplements that were supposed to be especially good brain support, but they didn't really seem to do a lot, so instead, I decided to make all her food.

I used fresh or frozen ingredients as the base and then added salmon and salmon oil, pumpkin, eggs, leafy green vegetables, and sweet potatoes. Sometimes she would eat normally but most times it was a fight.

One day I decided to lay out a blanket, like a picnic in my office. I turned on some Classical piano music and just let her walk around. Next, I offered Shamrock her favorite foods; one at a time. That finally got her eating. That controlled area in my office, gave me a better ability to keep her attention. By then, I also learned that if everything was given to her with peanut butter and apples, she would be willing to eat.

Shamrock's birthday at 16 years old was a milestone! Valentine's Day felt more like miracle day! She seemed to be doing much better, but unfortunately new problems were constantly cropping up.

We celebrated her birthday with her dog approved cake and candles, but Shamrock seemed more distracted. Nothing seemed to hold her attention, not even the ice cream she loved.

She had always enjoyed being outside in winter, when there was snow to romp and play in and lick, except now, she just stood still, but didn't want to come back in.

SHAMROCK'S STORY

She had never liked going out in the rain, but now she would just stand outside, getting soaking wet, and not move. The solution became, on rainy days she needed to be walked with a huge umbrella cover over her to keep her from getting soaked. Even with us next to her she kept stopping, so we needed to put her leash on and keep guiding her to walk.

As spring came, and the weather got nicer, I found myself walking with her even more, and waiting until she did what she was there for.

We would still take her for rides in the car to get ice cream, but now she shook all the time, so car rides were stopped.

With Shamrock being a Springer Spaniel, we had another issue to deal with. After years of jumping, and being very athletic, she developed back and hip problems. Even though I did "Doga" and manipulation therapy with her, there were days when the arthritis kicked in and she could barely walk. Thankfully, days like that were few and far between, and the doctors agreed that the daily "Doga" treatments kept her on her feet.

She now weighed approximately 23 pounds, having lost three pounds in a short period of time. Her doctors felt with everything going on and the medications, that the weight loss was understandable. They wanted to be sure Shamrock was getting her needed gentle exercise, but at times it was difficult as she was having more difficulty getting up and down. She did not like being carried, so my husband built a ramp for her to get to her bathroom area in the yard, which we called her "sandbox." Also, her issues with her hind quarter and back made it harder for her to get on or off the couch. We set up a ramp there and another for her to get on and off the bed. These all helped, but they signaled us to look at other areas that needed what we termed, "dog im- 'proofing!'"

It was difficult to recognize what a medium size dog might get into, so I got down on the floor for a "dog's eye view." I tried to see every place she could have trouble getting into, or out of.

The kitchen, which I thought was safe, became her enemy. Her food and water dishes were there, and she was always around when food was being prepared. But I would never have imagined that just walking across the ceramic floor would cause her legs to slide out from under her.

CANINE COGNITIVE DYSFUNCTION

One day she was drinking her water and as usual dripping it onto the floor. I turned to go into my office when I heard her cry out. I quickly ran into the kitchen to find her on the floor, in the water, not able to get up. After helping her onto my lap and drying her off, I just sat with her to calm her down.

That incident sparked us to move her water dish onto a floor mat on the carpet in the living room. That same day my husband built a gate system, and after that Shamrock was unhappily, barred from the kitchen.

Stairs were easy...or so we thought! They had to be blocked, but who knew that she could get her face under the gate and get stuck? Even when we thought we had protected her from everything, somehow, she would manage to find spots I never believed she could get into...like behind a toilet.

One day when I couldn't find her. I called out throughout the house...my heart was racing and then suddenly I heard a slight whimper. She had gotten herself stuck between the wall and the couch and couldn't get out! There didn't seem anyway for her to have gotten into such as small space, but again, another realization and another move of furniture to better protect her.

The next few months seemed much better and then around mid-June she totally changed. Shamrock had started walking constantly, non-stop, and not much could distract her. I would sit with her and do "Doga" or just massage her and that seemed calming, but as soon as I stopped, she would start to pace again.

I decided to let her work off her anxiety for a while and then go back to distracting her. Sometimes I would watch her walk...she seemed totally exhausted, and then suddenly she would slump down and be fast asleep, and she'd sleep for hours.

One night, things got very scary. I had been watching her walking and at one point she went to lie down but almost out of sheer will, got up and came over to me. I thought she was okay and sat on the floor with her. I hugged her and petted her, until she got up and walked the short distance from my office into the hall; just a few feet, and then, she just collapsed!

I ran over to her and thought she had passed out from exhaustion as she had done other times, but this time seemed different. I couldn't seem to wake her. She was still breathing, and her breath was steady and not labored. I held her in my arms and tried to comfort her. My husband picked her up and carried her to the bed. We wrapped her in a blanket and just held her and let her sleep; not knowing if she was ever going to wake up.

After about three hours of her being still, my husband decided to try something. He got a piece of bread and smothered it in peanut butter, then put it under her nose. In less than a minute, she opened her eyes and took the bread. I guess she was just hungry. The relief we both felt was incredible!

To help with the possible hunger and sleep deprivation or exhaustion issues we put in some new routines. I talked to Dr. Faust, and he suggested we add to her supplements and medications.

I added vitamins E, C and Brewer's Yeast and doubled up on the salmon oil which she loved. To encourage her to eat; peanut butter became a staple... so anything she ate got peanut butter added to it. I fed her something every three hours and would have frozen or lightly cooked vegetables and apples all with peanut butter ready for her at any time she seemed relaxed enough to eat. I made sure to always have calming music in the background and to use her favorite food games. Everything we did was to ensure that Shamrock was getting enough nourishment.

To help with her sleep issues, Dr. Faust suggested increasing the GABA and adding Trazodone, which he felt might help with her anxiety. He told me the medication also has had good results when used for behavioral stress.

After the medication change, I noticed Shamrock was having better sleep. The mild sedative in the medication seemed to help with her insomnia and allowed her to get a good, restful sleep.

In order to deal with her cognitive dysfunction, I was learning it required patience and trial and error. But that isn't always easy! At times it was so frustrating and left me feeling helpless; then something would happen, and I just had to deal with it. Like at two AM one morning. I was standing outside with Shamrock waiting for her to finally finish and be ready to go to sleep. After about an hour, she finally did go to the bathroom, but I wasn't quick enough to stop her from stepping in it. I led her to a safe place on the deck and ran inside and got a pot of soapy water and paper towels. I stuck her paws in the water and dried each one, but for the first time in her life, she was not being cooperative, she kept pulling her paws away. I was half asleep and had to concentrate on not getting upset.

CANINE COGNITIVE DYSFUNCTION

After another hour, I finally got her to sleep, and when I got into bed all I could think of was, *I am so very lucky that I work at home*. I cannot *even* imagine having to go to work within a few hours of that night.

Caring for an older dog with dementia, make family support essential at each stage of this disease. I was incredibly grateful that my husband was there to help both her and me!

Even with a great support system, this is a devastating disease that takes its toll on everyone; both physically and emotionally. It was so hard for us to watch our beloved baby Shamrock going through so much. All we could do was put on a thick skin and be prepared for wherever the journey would lead.

The days were filled with cooking for her, trying to get her to sleep as much as possible, making the house even more puppy-proofed, being sure to take her out, before she indicated she needed to go.

I called her veterinarian and kept him apprised of her progress, or lack thereof. We tweaked her meds and when she would show new symptoms, we would change them. We hoped each time her symptoms would get better...and sometimes they did. But the early morning hours, standing outside with her...just waiting, not knowing what would happen next, was the loneliest feeling in the world.

As the summer days were getting longer, I saw that I was going out with her more and it was getting later and later each night.

One night when she didn't want to sleep, I sat and held her until she started to fuss. I put her down and let her do her walking. She had gone into the other room, and I followed. To my surprise she was standing at the back door. I knew that meant she wanted to go out, but in the past, at least until that night, she had ALWAYS come to tell me.

I went outside with her and helped her down the ramp and into her sandbox area. She went immediately, but then walked around aimlessly for another 40 minutes. I tried to bring her in, but she kept heading back to the ramp. I thought she still had to go again. I didn't want to take her in, just in case, as she never had accidents, but as the long night faded into morning, I finally gave up. I got her leash and brought her back inside. I got her back in bed, but that only lasted fifteen minutes. Little did I know this was to become the norm.

SHAMROCK'S STORY

Because of these changes and not wanting her to have accidents, we put in a system where we wrote down when she would go to the bathroom. That way we got to see a pattern of sorts and could tell when we should take her out.

The biggest challenge was a week of torrential summer rain, lightning, and thunder. It pretty much rained day and night. The ground was muddy, and Shamrock was not always aware anymore of where she went. So now after a bowel movement my husband would have to go and shovel it out of the sandbox. That seemed to be the only way to limit the possibility of her stepping in it.

By the beginning of August, Shamrock had really become unsteady on her paws. Trying to take her out, while holding her leash and a large umbrella to cover her, was more than a challenge. Many times, we would walk and walk and usually come back in when she didn't do anything, and then have to walk her again.

The hardest time to deal with Shamrock's need to go out was right before she went to bed. Since her sleep was still erratic, I didn't want her constantly being disturbed thinking she had to go. No matter how long it took, we would wait for her to finish.

Sometimes it felt like a losing battle. But eventually we would get her in and put her in bed. Many times, within 15 minutes she'd be up again, standing at the back door, wanting to go out again.

To make matters worse, because at times, she was having trouble standing when she would go to the bathroom, she would leak on herself. I would use baby wipes when she came in, but that didn't prevent an infection on her tail. This area needed to be treated every time she went to the bathroom. First by washing her with a gentle baby soap, then applying an antibacterial cream. Shamrock hated to be washed, but again being a pet parent meant doing what needed to be done.

But That Was All Before Thing's Changed!

CANINE COGNITIVE DYSFUNCTION

Everything Is Spinning Out Of Control!

CIRCLES

Just when we thought everything was difficult enough, then the dreaded circles began! That changed everything. Instead of constantly walking, Shamrock was now turning in circles! The circles appeared to be more confusion or disorientation than anything, and we could see that she was becoming very agitated. During her circling, she had stopped responding when called and appeared totally unaware of anything. She walked in circles for hours without stopping, except occasionally to stare into a mirror or at a wall. There seemed to be no way to distract her.

For her protection, we closed off all the rooms and filled in all the areas where she might get stuck or hurt herself.

This new change only appeared to exacerbate her previous problems. There were more eating difficulties and constant thirst which resulted in her needing to go out more. But outside she would continue her circles instead of understanding the reason why she was there.

Another major problem that developed was the foods she had finally been happy eating, she now refused. I realized that food was another dementia issue that needed to be monitored closely. Shamrock originally had weighed 26 pounds throughout most of her adult life. Once her symptoms evolved and her appetite decreased, she dropped to 23 pounds and now, in less than a month, continued the weight loss, from 21 to 20 pounds. That signaled deep concern. Dr. Faust had made a point of wanting me to keep him alerted to her weight and once she went down to 19 pounds, more red flags went up!

These weight loss issues were very difficult to deal with as a pet parent, when you know your dog needs to eat, but you can't seem to find the way to encourage them to eat enough.

Dr. Faust had said Shamrock's lack of appetite, might be the disease, but also might be the medications which could cause her eating issues. Since regular food wasn't enough anymore, he advised me to add baby food, or canned mushed puppy food to Shamrock's home cooked foods. I discussed with him a menu that included healthy carbs and protein. He also recommended adding non sweetened cranberry water, to help flush out any toxins in her liver and to give Shamrock a small amount of sugar for energy.

In addition to hand feeding, I liquified many of her foods and used a syringe dropper to feed her. This helped me keep track of how much food she was actually consuming. I also had to put her on a leash to feed her so she couldn't do her circles and avoid me. Even all that didn't ensure that Shamrock would eat. It was still a fight....one which I had to win, even when it didn't make her happy!

Dr. Faust also mentioned another medicine that he said was more of a final try, Xanax. After discussing Shamrock's current issues, we decided to make the food adjustment and see if there was any change first, and then, if needed revisit adding the Xanax.

I knew that getting better sleep might even help Shamrock with her appetite. I approached the problem in the same way I did when my children were babies. I set up a sleep schedule for her and hoped that having a set routine might be of benefit.

I finally figured out after six hours of walking, she was ready for a nap. I needed to segregate her and lie down with her. I would hug her, rub her belly, and head and rub my hands very gently over her eyes. I would hum quiet music and stay with her until she totally fell asleep.

That could take 10 or 15 minutes, but when it did work, she would sleep for a couple of hours, except it didn't work all the time. Sometimes she would fall asleep, then suddenly wake only a few

CANINE COGNITIVE DYSFUNCTION

minutes later. When that happened, I would let her walk around to get sleepy again, then go through my routine to encourage her to sleep. Sometimes she would totally refuse, but I would keep trying because I knew she needed her nap.

Watching her patterns, I realized on the days when Shamrock napped for four or five hours, she would be up almost all night. Her total hours of sleep were still not enough and even after a good long nap, she would wake so drowsy, she didn't want to eat, or even go out.

I knew how important it was to keep up with her exercise routine, both for physical as well as emotional benefits. I would put Shamrock's leash on and walk her in a straight-line pattern; not allowing her to walk in circles. I hoped this exercise might help retrain her brain. We would walk to the end of a small area, then turn to the right, not to the left, which was normal for her to turn in her circles, then walk another straight line, never stopping. We would do laps, at least once a day or more. I kept hoping when we went back into the house, and I took the leash off, Shamrock would be fine. Instead, she would go right back to walking in circles. At least during our outside walks, she seemed more like herself again and it was wonderful to watch.

Dealing with her in the throes of this disease, I learned the importance of consistency. Having routines at set times, that she could count on, helped establish some normalcy, and at the very least, did not add to her confusion and frustrations.

As a pet parent, I would do anything to help my Shamrock, but I need to convey to you, the pet parent, that it is very hard to watch what this disease can do to your beloved baby.

Therefore, I stress again that prevention is the key and if signs do appear, be aware and don't wait...speak with your veterinarian

DEMENTIA & ALZHEIMER'S COGNITIVE TREATMENTS & THERAPIES

How To Deal With This Horrible Disease!

Once you understand and accept it

There are things that can be done

CAININE COGNITIVE - Treatments & Therapies

Treatments & Therapies - Who Does What?

When we start to look at treatments or therapies which can be used when dealing with cognitive issues, such as, dementia and Alzheimer's, we first need to look again at the different veterinary practices, but this time with an eye toward some of the tools they might utilize.

Conventional or Traditional - blood work, x-rays, ultrasounds, prescription drugs

Integrative – combines traditional with holistic – therefore uses less medicines, more diagnostic and testing tools

Holistic – treats the whole pet rather than specific symptoms, uses tools such as chiropractic and more

Homeopathy – uses natural sources in diluted amounts to treat the causes, remedies are based on the idea, "like cures like"

TCM - Traditional Chinese Medicine - herbal therapy, with Chinese herbs, compounds and Acupuncture, Traditional Chinese massage, and manipulation

And Additional Categories of Veterinary Specialties

Behaviorist – behavior determines treatment

Dental – non anesthetic cleaning procedure

House Call – environment determines requirements

Neurologists – possible MRI, prescription medications

Nutritionists – dietary and or supplemental changes,

Researchers - studies to determine treatments

SHAMROCK'S STORY

This list is just a basic idea of veterinary practices and so I questioned some of the veterinarians I spoke with to get a better understanding

How Veterinarians Approach Treatments For Cognitive Disease

Although Dr. Fallek trained as a conventional veterinarian, she now uses more holistic modalities, such as acupuncture, homeopathy, and herbs. Her treatment plan for pets is highly individualized and considers, not only the conventional markers of disease, such as bloodwork, X-rays, and ultrasounds, but also uses the animal's mental and emotional makeup, and their relationship to their environment. She said, "Normal aging may play a part in dementia, both body and mind can deteriorate with time, and added stressors can speed up the process." During her 25 years practicing holistic medicine, she has found that emotions can play a big part in cognitive dysfunction. "Checking out" can be the dog's mechanism to cope with physical or emotional issues.

Dr. Mar spoke about her concept of pet care. She utilizes both contemporary and alternative medicine to ensure that pet parents are educated on pet health and pet care, especially regarding the benefits of integrative medicine and how it can treat a variety of conditions in pets.

She clarified, "I want to help people directly by giving them practical steps to improve their pet's mental, physical and spiritual health."

She continued by explaining that because dogs have different stages of cognitive decline, she doesn't usually see pets until they are in the latter depths of the disease and sometimes that doesn't leave enough time to prevent further progression.

During the Pandemic and with the Covid restrictions, pet parents were home more, so they tended to identify a lot of signs early which they wouldn't normally have noticed. This led to pet parents bringing in their dogs sooner, which gave Dr. Mar a better chance of using integrative techniques to slow, or even prevent the disease.

CAININE COGNITIVE - Treatments & Therapies

Because Dr. Tynes is a Veterinary Behaviorist she helped me understand how looking at a dog's behavior was an approach to treating dementia in dogs. The term, "Behaviorist," refers to a veterinarian who looks at a pet's behavior to diagnose and treat medical, and or behavioral conditions, and that Dr. Tynes has trained in both sciences to evaluate conditions from both components.

As a Pitcairn Institute Instructor, Dr. Melling offered, "The Pitcairn Institute teaches 'Classical Homeopathy,' a practice which uses one homeopathic medicine at a time, rather than combination remedies, which is more accurately known as homotoxicology. Classical homeopathy is a very precise form of treatment that allows us to give one medicine and observe the patient's response."

After that conversation, I was extremely interested to speak with Dr. Wendy Jensen of the Pitcairn Institute of Veterinary Homeopathy because her journey in veterinary medicine took her from traditional medicine to homeopathy. She said, "When a pet presents with a problem, traditional medicine prescribes a drug, the homeopath looks for causes and zeroes in on the dog's whole life, early trauma, digestive problems, or anything that might have an effect."

House call veterinarians are becoming more a norm and there are a few that I spoke with that gave me more insight into why.

Dr. Fraser takes advantage of this unique approach in her practice; meaning she goes to the pet patient's home, instead of them coming to her, and uses integrative/holistic veterinary medicine as her guide to help both the pet and the family.

Dr. Jensen told me she also has a busy "house call" practice that uses hands-on techniques in homeopathy that she learned during her training at the Pitcairn Institute. These techniques help her bring dogs to better health and pet parents to better understanding.

SHAMROCK'S STORY

Dr. Mahaney also has a "house call practice," and he stated, "The importance of seeing the pet in their home environment gives him a perspective that most veterinarians never have."

He explained why the house call visit is so important for a dog and their family. "When he spends time seeing the dog's household, it is like a 'big breath' of information that he cannot otherwise get from an office visit. He can examine the dog's environment from a veterinarian's eye and see the adjustments that can be made to make the dog's home life as safe as possible. These visits give him an opportunity to look closely at the house and talk to the parents in terms of pet health and pet safety. Then he can suggest procedures they can easily implement that will help eliminate the causes of pet and family distress and struggle, especially during the difficult days of navigating this disease."

But the house call is not the end of how he helps these families and pets dealing with CCD. He mentioned the incredible resources of the technology age, whereby the pet parents can keep him apprised of changes with videos, or zoom video conferences, so he can easily see what's going on.

Through this technology, if a dog does begin to show signs, Dr. Mahaney is better prepared to spot changes in their routines and their family interaction, such as distancing, anxiety, changes in appetite, elimination and being up at night. He feels this is one of the differences and advantages of being a "house call" veterinarian.

The more I talked with these, "House Call" veterinarians, the more I realized what an incredible tool this is. I can see how the house call method would be so helpful for pet parents dealing with this disease and I wished I knew that something like that was available to me for Shamrock.

I told Dr. Mahaney that when I started to notice some of her issues, such as: slipping on the kitchen floor, unsteady gait, bumping into furniture, and standing and staring, I knew I had to do something to ensure her safety in the house she grew up in; that now, at age 16, was no longer safe for her.

When Shamrock was going through her worst days, her veterinarian suggested a video would help him see what she was doing, but I couldn't seem to catch her at the right times. I know that might have helped him to better understand what I was trying to explain…and in turn better help her.

CAININE COGNITIVE - Treatments & Therapies

But after speaking with Dr. Mahaney, I realized how each step: the phone call, the office visit, the home video, can also be taken another step when a veterinarian can visit a dog like Shamrock in her home.

Having a new set of eyes in your dog's home environment may be one of the most significant changes a pet parent can make.

I now know that my pet protection home issues, were only solved by the blind leading the blind, and trial and error. If I had had a "House Call," veterinarian visit Shamrock in her home environment, issues we experienced might have been prevented

Seeing a dog that is developing dementia in their home is very advantageous. But visiting the dog throughout the stages of the disease and seeing how the dog responds in its environment, can be even more helpful. It can keep the pet safe; notice the unnoticed and help the family to make a better, safer setting for the dog and themselves.

Next, I explored what the Homeopathic and Holistic position on treatment for this disease might be. I asked Dr. Melling, "How do you approach treatment of a dog that presents with signs of CDS?"

She responded, "We consider the emotional, mental, and physical symptoms and also evaluate the diet, exercise, and living environment. Homeopathic veterinarians are holistic practitioners that look at all the symptoms in a patient to identify a matching medicine that will stimulate a healing response. Instead of naming diseases, homeopaths see each patient as having their own unique illness, because even patients with the same 'disease' such as CDS do not all have the same symptoms. Some dogs have altered appetites, while others demonstrate confusion and forget their training. So instead of having one homeopathic treatment for CDS, we make a list of the characteristic symptoms that make one dog's CDS their own, unique demonstration of the illness, and identify a matching homeopathic medicine to treat their symptoms. Therefore, we see each patient as having their own unique disease."

I told Dr. Melling, I had nine dogs, and until Shamrock, never had any experience like this...So I asked, "What do you recommend for the pet parent going through this horrendous disease?"

Her answer was, "A pet parent should seek treatment from a veterinarian who has seen this condition before. CDS may be blamed on a patient getting old when there is more to the condition" She continued to explain, "I did not learn about CDS in my vet school classes, I learned about it because my own elderly dog developed behavior changes and a smart clinician at my vet school gave me a quiz to take about her symptoms. Based on the results, she concluded that my dog was demonstrating signs of CDS at fourteen years old. A combination of medication, the only option I knew about at that time, slowed the progression of symptoms, but ultimately, she died from this condition at sixteen years of age. While I do not know whether homeopathy would have altered the path of her decline or improved her quality of life, it has been my experience that this powerful method of healing improves symptoms and when used appropriately by a trained homeopath, can stimulate healing and remove disease."

Dr. Rivera added, "There are also other treatments that may be helpful, Chinese herbs, rehabilitation, magnetic therapy, and acupuncture. These can all be very excellent tools for brain stimulation. Again, these things should be done only under the proper circumstances with trained professionals, so, speak with your veterinarian for a referral."

More Treatments Therapies & Home Care
I was curious about how a veterinarian decides on the best combination of treatments for dogs with CCDS. The response from questioning many different veterinarians was sometimes you just need to combine traditional and holistic practices, Chinese Herbal treatments, or other needed therapies at each different stage of the disease. This type of medicine is called "Integrative Medicine." When physicians use these methods, they don't need as much traditional medication, because they have more tools to work with. One such tool is a test to determine where there is a weakness. This "muscle testing" can find the weaknesses in the body and the stresses on the different organs. With cognitive problems it may be the liver, not the brain that needs support. These tests can also help determine if there are viruses, parasites, or heavy metals in the body, which are things a veterinarian might not readily see on regular blood tests.

CAININE COGNITIVE - Treatments & Therapies

Dr. Bartner told me, "Once there is an understanding of whether the dog may have CCD, then it is a matter of looking for treatments that might benefit, but also will do no further harm."

Dr. Tynes said, if she can make a diagnosis of CDS, she will the discuss options with the pet owner regarding their relationship with their pet and any treatments she might recommend, which include treating the entire pet and reviewing the influence of everything in the dog's environment. "Treatment of CDS is aimed at prevention, slowing decline, and improving clinical signs. This treatment relies on early recognition and intervention. Because cognitive therapeutics are most effective at maintaining brain health and preventing or slowing cognitive decline, early intervention is optimal."

Her recommendations for this treatment might begin with including good age-appropriate exercise, and best diet choices.

Dealing with cognitive dysfunction, Dr. Haghighat uses treatments based on Chinese Medicine, acupuncture, and spinal manipulation.

Dr. Mar told me that she will also use medications such as Trazodone before bed, to help sedate the pet, as a medicinal trial. "The reason for this trial would be that if there was a tumor, it wouldn't necessarily respond. However, patients with cognitive dysfunction syndrome will be calmer at night from the sedation as it helps regulate their cognitive function."

Dr. Baker provided the following information. "It is important to remember that we don't have one treatment for every patient. In my experience, the best we can do once we have made this diagnosis is to treat the most prominent symptom. For instance, a dog that keeps the pet parent awake all night because the pet is pacing, and whining will need to focus on anti-anxiety medication or sleep aids. The bond with the pet will be disturbed if the parent is sleep deprived and frustrated.

"Logging the effect of medication, herbs or supplements is critical so the veterinarian can alter things as needed. In the example above, the dog may sleep, but be stiffer in the morning from not moving during the night. If the dog is more painful, then that needs to be addressed."

Dr. Baker concluded by stating, "There are also other alternative approaches for cognitive dysfunction including pulsed electromagnetic field therapy, LASER, acupuncture and behavioral therapy which uses new tricks, complex food toys, mazes, etcetera."

I discussed Shamrock not being able to be calmed with Dr. Dodds and she suggested using lavender oil for calming. She said, "At the first signs of the disease dogs might become very hyper, especially when not recognizing people and not being able to be calmed." Dr. Dodds also mentioned, "Animals are also very intuitive with their pet parents and when the parents are getting anxious, dealing with this disease, the pets feel that same anxiety. Putting lavender on their nose and behind their ears does a lot to calm them. Also looking your pet in the eyes and speaking in a calm, slow manner does a lot to relieve their anxiety."

Dr. Fraser said, "To specifically treat dementia, we address all the issues and the pet as a whole. A plan is made, and acupuncture or light therapy can be started, if these treatment modalities are indicated. We will also discuss healing modalities that pet parents can do at home in between appointments."

These treatments all seemed so positive that I wanted to dig further and understand how CCD is managed in dogs? Dr. Gardner told me, "A combination of diet, medication, and supplements can be effective in improving signs, and slowing the progression of cognitive dysfunction. Mental stimulation, such as training, play, exercise, and puzzle toys, are also essential for maintaining brain health. Discussing a personalized management plan with your veterinarian or veterinary behaviorist is important for the best outcome for your dog."

Dr. Villalobos explained, "If however, the veterinarian does feel it is CCD, they might suggest exercise, changes in diet, strict maintenance of routines or adding prescription medications. Depending on what they see they may also suggest further testing including blood work or MRI's."

CAININE COGNITIVE - Treatments & Therapies

The following outlines specific treatments, therapies and home care procedures.

Exercise & Games

An essential element in combatting cognitive decline is to first realize the need to stimulate our pet's brains.

Dr. Bartner said, "Physical therapy has shown many benefits. Humans with Alzheimer's seem to slow progression through completing mental exercises such as Sudoku and learning new things." She believes there is a similar rationale to using rehab for dogs.

Dr. Kass spoke about the need to stimulate our pet's brains. She recommended, "Mental stimulation exercises and physical exercises can keep the nerves and the brain stimulated and growing new connections. And don't forget that dogs need healthy sleep and lowered stress as much as we do."

Dr. Torraca stated, "With dogs that have CCDS, in addition to relieving any pain, they should be engaging in exercise and games."

Dr. Landsberg encourages pet parents to care for their pet's physical, mental and social needs with exercise. He told me, "An effective way to do this is by taking dogs for walks, sniffing and play, as their health can handle. Also engaging in brain enrichment, which includes feeding, and exploring for food and treats from food puzzles and toys." Dr. Landsberg believes in training based on rewards and feels that all of these can help with mental and behavioral health and quality social time. He recommends house proofing and modifying the environment to make the household, stable, safe, comfortable and secure.

For dogs like Shamrock who begin to get stuck in corners, slip on the stairs, slide on the kitchen floor and bump into objects, house proofing and comfort modifications are essential to address their safety needs. I looked around the house and in the same way you would, "baby proof," the house was made, "Shamrock proofed!" This included the outside: a ramp was built for her backyard so she wouldn't have to navigate the two steps to go to the bathroom and we secured all the fencing to limit the access from other animals.

Dr. Radosta said, "It is important to note that exercise is also a great stimulator for brain enrichment. Walking, if the dog is able, is best!"

Dr. Rivera told me, "Like people, dogs also need to decompress and enjoy their life, but that doesn't mean a lazy, 'couch potato' dog. Their activity level should be based on their growing needs, so give them a job. If your dog is constantly learning, moving, and developing new interests, all these things can help the body and the brain slow the onset of diseases like dementia."

I told Dr. Rivera even at 15 years of age, Shamrock, was still able to jump at the door and onto the bed or couch. But after that, toward 16 she did start to slow down and not even attempt these feats of athleticism. In areas where she could no longer get up or down, instead of lifting her we built her a platform she could easily use to get from one place to another, but which would still use her push and pull muscles. But when her brain started to misfire and the dementia got worse, she even became more hesitant and needed to be led.

Dr. Rivera responded, "A dog being mentally and physically active, will keep their brains stimulated. When they are not exercising their body, mind and spirit, dogs will tend to go down-hill faster."

The one theme that was constantly being repeated during my research was how important it is to keep your dog mentally stimulated and physically active!

I loved to play games with Shamrock and found they helped keep her engaged. Here is an easy way...play games with your dog like you would play with a baby: peek a boo, which hand is the treat in, I spy a..., hide and seek and so many other activities. These games are exercises that also keep you bonded, while stimulating your dog's mind...and are fun for both the dog and the pet parent.

I must admit that there were times when Shamrock seemed like her old self again. She would still attempt jumping; and many times, acted perfectly normal...then later, she might return to slightly limping again.

CAININE COGNITIVE - Treatments & Therapies

Dr. Rivera added, "Even in the case of an injury, the goal is to return the dog to functioning as optimally, and as soon as possible. But during their recovery the pet parent should maintain stimulation of their brain, muscles, and bones or they will atrophy, but again, caution must be taken as to not physically exacerbate the injury."

Alternative Modalities - Acupuncture & Body Work

I investigated many treatments that might help with CCDS and learned that acupuncture can help calm the mind and let the pet slow down enough to be able to relax, which in turn, helps with eating, sleeping and healing.

Dr. Bernard suggested, when the signs indicate a Qi or Yin Deficiency, there are many great acupuncture points and herbal formulas that can be used once a particular pattern is identified.

Dr. McKinstry also uses acupuncture and has seen remarkable results, especially with sick animals. She said, "Anesthesia can have adverse effects on the liver and acupuncture can help detoxify this organ." Additionally, she uses a combination of acupuncture, herbal medicine and diet before an operation, to help strengthen the body's immune system and as a preventative, guarding against issues that might arise from the anesthesia.

Dr. Dodds gave me some suggestions of what can be done to help your dog at home. Pet parents can experience helping their dog with acupressure spots, such as behind the ear that are very soothing. She added, "Acupressure points exist throughout the body and any pet parent can perform this procedure with the help of a dog acupuncture point chart." *(Note: See Recommendations, - pg 250) you can also Google these charts.

Dr. Bassingthwaighte is a holistic veterinarian with a passion for hands on bodywork and healing for animals. He encourages this type of body work which can be begun from a very early age and has many benefits.

He developed The "WEBB" Five-Minute-Deep Pressure Technique. "WEBB" stands for "Whole Energy Body Balance." He told me, "I had been focusing specifically on creating the 'WEBB' method for the last fifteen years. I have seen many positive changes in the thousands of pets I've done 'WEBB' sessions with, physically, mentally, and emotionally.

"One thing to be aware of is your dog will have trained you very effectively to give them the sort of touch they enjoy the most, pats, strokes, ear scratches and so on. What you're about to learn to do is a very different quality of touch. This firm, deep pressure, intentional touch that we use will be something completely new to your dog. In fact, most dogs find it strange, and will wriggle, jiggle, gently complain, roll over on their backs, hoping for their usual tummy rub, or they might try every doggy trick in the book to escape this weird stuff you're seemingly trying to torture them with. You will have to gently persist through this, whatever you do, don't let them bluff you into stopping the process.

"It's also a wonderful exercise to build your dog's level of respect for you, as this is a brief time when you're going to be asking your furry friend, and well-loved member of your family, to do exactly what you ask them to do. So don't let them run away from what you're doing, gently persist, and keep gently persisting until they let you practice the technique. If your dog is particularly reactive to intentional touch, it's still vitally important to persevere until you attain at least a small win. It can take a while.

"Before beginning the WEBB therapy, make sure you have your dog fitted with a collar that can't slip off, and on a leash, even if it's in your home. Most dogs are much better behaved on a leash than at liberty, it lets them know that you're doing something with them, and not just playing. Of course, you may have to work through a bit of 'Wahoo, we're going for a walk!!!' excitement, and some puzzled or maybe even resentful looks when they realize that no, this isn't walk time.

"Hands on body work can help release pain and tension from your pet's body." Dr. Bassingthwaighte continued, "Did you know that ninety-three percent of the dogs I assess are suffering from back and, or body pain and tension? I've discovered this in thousands of dogs that I've assessed! The scary part is that more than half of the people who parent these silently suffering dogs have no idea their best friend is in pain. That's forty-seven-point five percent of all the dogs, yours included, who are hurting and could do with some gentle, supportive, healing hands work.

CAININE COGNITIVE - Treatments & Therapies

"This simple, five-minute deep pressure bodywork technique makes a big positive difference if used consistently over time. People have seen big improvements and have told me how much calmer and happier their dogs are. It is best to do at least five minutes twice a day for three to four weeks to embed permanent positive shifts. This practice is a great support mechanism for any dog with phobias, post-traumatic stress, and of course, those crazy, over the top, highly driven working dogs and competition dogs."

Dr. Bassingthwaighte offered this example of how you can begin "Whole Energy Body Balance" with your dog. "WEBB is all about loving touch. If you want to learn how to find silent pain and relive that pain, it takes a little while to learn. That doesn't mean you can't get started making a difference with your pets right now. All you need to do is to gently, lovingly touch your pets. The more presence and love you bring into your touch, the better for your pet - so put your phone down (better yet, put it on airplane mode for a short while), then set a timer for 10 or 15 minutes. This will help you give all of your attention to your pet for the next little while. Take a moment of stillness and quiet to connect with your pet, while you bring all of your awareness into your body. Gently slow down and deepen your breath just a little and bring your heart into your hands. By this I mean to bring the loving energy of your heart into the expression of how you touch your pet. And, then start stroking and touching your pet, but make the movements very slow and gentle. Most humans have a habit of using quite a fast 'hand speed' when they are touching their pets. The more you slow down the speed of your hand movement, the more this will cause a deep, profoundly healing relaxation response in your pet's body. You can use all of your normal patting motions, but make them half your normal speed, then half again. Then you can try new movements, such as, long straight strokes, wavy strokes, short strokes, long strokes, and perhaps a time with stillness, holding your hand or hands still on one part of your pet's body. This is a short, simple version of 'WEBB' Loving Touch, which is just one of many skills you can learn with 'WEBB'."

Dr. Bassingthwaighte also recommended techniques such as acupuncture, and other alternative treatments which are good for older dogs seven or eight years old.

SHAMROCK'S STORY

Using Your Dog's Senses - Smell & Sight

I asked Dr. Rivera, when a dog like Shamrock is getting older and showing more signs of cognitive issues, what is the best course of action?

His response was, "Use the dog's senses to help them. One of their best senses is smell. This sense develops from the time they are born and helps to stimulate other nerves. Dog's sense of smell can be ten thousand to all most one-hundred-thousand times better and more acute than humans. So, providing different smells, will create more brain stimulation, as dogs associate smells with memories."

I asked him, "What are some of the ways to create this stimulation?"

He gave me a powerful list of suggestions. "This can be done by several methods. You can dilute essential oils, but just be sure the scent is not overpowering. You only want to stimulate the nose and not overwhelm the body. Another way to encourage the senses is to combine different senses, for example, hearing and smell. Music can be very calming, but also very stimulating. Classical music or popular music should be background and not blaringly loud, which can overwhelm the senses."

I told Dr. Rivera that Shamrock responded well to beautiful classical piano pieces as soft background music.

He indicated that playing music to bring in another sense and then adding touch brought the senses to good stimulation. Other tricks of stimulation, that he discussed, included vibrational, from a stimulator to different body parts, but only for a few seconds each. You can even use things like a loofah, a rough sponge on the fur." *(Note: If you do use a loofah, please be sure you properly clean them after use. Find ways to clean loofahs on the internet).

I expressed my delight that he recommended body stimulation. It reaffirmed my commitment with Shamrock to our daily "Doga" sessions. I found she loved that time and I believed that her reactions told me her body was stimulated through the touch and gentle movement and massage. But the added benefits for her were the range of motion for her legs, and, I believe, the effects of emotional stimulation through the close contact.

Dr. Rivera then spoke about another sense; sight and how important visual can be. He proposed changing the brightness in a

CAININE COGNITIVE - Treatments & Therapies

room. "We must remember that light lumens, can overwhelm the visual system and body, and depending on the dog, may be counter-productive. Other conditions to consider when trying to influence the visual system include, but are not limited to, cataracts, and corneal changes, among others." To be safe, this should be discussed with your veterinarian before starting.

"Sleep is another crucial factor for dogs. Therefore, where they sleep, if they actually do sleep for a significant amount of time, you do not want them to be too cold, or too hot.

"Using olfactory stimulation that engages their sense of smell can also help sleep patterns. Adding potpourri in their bed or putting lavender under their pillow is calming and results in long range effects of brain stimulation and learning.

"No matter what age or stage of disease your dog is in, you can start with these steps and then can add other things if needed to improve quality of life."

Anxiety A Major Issue-What Are the Remedies?
Watching your dog having anxious moments and experiencing anxiety can rip at the heart of any pet parent. I know how gut wrenching it can be, therefore the first thing I tried was to comfort Shamrock, but when your dog is in the midst of canine decline and anxious, they don't want to be comforted...so what is a pet parent to do?

Dr. Torraca helped me to better understand options available. "Even with minor anxiety like thunderstorms or car rides, you can assist your dog with anything that might work, such as thunder shirts, anxiety wraps, calming agents or even a prescription medication like Chroniquin, which is a full spectrum hemp oil extract." She added that if you give anxiety medication they should be given ahead of time as they can take about an hour to work. These remedies can reduce anxiety in about eighty percent of dogs. Pet parents should use anything that works to help relieve their dog's stress, but they must also be careful how they approach their dog. Don't suddenly grab your dog as that can feed into their fear. And remember if you are upset, your dog will pick up on your anxiety. Anxious people cause anxious dogs

SHAMROCK'S STORY

"Canine cognitive dysfunction causes many similar anxieties. Dogs tend to pant, pace and spin in circles. Anxious dogs that tend to spin, should not be crated, which will cause further stress. The pet parent can instead try simple exercise, like walking which works to reduce stress for both the pet and the parent both physically and mentally.

"Walking in water on an underwater treadmill helps a lot, but even if you can fill water to your dog's hips, in something like a small pool, they can get active, and the water can be very calming. Calm stimulating activity, burns off nervous energy."

Shamrock didn't really like water, but she did love walking, which seemed to be calming for her. When I would walk Shamrock in straight lines, she seemed herself. It was time together for us, in fresh air and good exercise for both of us.

Dr. Torraca gave me other suggestions which I was unaware of, such as, "Lick Mats." She said, "These mats have grooves and can be filled with healthy treats like yogurt, peanut butter, pet food, canned food, freeze-dried food, and any spreadable foods or snacks. The benefit of these mats is that they keep the dog busy 'licking' a healthy treat and aid in reducing stress and anxiety. They can also be used for any situation that can cause your dog stress.

"Another great tool is a 'Snuffle mat.' These mats are usually shaggy, and the pet parent can hide healthy treats in the shag to keep their dog busy and distracted from stressful situations.

"These are great mental stimulation and distraction tools, but it should be noted that pet parents should never leave their pets unattended when using either of these mats." *(Note: some mats may have straps that when chewed can come loose and can be swallowed causing choking issues).

One unexpected piece of advice from Dr. Torraca was that as great as puzzles are for mental stimulation, these may frustrate the dog and therefore aggravate their symptoms. She suggested instead to play games that offer the dog a reward with food."

I mentioned that Shamrock always responded well to food games. She loved to play, "Catch the Spaghetti." I would put a piece of long spaghetti on a fork in front of her and then count to three and say, "Okay you can have it!" Then she would grab hold and pull it into her mouth.

CAININE COGNITIVE - Treatments & Therapies

Another fun game was "Lick the Stick," in which I would put a thumbnail amount of frozen yogurt, or vanilla ice cream in a cup, then take a smidgen on a popsicle stick; ensuring it was smooth so she wouldn't get a splinter. Because the yogurt or ice cream was frozen, it stuck to the stick, and she would have so much fun licking it away until there was nothing more to lick. Then, she'd patiently wait for more. When it melted to liquid, I would let her lick the cup from all different angles, until it was all gone.

Dr. Torraca added the following statements, "Even when I see a puppy who may not be predisposed to be an anxious dog, my advice is to show the dog good behavior traits to emulate. A calm voice, soothing speech, or tone of voice, all help create a calmer environment. How you approach your dog also makes an enormous difference. Never come at them, try to be at their eye level and speak softly, not in a high-pitched voice. Then you can begin using long calming strokes down their back to keep them in that calmer state."

Other Therapies & Treatments

When Dr. Buchoff sees a dog with possible cognitive problems he first does testing to rule out other issues. Depending on what the tests show and the pet's cognitive needs, he has many different therapies to use: Chiropractic, Acupuncture, Aromatherapy, Homeopathy, Herbs, and Nutrition. If he then believes there is still a need for more extensive therapies, he can use a treatment called, "Biophotonic Blood Treatment," which involves a combination of sodium chloride, ozone, and a small amount of blood, and then the mixture is run through UV lights before injecting it back into the patient. This treatment can have good results on the body to help eliminate toxin effects and assist in the body's oxygenation, while balancing the microbial effects. Dr. Buchoff also recommends a treatment called, "BEMER," this treatment uses a gentle pulsating electromagnetic field energy pad to improve microcirculation within the blood vessels, promoting self-healing and supporting the immune system. *(Note: Both or either of these treatments should only be performed by a veterinarian that is knowledgeable in this type of procedure).

SHAMROCK'S STORY

Because CCDS can manifest itself in many ways and at varied ages, I wanted to know what else could be done at these different stages.

Dr. Brugliera told me that when she sees a pet with early onset of cognitive issues, she typically uses antioxidant therapy, or the appropriate herbal therapies, as well as melatonin, which can help with sleep at night. But when the pet is already in the mid-stages, meaning signs of cognitive decline are increasing, treatments would also include acupuncture therapy or Ozone Therapy. She added, "We also need to make sure that we are checking for other signs of disease processes such as internal disease or metabolic disease. Typically, these older dogs will also have arthritis or pain in multiple areas and that can make them more uncomfortable and agitated. So, treating their discomfort can give a lot of peace and comfort."

The worst-case scenario of course is to see a dog only when they are in the latter stages of CCDS. Dr. Brugliera said, "There are prescription medications that can be used at that stage in addition to the items mentioned previously."

Of course, there is always the desire to delay the advancing of the disease, and I wanted to know what was possible.

Her answer gave me hope! "Yes absolutely! The treatments we talked about have been used with my older patients, and the results for some have been a very long and happy quality of life."

Part of the reason that Dr. Brugliera has such good results is her concept of treatment for this disease. She uses Integrative care as one of her specialties. "This means that each pet patient is different, so we always have to address all of the issues together. That's what makes us holistic! With a focus on the complete, whole health of the pet!"

Since oxidative damage is a cause of aging, Dr. Katz uses a treatment of ozone which floods the system with oxygen. This process can reverse oxidative damage and turn mitochondria back on. "This treatment can be inhaled, or blood treated. It is not used specifically for canine cognitive dysfunction, but it might help."

Again, it is important to note that any and all of these treatments should only be performed by a veterinarian.

CAININE COGNITIVE - Treatments & Therapies

Still More Treatment Options
Animal Communicator, Ayurveda & More

When Shamrock was in the grip of the disease it was hard to reach her. She became more distant, didn't want to be held, or comforted. From my research I have learned that some pet parents turn to an animal communicator to help better understand what their pet is feeling and going through. I had no idea about how to reach one, but many holistic veterinarians told me they have animal communicators they are familiar with. For pet parents interested in animal communicators *(Note: See Recommendations-pg 250) or do an internet search.

Dr. Frick said, "There are also many ways to help your dog from an early age. If the pet parent is interested in pursuing balance to support their pet's body function, getting into their mind pattern, and learning how the mind works with the body, then Ayurveda may be an option. Ayurveda means, 'signs of life,' and it is considered the traditional medicine of ancient India and the Hindu culture. Its philosophy is that life's imbalances occur with several factors such as, change of seasons, diet, viruses, environmental toxins, stress, aging, and other influences that attack the body. Ayurvedic practitioners can help guide pets back to healthy living."

I was told by many veterinarians that the best treatments are those that are proactive; working with the veterinarian and the pet parent to stop the advance of the disease. Sometimes it is necessary to give preventative medications, like heartworm, but which have many risks associated with them. The best way to approach this subject is with an open dialogue. It is important to understand when these medications are necessary, and if they need to be given, how then to support the immune system so the dog can better manage the stress of the medications.

During Shamrock's journey I tried many different treatments, some worked, some didn't. But along the way I have learned there are sometimes more natural ways to do things, and at other times diverse treatments and or medications might be needed.

The best way to start is to learn what the options are for your dog and then discuss these with your veterinarian. Pet parents can then better understand whether these treatments should or shouldn't be used as the first line of defense. The idea should be to find the best way to help your dog in a supportive way; to make the dog stronger, so your dog can be its own first line of defense.

BEAM - "Behavior, Energy, Appetite, Mood"

My discussion with Dr. Jeff Feinman, a veterinary Homeopath, was about, "Dog Happiness."

Treatments for our pets should be based on individuality, vitality, and balance. He said, "'Dis-ease, imbalance,' is a way of stating that 'disease' is really the body not at ease with itself. Dis-ease is associated with the amount, and balance, of cellular energy and information flow. Intercellular communication, or the way that cells 'talk' to each other, is key to maintaining and regaining health for pets."

He has been using a method for understanding dis-ease for over a decade called the "Vitality and Balance System." This system helps to evaluate dogs based on their Quality of Life and is not primarily for management of their symptoms and can also help dogs that have not responded to medications.

"Every pet, just like every person, is an individual. The 'paint-by-numbers' approach prevents pets from receiving truly customized care based on their unique biology, life history, and symptoms."

Dr. Feinman spoke with me about the exposome, (how a dog reacts to the exposure in its life and how it affects its health), and BEAM.

"The exposome allows us to assess a pet's individual exposure to things that can make them more susceptible to dis-ease: either exposure to negative things, like toxins, abuse, neglect, and so forth, or a lack of exposure, or access to positive things, like sound, nutrition, adequate exercise, enrichment activities, and much more.

"BEAM" is an acronym for "Behavior, Energy, Appetite, and Mood," which pet parents, who know their pets best, can use to identify and track symptoms across these four categories.

"Almost everyone agrees with and understands the concepts of cellular energy and vitality. And we know that internal homeostasis, balance, is how we stay healthy. This is super important in the brain and heart because they are the two most energy-consuming organs in the body."

CAININE COGNITIVE - Treatments & Therapies

Dr. Feinman stated, "Wellness care based on the Quality of Life of our dogs improves pet's lives better than concentrating on any individual symptom. Therefore, it is useful for pet parents to focus on BEAM to 'shine the light' on better balance and health. BEAM can be easily monitored through observations by the pet parent. By using BEAM, the course of treatment becomes targeted at eliminating isolated signs and symptoms, instead of treating the underlying problem.

"This also helps pet parents put all their dog's symptoms in context. By basing their dog's care on vitality and balance, pet parents become more involved. They can make better decisions while 'Avoiding' triggers like allergens that can cause immune imbalances. 'Supporting' the body while it heals using any holistic modality, and 'Curing' the underlying imbalance energetically using Traditional Chinese Veterinary Medicine homeopathy." Dr. Feinman suggested before using homeopathic treatments, pet parents speak with their veterinarian.

"Also, if a dog has a strong immune system, it may still get some disease, but the pet will get over the problem more quickly.

"The other benefit is that actively engaged pet parents are more focused on a wellness model and will see the veterinarian more often to support this system, instead of just for sick only visits."

After speaking with Dr. Feinman I researched using "BEAM." I delved into each of the subjects of the acronym, "Behavior, Energy, Appetite, and Mood," and found that when using this system, the pet parent is better able to be aware of changes so much sooner.

"BEAM gives the pet parent the easiest way to look at 'Behavior' and consider any changes, day or night, no matter how small or seemingly insignificant.

"Next, 'Energy'. Compare what you know as your dog's normal energy levels and monitor any changes. "'Appetite', should be easier to calculate. Look at the amounts, more or less, and, or favoring a particular food.

"'Mood' is harder. Is there new sadness, or is the dog more withdrawn? Pair this with behavior.

"Once you begin keeping track you will be able to see if the changes are temporary or developing a pattern. Either way changes should signal concern and concern should prompt talking with your veterinarian. Use BEAM as your guide and bring all the documentation you've kept showing what has been happening with your dog."

If I had such documentation when Shamrock stopped wagging her tail, I might have understood that as an early warning sign. Even when we started different medications and treatments, I believe using BEAM to keep track of her progress would have given me a better handle on how well, or not well the treatments were working and changes could have been made so much sooner, or changes that were made quickly, might have needed more time.

In the midst of your dog's illness, I realize the goal is "immediate results." All you feel is your "baby" is having a difficult time and you need to fix it...now!

Unfortunately, especially with cognitive issues, that might not be possible. In which case having BEAM as a tool, can help a pet parent be better informed, to make more proactive and involved choices and in these times of stress, see the changes more clearly. This is a great tool for both the parent and the pet, to help produce an environment of calm, associated with the knowledge that the goal is good health and good quality of life.

What Else To Be Aware Of...What Else Can You Do?

Dr. Gardner suggested that when pet parents want to continue at-home care, they should be sure to include easy access to food and water, and a comfortable location for sleep. Be consistent with medications and supplements. Some parents may also want to try prescription diets that promote brain function. Separation from other animals, may be needed to avoid altercations or injury. Predictable routines are very important, such as daily gentle exercise and activities for brain stimulation, with modified surfaces to increase traction, night lights, ramps or stairs, and safety gates. She also recommended having on hand, doggy diapers and potty pads, if needed.

I was curious as to what these home care CCD treatments look like.

Dr. Gardner explained, "Although there is no cure for CCD, there are many therapies that can help your furry friend feel themselves again. Your veterinarian may use a multimodal treatment approach that includes:

CAININE COGNITIVE - Treatments & Therapies

Cognitive enrichment —Regular mental stimulation can help keep your senior dog's mind clear. Activities that encourage thinking and reasoning, such as solving food puzzles, learning new tricks, and playing with a new toy, can improve cognitive function. A short daily walk or wagon ride provides sights, smells, and sounds that will stimulate your pet's brain.

Environmental modifications — Your pet's anxiety and restlessness may be alleviated by calming pheromones, some are provided as a sprays, plug-in diffusers, or impregnated collars. *(Note: See Recommendations-pg 250). A white noise machine may calm pets who are up at night and anxious about unusual, strange noises.

Supplements — Dog foods and products containing supplements that support brain health, such as antioxidants, omega-3 fatty acids, and medium-chain triglycerides (MCTs), can improve cognitive function in dogs with CCD.

Medication — Your veterinarian may prescribe medications to help manage symptoms such as anxiety and restlessness."

Dr. Mahaney spoke to me about the importance of good blood flow saying, "Acupuncture and massage can help with CCD, as there can be problems in the body's internet energetic flow, delivery of nutrients and oxygen, and removal of cellular breakdown products and metabolic wastes. Generally, when the body's fluids are moving well the dog has more energy and a greater ability to fight illness."

I told him that it in addition to helping Shamrock get better blood flow through massage, it also helped me to feel good about the home care I was providing. Since Shamrock was a Springer Spaniel, and used to high jumps and runs, I could see the difference doing daily "Doga" and body massage made for her; especially regarding her new difficulty with jumping and her occasional limping.

Signs and symptoms in a patient's history, as well as the dog's physical exam findings, which include evaluation of the tongue and pulse help Dr. Landau map out a direction for treatment, which will help balance the body's Yin and Yang. To explain, "Dog dementia patients will often have signs of yin and yang separation which is expressed as yin deficiency and qi deficiency. Yin deficiency will present as evening confusion, 'Sundowners syndrome' and anxiety. Qi deficiency will present as weakness to the back and hind legs, increased thirst and urination and muscle wasting to hind legs. This condition can be helped with a combination of Chinese Herbs, acupuncture and nutritional supplementation."

I told him that his description mirrored what the disease looked like with Shamrock, and even though she was on supplements, they were not paired with acupuncture or Chinese Herbs.

Dr. Mar said, "Because integrative medicine is becoming more popular in veterinary circles, pet parents are becoming more aware of other types of treatments."

I asked her, what type of therapies she might use on a pet with cognitive decline.

She replied, "Depending on the patient, physical rehabilitation, homeopathy, herbal medicine, therapeutic massage and spinal manipulation therapy might be the best course of action."

Dr. Mar also uses acupuncture to calm pets, but rarely uses that treatment for those with cognitive issues.

Pranayama- Breathing Practices - Better Quality Of Life

I again spoke with Dr. Feinman about what happens when a dog develops dementia. He responded, "The Quality-of-Life changes, and regarding Quality of Life, breathing is number one."

Human beings understand the life-giving force of breath. We also know there are different types of breathing:

Normal – which we are usually not even aware of
Fatigued– faster, harder breaths like after a long run
Anxiety Driven– sporadic, from worry, fear or pain
Relaxed– slow, deep breathing

But whatever breath you take it is necessary for life. So why wouldn't it be just as important an issue for dogs? This all may sound very, very strange, but here's the question...how do we get our dogs to breathe better?

Dr. Feinman provided an informative explanation. "Pranayama, or breathing practices derived from yoga and Ayurveda, can be

CAININE COGNITIVE - Treatments & Therapies

effective for animals to help maintain their bodies stability and increase longevity, while helping with the growing incidence of chronic diseases. In addition, dog's quality of life can be improved by using breathing methods that help to optimize health, delay aging, and speed efficient recovery from injury or disease.

"Once a dog is going through dementia, they can become very anxious, anxiety stricken, fearful, confused and even aggressive, and can pant excessively. The use of breath control can improve their Quality of Life and reduce many of these issues. One specific approach is to teach the dog to slow down its breathing and induce calm.

"When sitting with your dog use a calm voice and a high value treat. Gently massage them, if you already know a spot that calms your pet, gently stroke them there. If not, slow rhythmic stroking under the chin is calming for many dogs. Use their name preceded by the word 'good,' using a long 'gooood' in a soft, soothing tone. Maintain eye and physical contact with your dog, if tolerated but avoid this technique with dogs that exhibit fear-or aggressive behavior. Do not stare at your pet, instead, use a soft gaze."

Dr. Feinman continued, "The whole concept is to work with the dog's body to raise energy. Therefore, immune resilience and resistance to infectious diseases improves by focusing on vitality and balance. The Therapeutic 'Sniff Walk' is a great way to turn genes on and off through 'C.H.E.,' pronounced Chi, which means, increasing 'Connection, Happiness, and Engagement,' which in turn improves the Quality of Life.

"These connections are created through 'sniffing' and learning about the world. At the same time, they are also engaging with their pet parent and the environment. Perhaps the most powerful proactive application of pranayama for pets makes use of their keen sense of smell during the sniff walk. 'Sniffing' activates the relaxation response and improves Quality of Life and longevity by optimizing aerobic respiration, mental stimulation, and engagement.

"A dog's ability to regularly exercise their sense of smell has enormous implications for their health and cellular energy. If they can do so in the sunshine and open air, even better! Most pets would spend most of their time on walks by stopping to sniff every few feet. Parents should avoid tugging on the leash to keep their dog moving in order to maximize the potential benefits of their sniffing. Even animals unable to do much exercise, such as those that are older or have arthritis or pain or other health challenges, can benefit from slow sniff walks.

"Pets benefit from safely being able to explore new things to keep their brains sharp and to help them heal their bodies. Whether it's a new toy, a new friend, a new park, a new agility course, or a new healthy treat, your pet's happiness and well-being will increase through exposure to these novelties. This can be especially powerful to help 'tune-up' pets who have early warning signs of cognitive decline.

"Two other ways to harness the power of increased airflow are physical exercises, such as running and playing, and doing nose and scent work. Like the sniff walk, nose and scent work does not slow the breath, but rather induces calm and improves focus both during and after these activities. Breath work also improves cognition and reduces distractibility for nervous dogs, which facilitates training and increases learning.

"Exercising by running, playing, fetching, etcetera, increases the rate and depth of breathing in addition to the other known benefits of exercise. Even pets that cannot exercise on land due to arthritic conditions or obesity can benefit from the effects of prana-building; life force energy and building better breath force energy. Methods that increase respiration include swimming, using an underwater treadmill, and low-impact core exercises such as ball work, which improve healing and Quality of Life. Even just walking outside in nature has shown improvements. Breathing and exercise have separate and additive effects on the improvements seen in animals

"If this is not practical because of your pet's limitations, a 'snuffle mat' is a great tool for indoor pranayama, breathing exercises. The snuffle mat is like a shag carpet in which you hide treats which your pet then sniffs out. This 'exercises' their brain, similar to the sniff walk. Daily therapeutic 'sniff walks' should be loose leash walks that help the body heal and support vitality, cellular energy, by providing it with more oxygen and, life force energy."

Because of Dr. Feinman's advice about how breathing can increase the Quality of Life and how teaching your dog through breathing exercises cab be calming, I was led to Dr. Overall, and her technique for better breathing in dog's.

CAININE COGNITIVE - Treatments & Therapies

Dog Breathing

The following step-by-step techniques for teaching your dog how to breathe better have been provided by Dr. Karen Overall, a Professor of Behavioral Medicine and author of over 100 scholarly publications.

Protocol For Dog Breathing

Protocol For Teaching Your Dog To Take A Deep Breath And Use Other Biofeedback Methods As Part Of Relaxation
By Dr. Karen Overall

"Dogs, like humans, cannot learn new behaviors if they are distressed. In fact, we all best produce the needed brain chemicals to make lasting memory if we are attentive enough to watch carefully but not so attentive that we are overly concerned. Most dogs about whom clients are concerned and/or who have truly pathological behavior are not calm enough to learn and use new information, especially if part of that information is learning to be calm.

The purpose of this protocol is to teach you how to teach your dog to take a deep breath and how to use other biofeedback tools to prepare your dog to relax so that the dog can learn how to change his behavior in a way that makes everyone happier.

The 3 important signaling tools used here that involve biofeedback are:

'look', 'breathe', and 'petting' a dog in a manner that avoids unhelpful arousal and encourages useful focus.

These 3 signaling tools are demonstrated in the video, *Humane Behavioral Care for Dogs: Problem Prevention and Treatment.*
*(Note: See Recommendations -pg 250).

'Look'

You will make the most progress with your dog if you work with this protocol together with the other 2 foundation behavior modification programs, the *Protocol for relaxation: behavior modification tier 1, and the Protocol for deference,* *(Note: See Recommendations-pg 250). Both of these protocols require that your dog 'look' – meaning look at and – preferably - make eye contact with you and work best if your dog can hold his breath for a second or two.

SHAMROCK'S STORY

The nine steps for teaching 'look' are as follows:

STEP 1. First, you want to couple your dog's attention to the word when giving the dog a food reward. Start by holding the treat in your hand with fingers closed, palm up, and then opening the hand to deliver the treat. The open hand prevents shying in some fiercely treated dogs and also promotes treat delivery that is gentle for the human. Your first step in teaching deep breathing may be to teach the dog to take a treat calmly. Feel free to get professional help with teaching this. You will need to ensure that you are not triggering any signs of anxiety, as this will not help the dog to be calm (See Box1).

BOX 1

Non-specific Signs of Anxiety

- Urination
- Defecation
- Anal sac expression
- Panting
- Increased respirator and heart rates
- Trembling/shaking*
- Muscle rigidity (usually with tremors)
- Lip licking
- Nose licking
- Grimace (retraction of lips)
- Head shaking
- Smacking or popping lips/jaws together
- Salivation/hypersalivation
- Vocalization (excessive and/or out of context)
- Frequently repetitive sounds, including high pitched whines*, like those associated with associated with isolation (see Yin and McCowan, 2004).
- Yawning
- Immobility/freezing or profoundly decreased activity
- Pacing and profoundly increased activity
- Hiding or hiding attempts
- Escaping or escape attempts
- Body language of social disengagement (turning head or body away from signaler)
- Lowering of head and neck
- Inability to meet a direct gaze
- Staring at some middle distance
- Body posture lower (in fear, the body is extremely lowered and tail tucked)
- Ears lowered and possibly droopy because of changes in facial muscle tone
- Mydriasis
- Scanning
- Hyper-vigilance/hyper-alertness (may only be noticed when touch or interrupt dog or cat – may hyper-react to stimuli that otherwise would not elicit this reaction)
- Shifting legs
- Lifting paw in an intention movement
- Increased closeness to preferred associates
- Decrease closeness to preferred associates
- Profound alterations in eating and drinking (acute stress is usually associated with decreases in appetite and thirst, chronic stress is often associated with increases)
- Increased grooming, possibly with self-mutilation
- Decreased grooming
- Possible appearance of ritualized or repetitive activities
- Changes in other behaviors including increased reactivity and increased aggressiveness (may be non-specific)

---

*(The most commonly recognized signs of anxiety recognized by clients)

STEP 2. Start by giving the dog a treat so that he knows what the reward is and so that you can be sure the dog loves the treat. Remember that dogs work best for information about expectations.

CAININE COGNITIVE - Treatments & Therapies

A really good treat tells them that their work with you will be appropriately rewarded.

STEP 3. Once you are sure that your dog likes the treat, take the treat in your hand, close your fingers over the treat so that only your fingers-not the treat- show and move it to your eye. (See Photo 1 and 2)

Fingers closed over treat in hand

Distance to stand from the dog (Picasso) with the dog looking at a closed hand that is held near your eye

STEP 4 When you get the treat to your eye, say 'look'.

STEP 5 As soon as the dog looks at your eyes, however briefly, tell him he is great and quickly move your hand with the treat down and open it flat under their chin so that he can have the treat.

STEP 6 Then, continue to practice the sequence above where you reward eye contact with the treat to further promote the coupling of the word "look" to actually looking up to your eye.

STEP 7 Next, reward better eye contact with a signal that draws the dog's attention to the human's eye (e.g., moving a finger to the eye while saying 'look'). You can do this by hiding the food behind your curled index finger and thumb so that your dog is watching your finger and not the food. This action helps dogs to follow a target – your finger – not a lure – the treat. See photo 3.

SHAMROCK'S STORY

STEP 8. Ideally and ultimately, your dog should be able to respond to the non-verbal signal and to sit and relax when he sees your finger go to your eye. It takes practice to get this amount of progress but it's achievable within a few practice sessions. See Photo 4.

Fingers hiding treat brought to eye   *Picasso sitting and looking with relaxed face*

STEP 9 Finally, as soon as you say the dog's name and begin to move your finger to your eye, your dog should sit and look at you.

  A really smart dog figures out that since we are working with deferential behaviors, every time you say their name, they will look at you and if you are close to them, they will sit. This is a desirable outcome because it means you are meeting their needs for information, and you are communicating well.

*(Note: If you are using these instructions for teaching 'look' and 'breathe' so that you can begin the *Protocol for relaxation: behavior modification tier 1,* See Recommendations). Please go slowly until you are sure that the dog responds as described above. It is very easy to teach dogs to be obedient, but they can become more anxious if you rush any of these programs.

The single biggest mistake pet parents make in working with true behavior modification is that they move through the process too rapidly without paying attention to the dog's signals about whether he is calm, scared, or simply overwhelmed. It's best to pretend that all dogs have special needs and go slowly... there is no cost to going slowly enough so that the dog is always rewarded for clearly showing you they are calm and attentive.

On the other hand, there is a huge cost in confusion and anxiety on

CAININE COGNITIVE - Treatments & Therapies

the dog's part - and frustration on the human's part – when the human goes too fast for that dog's particular comfort level. Frequent, short sessions are preferable to long, drawn-out sessions for both the client and dog. Working for a few minutes 4-5 times a day actually may help the dog to learn and use the behaviors better than would 1-2 long sessions. This work schedule also allows everyone to incorporate the behavior mod into for completeness.

'Breathe'
Heart rate, attentiveness and respiratory rate are all linked. If we can teach a human or a dog to take slower, deeper breaths, they relax, their heart rate decreases, and they can be more attentive to focusing on the task at hand. These responses are all coupled to changes in hormonal and other chemical signals that shift the brains and body's reactivity from a system ready to act on a threat to one ready to focus on learning, not reacting.
The first step for dogs is to teach them to hold their breath as a way to learn deep breathing and focus.
The trick to getting this to work is to teach the dog to breathe deeply and to incorporate this breathing into all encouraged deferential behaviors. Understanding how dogs breathe will help in understanding how we can teach them to hold their breath.
Dogs cannot simultaneously pant and smell or breathe through their nose, and they have alar folds/flaps on the sides of their nose that move up and out when they take a deep breath.
This means that you can use the movement of these folds – the dilation of the nostrils – to indicate and confirm when the dog is holding his or her breath. With small or thin and short-coated dogs you can also watch the ribcage to see if the rate at which it moves, slows. The steps are as follows.

1.You can start to teach the dog to take a deep breath by asking the dog to sit and 'look' at you for a food treat, as explained above. See photo 5.

SHAMROCK'S STORY

**Picasso sitting and looking as he is beginning
to relax and take a deep breathe**

2. Next, as you quickly move the treat from your eye region (where it is hidden in your curled finger) and while the dog makes eye contact with you, stop moving your fingers a few centimeters in front of the dog's nose without giving the treat. Say the word 'breathe'. See photo 6.

If your dog is reactive or aggressive when food is available, you will want to watch carefully here to ensure that the dog remains calm.

*Changes in Picasso's mouth and nose as the
treat is lowered to his face and he inhales*

3. The dog's nostrils will usually flare as he smells the treat, and because he cannot sniff something and pant at the same time, the dog will hold his or her breath. See photo 7.

CAININE COGNITIVE - Treatments & Therapies

4. As soon as you see that the dog has held his breath and/or flared his nostrils, immediately deliver the treat with the phrase 'good breathe, Picasso'
*(Picasso is the name of the dog in the photos; you should use your dog's name.)

Nostrils begin to flare as Picasso closes mouth and inhales in response to the request 'breathe'.

See photos 8 and 9. If your dog does not flare his nostrils you will have to shape the flare. Simply reward any movement of the nostrils at first. Then reward them only when the nostril is larger. Then, move towards only rewarding larger, flared nostrils once they are held still, round and open. Most dogs can figure this out in a few minutes, but the changes can be hard to see. By only using positive rewards in this activity, mistakes are recoverable and it's okay that both the human and the dog are learning.

Deeper breath with flare of sides of nostrils   *Deep breath and fully flared nostrils*

5. Practice this for a few minutes until you are certain that you know what you are looking for and that your dog is giving it to you. It can be difficult to see nostril flares in dark faced dogs, but once you learn what a nostril flare looks like on your dog, you will know it.

6. As your dog gets better at responding to the 'breathe' request, start to delay the provisioning of the treat a few   seconds at a time.

SHAMROCK'S STORY

7. Within a short while you will have a dog who holds his breath and slows his heart and respiratory rate, and so becomes more focused and relaxed. If you only reward the most focused and relaxed states, your dog will come along quite nicely.

It does not usually take more than 5 minutes to teach a dog to hold his or her breath, even if the dog is very hairy, making the nose tough to see (Photo 10 A) or the nose is dark (Photo 10 B), but it may take longer for you to recognize and encourage the behavior. You will need to be observant and quick, and not linger with presenting the food as an olfactory stimulus.

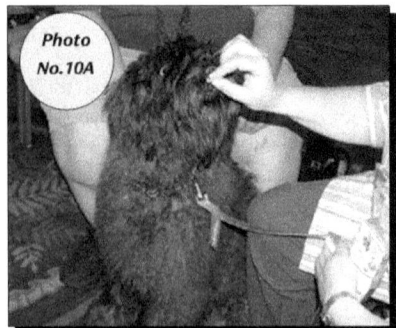

Naïve dogs being taught to 'breathe' and flare their nostrils. Very hairy faces (Photo 10A) and dark noses (Photo 10B) often make it a bit harder for people to see the nostrils move, but veterinarians in this laboratory class had no difficulty.

If you videotape yourself, you will learn to teach the dog to take a deep breath upon request because you will see when the dog takes a breath and learn to look for the associated behaviors in your dog.

How to pet a thoughtful dog

Finally, people pet their dogs, but few calm them by petting them. In fact, people usually arouse their dogs when petting them by petting in quick, short strokes all over the dog's head, face and shoulders.

Instead, if we want a thoughtful, calm dog who looks to us for information that is helpful to him, we need to replace conventional petting with long, slow strokes, deep muscle pressure, and massage.

'Smart-pet' instructions:

1. To start, the next time you touch your dog, don't move your hand. Instead, touch him and press firmly but gently. Most dogs will move

CAININE COGNITIVE - Treatments & Therapies

into your hand.

2. Then, gradually, using constant, gentle pressure, move your hand from his head, down his neck and slowly down your dog's spine. If you move too quickly to be able to identify and count the vertebrae (back bones) you are going too fast (or the dog is too plump).

3. Then press and massage the front of your dog's chest in a circular motion. Concentrate on the area just above where the front legs attach. Use one hand at first until you get used to slow, firm pressure. Slowly extend your circular massage movements to the dog's shoulders and neck and work your way back down the dog.

4. The dog will relax if he is not worried about you (see Photo 11), there have been no traumatic handling experiences, and the dog has no painful conditions.

Photo 11: Puppy after being petted and massaged slowly.

These 'smart-pet' instructions are demonstrated in the video, *Humane Behavioral Care for Dogs: Problem Prevention and Treatment.* *(Note: See Recommendations-pg 250). For most dogs this type of petting really helps them to focus when needed because they learn what it is like to be calm and to be able to take in information when calm. This type of handling and physical interaction also changes the dog-human relationship. The dogs get to have some seriously enjoyable downtime with their people and then seem more attentive to them in other circumstances.

What's after 'Look', 'Breathe' and Pet'?

Enjoy the calm and use it to help promote the dog's ability to learn the other 2 parts of the foundation behavior modification protocols: *Protocol for relaxation: behavior modification tier 1, and the Protocol for deference.* *(Note: See Recommendations-pg 250). These act as foundations for kind and humane rules by which you can guide your dog through more appropriate and desired behavioral responses.

If your dog has no behavior problems, these exercises will minimize the chance that any problems will develop. Most important - these exercises will ensure that you and your dog understand each other's signals and needs. That's priceless!

Reprinted By Permission From Dr. Overall - Originally from: Overall KL. Manual of Clinical Behavioral Medicine for Dogs and Cats, Elsevier, St. Louis, 2013. Copyright K.L. Overall.

This Protocol is supplemented by the following statement from Dr. Overall regarding this technique and CCDS.

"The breathing technique works well for any dogs who can either sniff or learn – or who have learned it, so it works with dogs with early to mid-stage cognitive changes, extremely impaired dogs may have problems.

"If they have learned this, they will retain it and if a very smelly treat is used, they should be able to learn it, olfactory learning skips the hippocampus at first, that part is top down for olfactory learning, unlike other learning. And, keeping a healthy ability to smell things, is related to cognitive ability and may either be a mirror or reflect early changes."

CAININE COGNITIVE - Treatments & Therapies

The following article was written by Dr. Stanley Coren, a Behavioural Researcher and Award-Winning Author.

Article:
Building a Better Brain Article –
By Dr. Coren

"Text taken from article, 'Building a Better Brain for Your Dog' You can actually change the physiology of your dog's brain."
Posted November 5, 2008, By Dr. Coren"

"It may be hard to believe, but you can actually change the physiology of your dog's brain. You can make it larger and more efficient simply by providing certain experiences for your pet. The same process will make your dog more intelligent and give his personality an added degree of stress resistance.

"... dogs reared in the more complex home environment not only learned faster but seemed to be less fearful and considerably less stressed...

"Over the years researchers have proven that these behavioral changes are the result of actual changes in the physiology of the animal's brains. The brains of animals that have lived in changing and complex environments actually become larger.

New connections develop between existing neurons in the cortex as a result of experience. Recent evidence demonstrates that it is even possible to grow new neural cells in important areas of the brain that are associated with learning, memory and the organization of behavior.

"The important aspects of the animal's experience which cause these positive changes in their brains involves exposure to a wide variety of interesting places and things that novel, and exciting experiences. It is best when these are combined with frequent opportunities to learn new things, solve problems and to freely investigate, manipulate, and interact with objects and environmental features.

... the benefits of such experiences are not restricted to growing puppies. Adults and even elderly animals, not only benefit from having richer environments, but these problem-solving experiences seem to help to offset the usual decline in mental efficiency that is seen in older dogs.

"For those of us who want to give our pet dog the advantage of a more efficient brain, the trick is simply to keep the dog's mind active, exposing him to new experiences, giving him new things to learn and puzzles to work out. Some different experiences can come out of just taking the dog to new places and on different routes on daily walks or including the dog on day trips or when out doing various chores. However, a little bit of effort to pose questions that your dog must answer will work even better.

"For most dogs, using food as the reward for solving problems and finding things will keep its motivation high. For example, there are a number of different dog toys that can be filled with kibble. When the object is rolled around or knocked about it will dispense bits of kibble. If you are willing to put up with a bit of controlled destruction you can put kibble or treats inside a cardboard box, old towel or rag, or crumpled plastic jugs and allow the dog to tear the item apart to get to the food inside. The cardboard rolls that toilet paper and paper towel rolls come on are great for this. Put some kibble in them, crumple the ends and let the pup tear apart the "toy" to get to the food. Many dog toys are hollow, such as Kongs and hollow nylon bones, and these can be filled with a dog biscuit, peanut butter, cheese or such like. The dog has to work at getting the food out. If you moisten some kibble, stuff the toy, and then freeze it, by the next day you will have a food stuffed toy that the dog will have to work at for quite a while before getting it out.

"One variation on this theme involves turning meals into searches. Simply divide the dog's meal into small portions, each in a plastic container. Now hide them around the house and let the dog search for them. At first you will have to make the hiding places fairly obvious, but later you can make finding the next portion of dinner more of a challenge.

"Actually, all forms of games based upon hide and seek are good. If you have someone to help you (I find visiting grandchildren are great for this), one person can hide and the other then encourages the dog to go and find them with

CAININE COGNITIVE - Treatments & Therapies

a command like "Find Becky". In the beginning the person who is hiding might have to actually call the dog from some place out of sight. Once the hidden person is found, the dog either gets a treat or gets a toy to play with. You a can actually play a form of "canine tennis" with the dog serving as the ball, by then sending the dog back to find the first person (who has now moved to a new place), and they send the dog back to the second person (who has also moved their hiding place) and so forth.

"Generally speaking, however, the dog is apt to find the environment in the house, where people are moving about, more exciting that the average yard. That means that if you want the dog outside you should go out there to play with it occasionally. Remember, you are not only building your relationship to your dog, but actually building him a better brain."

Reprinted By Permission from Dr. Coren.

Dental & Disease- Alternative Option
Non-Anesthetic Veterinary Dental

I never even considered dental alternatives for Shamrock. Probably because I didn't know any alternatives existed. When she needed a cleaning, which if I remember right, she had done three times, she was taken to her regular veterinarian in the morning, anesthetized and picked up later that afternoon.

However, during my research, I kept hearing about non-anesthetic veterinary dentistry and the name Kathy Shafer, from many of the veterinarians I spoke with.

One such recommendation was from Dr. Buchoff who said, care of dental issues is another top priority for our pet's good health. He recommended a procedure called "non anesthetic dentistry," only, as long as the pet does not have gingivitis. He said, "By eliminating the risks of anesthesia, regular dental care can be provided to most pets, including high-risk breeds, pets with medical conditions and those whose guardians want to avoid anesthesia."

SHAMROCK'S STORY

I have known that, as with humans, dental care for our pets is essential to prevent infection and inflammation that could lead to a growing number of diseases, like dementia. But I was unaware that there was anything except dental surgery with anesthesia.

When several of the veterinarian's I had interviewed mentioned dental anesthesia issues relating to dog dementia, I was extremely interested to learn more. These veterinarians told me they had been using a non- anesthesia procedure for over 10 years and referred me to Ms. Shafer.

Before my interview with her, I gave a lot of thought to the issue of pet dental. With my teeth I go to a "Dentist," or a "Periodontist" or an "Oral Surgeon. But I never thought twice about having a dental procedure done by any of my dog's veterinarians, nor did I ask if they had dental technicians, dental specialists, or special dental equipment. When I was told any of them needed dental work, I just had it done.

Ms. Shafer opened my eyes to the benefits of thinking about this procedure and asking questions.

She told me she specialized in preventative dental care for pets for over 30 years. She began as a teenager in the 1960's assisting with non-surgical dental at the veterinary clinic she worked for. At that time the procedure was called a "Standing Dental."

I mentioned to her that I have had 9 dogs in my lifetime, so far, and never heard of any alternative treatment to surgery for dog's teeth cleanings. I was intrigued to learn about both her and her procedure.

She told me that non-anesthetic (anesthesia free) dental cleanings have been offered for decades at holistic veterinary clinics that lean towards preventive and wellness care. Thousands of pets are regularly cared for this way at these hospitals.

"This level of dental cleaning is for 'Wellness care'. This type of care would be preferred for puppies, in order to ward off disease; as long as possible. But this care can also be especially helpful for pets that have previously had oral surgery. When the dogs are disease free, their veterinarian wants to keep their teeth in that condition."

The technique that she developed depends on gentle coaxing and patience. She told me, "The technicians are trained to

CAININE COGNITIVE - Treatments & Therapies

effectively clean both above and below the gum line and polish while your pet remains comfortable."

I was confused as I'd never been told about this alternative for dogs, or even recommended for this type of treatment, by any of the previous veterinarians that took care of my nine dogs; even those that were in holistic practices.

Ms. Shafer expressed to me, "Unfortunately, veterinarians have very limited exposure to dentistry in veterinary school.

"Dental Disease is a topic that veterinary education spends only a modest amount of time teaching. But upon graduation, every veterinarian is shocked to discover that dental procedures are the most regularly performed procedure a hospital will do and the one that they are most ill prepared to perform.

"Dental Wellness is a preventive care. Veterinarians, as are most doctors, are trained to focus on disease eradication. Veterinarians train to treat disease and that dental disease can only be located with oral surgery. Often, pet parents and veterinarians put off treatment until advanced disease has wreaked havoc on the pet's immune system; all because of the fear and serious risk associated with any major surgery.

"Many veterinarians don't have dental X-ray equipment. So, they have no idea of the extent of the pet's dental disease. Without X-rays the removal of disease will have a poor outcome. X-rays are a must. They will always reveal how far dental disease has progressed to bone disease.

"When veterinarians today perform dental cleanings and extractions, many don't even have dental x-ray technology or if they do, they haven't really been trained on using the equipment properly.

"Without dental x-rays as a baseline there is no way of determining the depth, or the progression of the dental disease. Without x-rays only teeth that are visually diseased may be removed. This can leave behind abscesses, retained roots and bone disease. This also results in poor outcomes for the pet's overall health.

"We know the damaging effects of poor dental health on the heart, liver, brain and kidneys. There has also been information associating various forms of arthritis and dementia to oral neglect and diseases."

SHAMROCK'S STORY

This is how bacteria is able to gain access and silently invade the body:

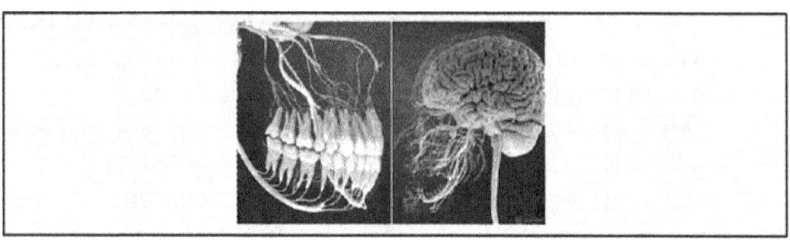

Ms. Shafer also advised me that in 1972 state laws permitted veterinary techs to perform procedures such as dental. Most of these technicians did not know how to do dental care without anesthesia. In many cases they tried but got bit by the dog, which raised insurance problems. They were instructed that the only way to perform dental care was to have the dogs anesthetized.

She made me aware of a shocking statistic that when anesthetics are used in human surgeries, especially with seniors, there can be up to a 30 % cognitive loss. Unfortunately, it is the same for pets. That is a good reason why our medical professionals are so cautious about prescribing major surgery.

I next asked her what pet parents can do from the time their dogs are puppies to avoid future problems?

She explained that the best care begins with understanding your dog's mouth. We have 28 to 32 teeth (depending on molar removal), dogs have 42 teeth; that is a lot for your pet's little mouth.

Her advice was, "Start by getting a baseline of the pet's mouth. Each parent can do this with a mobile device or ask your veterinarian; and be sure to update those photos regularly.

"For home care, wipe your dog's teeth every day. The plaque at that point is very soft and can be easily wiped off. When it's not removed quickly the plaque will build up and then gums can become red and swollen. Using a little diluted hydrogen peroxide on a cloth can calm the inflammation. This will also attack the bacteria levels that caused the inflammation in the first place. The gums will feel and look much better.

CAININE COGNITIVE - Treatments & Therapies

"Good dental health is also a result of the dog's lifestyle and their diet. Saliva keeps their mouths clean, so dogs that become 'couch potatoes' are likely to display dental issues earlier in their life.

"A dog should eat good foods; feeding raw is highly desirable. Their food should be starch and grain free. Therefore, a paleo-keto style diet works well.

"Chewing is good for oral health because it creates a mixing of saliva throughout the mouth." But Ms. Shafer warned against giving pets antlers, or weight baring bones to chew on. She clarified, "If a bone is strong enough to hold up a large animal, it is not designed to be chewed on."

I have seen some dogs with very severe gingivitis or periodontal issues, and wanted to know what can be done when dental concerns get to that stage?

She continued, "The pet needs an oral evaluation by a veterinarian, preferably one that is passionate about dental. This evaluation will determine and then categorize whether what is seen can be cared for with a non-surgical protocol. However, if dental disease is present, in which case, the protocol is surgical, dental x-rays must be done, first to discover the depth of the disease and then to remove the diseased teeth, tissue and repair the bone."

Ms. Shafer added, "I have witnessed pets after their dental care return to being a happy playful pup that pet parents say they haven't seen in months or even years. Oral neglect is a slow silent killer.

"When our technicians care for your pet, they may make several suggestions to help the pet's parent, understanding that each pet is an individual and we adjust our suggestion according to the needs of the pet and the capabilities of the caregiver."

But she alerted me to a problem most dog parents just ignore, "Doggy Bad Breath!" Most people pass their dogs bad breath off as something that is just, "Dog," or believe it's something that can be delt with in the future. Ms. Shafer commented, "Unfortunately, that happens far too often. The good intentions turn into a few months then a couple of years and what would have been resolved with a routine non-surgical protocol has progressed beyond that and may have progressed to a stage that is now damaging the heart or other organs."

SHAMROCK'S STORY

But my concern was what do you do when an older pet's blood work comes back compromised with health indicators that make it impossible for the pet to have a surgical procedure to remove their dental disease?

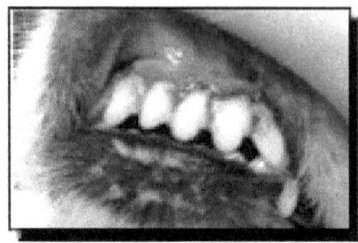

This advanced dental disease took years to reach this level

In these cases, Ms. Shafer advised, "We have a consideration, 'Quality-of-Life Care.' Or QOL for short. At that point, the dental tech will work with the veterinarian and the pet parent to develop an individualized plan. Depending on the dog's condition and the extent of the dental disease, they may not be able to remove the dental disease but can attack the bacteria's ability to go unchecked. Without this protocol most pets will eventually be at a state when a veterinarian will no longer be able to treat your dog's oral disease. Then, if the dental needs are totally unchecked, the bacteria will make the dog's breath smell so offensive that some pet parents will stop face to face love and affection. That makes the situation even worse for both the dog and the pet parent."

This protocol would be the perfect solution for dogs like Shamrock, whereby the medical reasons prevent an anesthetic procedure being used to remove the disease. So, the treatment becomes damage control, but the pet parent can still feel there is a plan to reduce the impact of the mature bacteria.

To sum up Ms. Shafer believes that both the veterinary community and the pet parents need to have better access to education about oral health and dental care. For years pet dental health has been treated as, "The Panty Hose syndrome, One Size Fits All!" She added, "That never worked with panty hose, and it certainly never worked with dental disease. But like panty hose, when we knew better, we did better...as it should be with dental care also."
Pictures provided by agreement with Ms. Shafer

TCVM-Traditional Chinese Veterinary Medicine

CAININE COGNITIVE - Treatments & Therapies

After reading about all these treatments and possible ways to help our dogs, I wanted to delve into an arena that is over 3,000 years old to find out how Traditional Chinese Veterinary Medicine looks at cognitive dysfunction syndrome.

I contacted the Chi University and they pointed me to this article by Dr. Ronald Koh, who specializes in Integrative Medicine, Sports and Rehabilitation, and Chinese Veterinary Medicine. This article provided a great deal of information about the disease and how it relates to understanding the body deficiencies, treatments such as acupuncture, Chinese herbal medicine, and food therapy.

The following information is being presented by permission from Dr. Koh and in thanks to him and the "American Journal of Traditional Chinese Veterinary Medicine."

Article:
Traditional Chinese Veterinary Medicine for Cognitive Dysfunction Syndrome
By Ronald Koh DVM, MS

"ABBREVIATIONS (terms used in this article)
AD Alzheimer's Disease
CDS Cognitive dysfunction syndrome
TCM Traditional Chinese Medicine
TCVM Traditional Chinese Veterinary Medicine
EAP Electro -Acupuncture
SLT Sai Luo Tong

"Cognitive dysfunction syndrome (CDS) is a degenerative brain disease that affects many older dogs.

Traditional Chinese veterinary medicine (TCVM) is being used much more commonly now as a sole or integrative modality in veterinary medicine and can offer potential benefits and safety for the treatment of CDS. Clinical evidence indicates that acupuncture and Chinese herbals may recover cognitive impairment, improve memory, ameliorate anxiety, and provide calming effects.

Cognitive dysfunction syndrome (CDS) is a veterinary term to describe the progressive neurodegenerative disorder of senior dogs and cats that is characterized by a gradual decline in cognitive function (learning, memory, perception and awareness). It shares some similarities with Alzheimer's disease (AD) in humans. In veterinary medicine, 68% of dogs older than 15 years of age demonstrated clinical signs consistent with CDS. Regardless, a learning and memory decline may begin in dogs as young as 6 and 7.7 years of age, respectively. Common clinical signs or behavioral problems in pets with CDS are often represented by the acronym DISHAAL (Disorientation, Interaction changes, Sleep/wake disturbances, House soiling, Activity changes, Anxiety, and Learning/memory). Additionally, signs of anxiety, phobias and aggression are also commonly reported by owners of senior pets. Diagnosis of CDS remains a challenge in daily clinical practice because the characteristic behavioral signs overlap with those of other medical and behavioral disorders. CDS is diagnosed based on clinical signs, obtaining a thorough behavioral history and ruling.

Traditional Chinese Medicine (TCM) has a long history for preventing and treating cognitive decline or dementia in humans. CDS in dogs' parallels AD in humans as they share similarities in the etiology, pathogenesis, and treatment. Traditional Chinese Veterinary Medicine (TCVM), which includes acupuncture, Chinese herbal medicine, food therapy and Tui-na (healing therapy that originated in China) can be a valuable and effective therapy. It can be a sole or integrative modality for the treatment of CDS as it has been used in animals for thousands of years in China. Clinical evidence indicates acupuncture and Chinese herbal medicine may greatly benefit patients with AD. Acupuncture has demonstrated significant improvement of cognitive impairment and memory along with ameliorating depression and anxiety in various neurodegenerative disorders in humans and lab animals. In addition, there are a number of Chinese herbs or herbal formulas that have been found to possess a calming effect and are able to enhance blood circulation and promote neurogenesis in the brain of animal models with AD and dementia. out other medical (e.g., intracranial, extracranial) causes of the behavior. Treatment of CDS is aimed at slowing the advancement of neuronal damage and cell death in the brain and improving the behavioral signs of affected animals.

According to TCM theories, AD belongs to the category of memory disorders known as Jian Wang (forgetfulness) and Dai Bing (dementia). Kidney and Heart are the two primary TCVM organ systems related to CDS. The Kidney is considered the center for vigor and strength with the brain viewed as more of a reservoir of the kidney. The functions of the brain, however, are regulated by the Heart so there is an intimate relationship between the Kidney and Heart and cognition. In a nutshell, Kidney provides the brain and Heart regulates its activities.

Deterioration of the brain is due to Kidney Deficiency of Qi, Yin, Yang, or Jing (Essence). In particular, Kidney Jing

Deficiency is commonly associated with CDS. Kidney Jing declines naturally as an animal ages resulting in the characteristic signs of gray hair, loss of teeth, rear weakness, impairment of memory, cognitive dysfunction and inability to reproduce. Kidney Jing is the origin of both Kidney Yin and Kidney Yang, so a Deficient Kidney Jing can result in Kidney Yin Deficiency or Kidney Yang Deficiency.

The Kidney Yin and Yang are always mutually dependent, so long-term damage to Kidney Yin will result in depletion of Kidney Yang and vice versa.

The Heart is the second main organ involved with cognition. Injury to the Heart through Deficient Qi, Yin, Blood or Phlegm obstruction can impair behavior, cognition and memory. The Heart also houses the Shen, which is equivalent to the spirit, soul, mind and outward appearance of the whole body. Shen rules mental activities, cognition, memory and sleep. It provides an animal with awareness and mental clarity. When Shen is healthy, the animal exhibits normal behaviors, sleeps well and is alert and responsive to environmental stimuli. On the contrary, an animal exhibiting a Shen Disturbance pattern displays poor memory, anxiety, restlessness, aggressiveness, disorientation, house soiling, insomnia, or hyperactivity. Shen requires nourishment from Heart Yin and Blood, therefore, when Heart Yin and Blood are Deficient, the Shen lacks anchoring and nourishment, leading to a Shen Disturbance and abnormal behavioral changes.

General Treatment Approach to All TCVM Patterns

The main treatment principles for CDS are to strengthen the Root, to harmonize Yin, Yang, Qi and Blood and to eliminate the Manifestation. Once achieved, this reestablishes balance in the body, which achieves the goal of a healthy mind. Before initiating treatment, a thorough Si Zhen (the Four exams) should be performed to determine the correct pattern differentiation. The treatment strategy should include acupuncture, Chinese herbal therapy, food therapy, and Tui-na massage.

The energetic effects of food can be used as an effective treatment to address the patterns of disharmony, therefore balancing the body and enhancing cognitive abilities as well as protecting the brain from damage in CDS patients. Bitter food is the taste associated with the Heart and the spirit (Shen). The following foods could be used to help: vinegar, turnips, gingko, seaweed, pig's liver, asparagus, bitter melon, cauliflower, kale, broccoli, and lettuce. Salty food goes to the Kidney: duck, pork, seafood (octopus, oyster, anchovy, clam and crab), alfalfa sprouts, barley, seaweed, kelp, beets, celery, and parsley. Beans such as kidney bean and black bean also benefit the Kidney. The author also adds berries, such as blueberries and strawberries, as a natural source of antioxidants.

The final deficiency TCVM pattern is Kidney Jing Deficiency, which presents as a Yin or Yang Deficiency. Yin Deficiency signs observed are poor memory, restlessness, Heat signs (panting, thirsty but drink small quantities of water, warm feet and ears), nighttime anxiety, trouble falling asleep at night and hind end weakness/lumbar pain. Clinical signs often worsen during late evening or at night. The tongue is red or deep red and dry with thin to no coating. Pulses are rapid, thready, and weaker on left side. Yang Deficiency clinical signs are depression, lethargy, hypersomnia, loss of coordination, weakness of all limbs, lumbar pain, urinary and/or fecal incontinence, poor appetite, loose stool, cool to cold back and feet. The tongue is pale to lavender, wet and swollen. Pulses are slow, deep and weak. Treatment strategy includes nourishing the Kidney Jing and Yin or Warm Kidney Yang along with tonifying Spleen (post-natal Jing). Acupuncture treatment uses common points along with adding a Yin.

Early identification of CDS signs is essential for treatment success. The existing evidence to support the use of acupuncture and Chinese herbal therapy is promising but larger blinded, controlled, randomized clinical studies of their effects are needed in veterinary patients.

Clinical studies of Sai Luo Tong (SLT) formula, which consists of the bioactive components of the three herbal extracts from Panax ginseng, Ginkgo biloba, and Crocus sativa, showed significant improvement in neurocognitive function, learning, and memory "

This information was taken from an article by Koh R. Traditional Chinese medicine for cognitive dysfunction syndrome. Am J Trad Chin Vet Med 2018; 13(1): 65-78.
Article is reprinted here by permission with Dr. Koh.

CBD OIL-A Cannabinoid Called Cannabidiol

I must admit what I knew about CBD for human's was only the word, "Marijuana," and my knowledge of that, was very limited. What I knew about CBD for dog's was non-existent!

First, I learned that the cannabis plant produces many compounds, some which are known as cannabinoids. That was a start, but I had a long way to go! My research revealed that the cannabis was a flowering plant with some sub-species that are referred to as cannabis something, I hope you are not as confused as I was.

When I was interviewing Dr. Kangas, about "Canine cognitive dysfunction syndrome," she mentioned the use of CBD oil. She was the first veterinarian I had spoken with that told me about using CBD for cognitive decline and the beginnings of dog dementia.

Dr. Kangas told me, "Using pharmaceutical medicines for pain can affect both the gut and the brain, as well as the liver and other organs." She wanted pet parents to understand they don't necessarily have to rely on pain meds to provide better comfort and quality of life for pets. There are many natural substances that provide anti-inflammatory and analgesic, properties to relieve pain. These include CBD oil and many other types of herbs and nutritional substances.

While discussing this issue, she revealed that there are still many veterinarians that do not; or will not, dispense CBD oil, due to either local regulations or due to the lack of knowledge and understanding of the general safety and significant benefits that this type of plant medicine can offer. She explained that cannabinoids have many versatile benefits which include anti-inflammatory, analgesic (pain relief), calming the brain and nervous system, anti-seizure effects, anti-cancer benefits, immune modulation, and more.

I questioned Dr. Kangas, about her reasons for recommending CBD oil for cognitive issues?

She replied, "In these circumstances, CBD products may help regulate the dog's mood and also relieve pain. These factors make it a worthy option for pets." She does also state that it is important to choose a quality product and use it with appropriate dosing for each individual pet.

"In many states the distribution of CBD oil by veterinarians, is still against the law." Her state of California is one and therefore she turns to certified cannabis advisor, Robbin Lynn. When dealing with your pet's health, Dr. Kangas feels the best approach is to go directly to a specialist in this area who also knows how to be an educator and how to guide people to not just a quality product, but also proper counseling regarding its use.

Dr. Kangas said, "Plant medicines are generally very safe if you have a quality product that is designed or formulated for pets." Specifically, regarding CBD, she expressed, "It can be a GAME CHANGER for many pets with different disease issues." She has also seen first-hand that CBD oil can help dogs with gut inflammation and inflammatory bowel disease, which is becoming increasingly common in dogs. "For many dogs this can be a remarkable tool, but there also needs to be additional steps to help support the pet's health." Dr. Kangas added, she would not use this as a sole treatment without recommending other (natural and dietary) health supportive measures. These generally come from other herbs and supplements; diet and the removal of toxins all to help bring your

CAININE COGNITIVE - Treatments & Therapies

dog back to better health. These can include specific herbal supplements, foods, and nutritional supplements, including MCT oils, vitamins, and antioxidants, etc.

Dr. Bassingthwaighte expressed, "CBD oil is one of the best choices for reducing symptoms. PEA, Palmitoylethanolamide is another non-toxic, natural medicine which can be used alone or in conjunction with CBD oil."

When Dr. Kangas referred me to Mrs. Lynn, a Certified Cannabis Advisor, I was very anxious to speak with her to learn as much as I could about CBD oil and its use for dogs with cognitive issues.

Mrs. Lynn told me she started using CBD Oil for people and later collaborated with Dr Kangas to help pet's and their parents dealing with dog ailments.

My biggest questions were about using CBD for dog dementia treatment and how to educate pet parents about its use for this disease. I began by asking, "What is the procedure when a pet parent is sent to you with a dog that has two or more signs of dementia?"

She told me, "It's rare that she hears the word 'dementia' with pets, the issue is often characterized as a behavioral issue, and what the veterinarian is looking for is help with signs such as, 'sundowners' or behavioral panting, pacing, disorientation and anxiety." The big thing pet parents tell her is that their pet used to love to do things, and no longer seems to enjoy life!

Her procedure involves first educating pet parents about CBD and what the endocannabinoid system is. This can help them to better understand the use of these products, and to arrive at their comfort level in giving cannabinoids to their dog. She pointed out, "It is important to remember, each condition and each dog is unique. There is no, 'One size fits all!'" The type and dosage of CBD she will suggest getting started will be determined by weight, age and if the approach will be conservative or aggressive. Unfortunately, treating dogs in the latter stages of dementia is sometimes the last resort, and Mrs. Lynn will generally suggest a more aggressive approach.

She also helped educate me about this product. "CBD is derived from the family of the cannabis plant scientifically known as Cannabis Sativa L., which is made up of hundreds of components,

SHAMROCK'S STORY

CBD being one of over 120 cannabinoids. Two most commonly discussed cannabinoids are Cannabidiol, called CBD, which is considered a non-psychoactive cannabinoid, which is non-intoxicating and non-euphoric, meaning it won't get you 'high'. Also, Tetrahydrocannabinol, referred to as, 'THC,' is the main psychoactive compound in cannabis. THC is responsible for the 'high' that most people associate with cannabis.

"Just those three letters can be very frightening to many pet parents. Many people still think of THC as the psychedelic drug that causes hallucinations and distortions of the mind." Mrs. Lynn explained that THC has many therapeutic properties, and when used properly, does not induce a psychoactive effect, and can also better assist CBD to activate.

Once the pet parent understands these differences, and Mrs. Lynn understands the dog's needs, she can proceed to measure the pet parent's comfort level. Based on all that information she can help the parent select products that are appropriate for the pet's condition and then choose an optimal dose. The use of CBD will usually, but not always, begin at the lowest dosage level and then after two weeks, increase to higher concentrations, allowing her to determine the results. This gives the pet parents an opportunity to monitor how the dog is doing and see how they need to continue.

I asked Mrs. Lynn what her prognosis was when using CBD products for CCDS? She reiterated, "CBD is not the 'magic pill' or 'cure all!'" However, she recommended using these products to re-balance the deficiency of the endocannabinoid system, which was discovered in the 80's. A lot of what happened then was disallowed because of the association to the word 'pot'! But over the years she has seen the benefits, not necessarily in reversal of this disease, but improvement in symptoms and more joy in life. She continued, "If the pet was a 'sundowner,' giving a dose one hour before their issues start can help to decrease the symptoms." She also specified that it is rare to see 100% difference, but 80% change is reasonable: better sleep, less pacing or panting, more wagging tails and more joy!

I told her if there was even a glimmer of change with Shamrock, I would have been so happy; but 80%; that would have seemed like a miracle!

If the pet parent is using just CBD products and believes there is no significant improvement, Mrs. Lynn might discuss adding THC, depending on the parent's comfort zone. But, when adding THC makes them feel uncomfortable, she can suggest other compounds like, "THCA," which is radically different in the way it affects the brain. THCA provides all the benefits of THC, but does not produce any psychoactive, or mind-altering effects, making it an ideal addition to the regime, without worry of intoxication

Any new compounds introduced to a pet's body can have deleterious responses, so she goes slow in the process and wants to see if there are any undesired results, such as, too lethargic or cotton mouth; or even if the pet's symptoms are getting worse. It is important to understand that everyone gets different responses, which need to be monitored and measured. Dogs, like all mammals, are the most sensitive to cannabinoids simply because they have the most endocannabinoid receptors. Therefore, there is a need to look at each case individually, and based on that pet's results, to get the optimum dosage for a good quality of life.

That led me to ask how pet parents with little or no knowledge of CBD products, who want to try these for their pet, would go about it in a safe manner; especially since there are no current regulations and products are being sold on-line and even in grocery stores?

The answer was, you can find a cannabis specialist, like Mrs. Lynn, or at least do research into products that contain just CBD, THC, or a combination of both. Just be aware that the dried flower that most people associate with cannabis contains both, though certain strains may have much more of one than the other, and depending upon the source, can contain very detrimental pesticides.

As far as side effects, she added, "These effects are less common in products containing more CBD than THC."

She also told me, "Per the federal government, products containing less than zero-point three percent THC are classified as hemp and this is a largely unregulated industry. Any products containing above zero-point three percent are classified as cannabis, also known as 'marijuana,' and those products are tightly regulated in many states." But she cautions, "There are many products out there that are simply hemp seed oil, which is a great source of omegas for humans, but not for animals. These products usually contain little or no CBD. And, if not organically produced, can also be loaded with pesticides. So, it is important to be aware of any toxins, and be sure that what you use is organically grown."

At that point, I wanted to know if there were any statistics of success in the treatment of dog dementia with CBD products?

Mrs. Lynn said that success is measured in many different ways. Dogs may start treatments at various stages and that can make a big difference as to the results. Improvement of symptoms like sleeping or pain relief, as well as overall quality of life are good markers of success. "You first have to ask what was the goal? Was it to rectify a deficiency, or to achieve a better quality of life?

"Endocannabinoid deficiency develops when the body's endocannabinoid system isn't functioning properly. CBD products can address, pain, and anxiety making a difference in the dog's quality of life."

She also told me that with dogs like Shamrock, if they get better sleep, eat better, and seem to enjoy life…pet parents consider that is a success.

But she stressed, "Buyer be aware! Become educated because there is so much information, so learn from reliable sources."

A Personal Look Into A CBD Consultation

I told Mrs. Lynn I wanted to become better informed about the process to give my readers a more accurate experience for choosing CBD products for their dog with dementia, She suggested we do an actual consultation. *(Note: Shamrock's history was used to simulate an actual experience).

We began with her explaining that dogs are very sensitive to many cannabinoids, and the key is to understand that endocannabinoid deficiencies exist. Then you can look at putting cannabinoids back in, like CBD which replenishes the system and helps natural endocannabinoids to function again. This can help with CCDS, as even a small amount of THC and rich CBD can have incredible benefits to the system.

Mrs. Lynn discussed the ways to restoration of the physical, emotional, and protective systems.

CAININE COGNITIVE - Treatments & Therapies

"First, we need to achieve a calm mind: relieving signs such as: sundowners, or hyper-activeness, getting stuck in corners, being dazed, or pacing, panting, sleep disruption. These are achieved by naturally decreasing stress and relaxing the mind to improve the dog's joy." She explained that with the right amount and the right combination of compounds, she does see up to about 85% improvement.

I was amazed at those figures and asked, if to achieve that percentage, does the dog need to be, "a druggy?"

Her response was that each dog is unique, and the ultimate goal for most pet parents is to reduce the undesired symptoms, and balance that, with any undesired effects of the CBD or other cannabinoids.

My goal was to make Shamrock happy and joyful, to reduce her agitation, anxiety, and combativeness.

Mrs. Lynn added "With the right products in the right amounts and combinations; this could be achieved."

I also wondered about other changes: diet supplements, routine, exercise, and whether those things would increase the success rate?

She told me we can get satisfactory results from tinctures. Today, most formulations of CBD "tinctures" are referred to as CBD oil or CBD extracts. She added, "I like tinctures best for pets because we can be very accurate with dosing and pet parents can pick the right concentration for the size of their dog. With low doses we can go slow to watch for any sensitivities and then see if other modifications are needed."

I was curious how this experience would change is I was not being guided by her expertise. I asked, "What should I look for if I was choosing a product on my own."

Mrs. Lynn explained, When selecting a tincture for your dog, always choose one that is organically sourced (cannabis is a bio accumulator) and contains just two ingredients: the cannabis extract and the carrier oil, (usually coconut/MCT, olive or hemp seed oil). Ensure the tincture actually contains CBD by confirming through the Certificate of Analysis, (COA), which is the lab report that the manufacturer should make easily available to you. If they do not, move on to the next product that will.

She told me, "Any other dietary or supplementation changes, should be a conversation to have with Shamrock's veterinarian."

SHAMROCK'S STORY

Also, because Shamrock walked around; sometimes 16 hours a day and I only got her to really sleep in the afternoon when I would lie down with her, Mrs. Lynn said that we should see whether we need to adjust for her daytime and nighttime symptoms.

Now that we had discussed the process, we were ready to pick a product with the understanding that we could go up or down based on what we would see in the first few days. The choice would be a product that has the highest concentration of cannabis oil, so that Shamrock would have to take as little volume as possible. We would start with twice a day for 14 days to saturate her system, after which, we would review the results and adjust as needed.

I wanted to know if there were things I needed to be aware of.

Mrs. Lynn advised because of Shamrock's CCDS, possible reactions to be aware of would be her becoming too lethargic, or if her anxiety was being exacerbated. She said, "There are certain things that she has seen in dogs, they can get cotton mouth and be seen drinking a lot more water or smacking their lips. If these effects happen with Shamrock, most of the time these issues will resolve as she gets more used to the product, but if not, we can change doses or switch products." Mrs. Lynn added, "We may even need to layer in other cannabinoids"

She told me the range of treatment many times is dictated by the pet parent. Lots of things also revolve around how aggressive or careful the pet parent wants to be in the treatment.

Because of Shamrock's symptoms of the disease, I wanted to be more aggressive, but not give her more anxiety.

She felt it would be a good idea to see how Shamrock did the first two days, while I watched for even the smallest change; anything different I observed, because any change could indicate good movement.

I did have one last question. I remembered in the sixties people talked about how marijuana affects the appetite. Mrs. Lynn responded, one reason for using THC in a compound with CBD products is, CBD can depress the appetite and Shamrock was already losing weight and not eating well. She was very aware of that and didn't want to add an appetite suppressant. So, THC and THCA could be added to help with the appetite.

Her message really came down to, "No one size fits all!" She also cautions, if you want to try CBD products without consulting an expert in the field, "Do your research and choose what makes sense to you."

But her best advice on this journey was, "Be patient, be consistent and don't give up! Give the pet's body time to let the system reboot, and then adjust as needed."

It is also important to note that cannabis is still illegal in many places, but in more and more areas that is starting to change, for both recreational and medical uses. But cannabis remains illegal under federal law in the United States. If you are interested in using cannabis for your pet, make sure to read up on the laws in your area first!

More CBD Information

I heard about Dr. Russo from Mrs. Lynn, when she referred me to an interview he gave. He discussed clinical endocannabinoid deficiency and ways to target the endocannabinoid system for therapeutic benefit.

Interview:

With Dr. Russo, a Neurologist, an author, and teacher.
Dr. Ethan Russo on CBD & Clinical Endocannabinoid Deficiency.

*During the interview Dr. Russo stated, "... cannabidiol, can counteract some of the less desirable effects of THC such as its tendency to produce anxiety and rapid heart rate. But at the same time, cannabidiol on its own has many properties that THC doesn't – as an anti-anxiety agent, as an anti-psychotic, and without producing intoxication, which can occur with too much THC.

"Also, in the endocannabinoid system one of its main roles in the brain is to regulate neurotransmitter function and again, if there's too much of one kind of neurotransmitter it will bring it down, if there's too little it will bring it up."

He then pinpointed this information regarding dementia and said, "One primary problem in Alzheimer's disease or other dementias is a lack of acetylcholine, the memory molecule in the brain. So, what would a deficiency of endocannabinoid function look like? Well, we already knew that. If you don't have enough endocannabinoids, you have pain, where there shouldn't be pain. You would be sick, meaning nauseated. You would have a lowered seizure threshold. And just a whole litany of other problems. It occurred to me that a number of very common diseases seem to fit a pattern. There seems to be pain out of proportion to what should be going on, in other words you can look at the tissues, they look okay, but there's biochemically something that's driving the pain.

"First and foremost, we need to better understand the role of the endocannabinoids in our lives and our health status. That's been ignored, possibly because of its name, having cannabis in the name of this has impeded education, even in medical school. Basically, it hardly exists. Let's consider this. There are more cannabinoid receptors in the brain than there are for all the neurotransmitters put together. That being true, and it is, recognizing that fact, why would one ignore this system? Why isn't this being taught? Our public needs to know about this and how lifestyle and diet affect this system, and how it could be brought to bear to improve their life condition."

*Interview excerpted with permission from ProjectCBD.org
Reprinted by permission with Dr. Russo

In our communication, Dr. Russo told me, "We need a little history first to indicate that cannabidiol has always been part of the capabilities of cannabis. It's just that it's been pushed into the background but, for the most part, the medicinal benefits of this substance have a lot to offer on many levels.

"Firstly, it synergizes with THC, so it complements the ability of THC to treat pain while in its own right it's an excellent anti-inflammatory without the liabilities that we get from non-steroidal anti-inflammatory drugs, with their tendencies to produce serious side effects like ulcers, heart attacks, and strokes, these just aren't a liability with cannabidiol."

To better describe the theory, Dr. Russo uses a familiar analogy. "Although this is overly simplistic, in Alzheimer's disease or dementia, we have a deficit in acetylcholine, the memory molecule in the brain. In Parkinson's disease, we have a deficit of dopamine function, another neurotransmitter. Although, again, this is much more complicated than that, there seems to be serotonin deficiencies in depression. I theorized, what would it look like if we had deficits in the endocannabinoid system? One might expect a constellation of different symptoms, above all pain, where we didn't expect it."

There is evidence that with more research, his theory could revolutionize how we approach and treat chronic disorders.

**Regarding Alzheimer's Dr Russo stated, "Alzheimer's Disease, AD, is a neurodegenerative disease and once the process begins, deterioration is unstoppable. Dementia and cognitive decline develop, and no treatment arrests the process. Intervention must begin at an early stage to have any hope of success.

"Endocannabinoid function modulates the processes of AD during the silent phase of neurodegeneration, protein misfolding, neuroinflammation, excitotoxicity, mitochondrial dysfunction and oxidative stress.

"The study of AD is fascinating. North America and Western Europe have the highest rates, (6.4% and 5.4% at age 60), then Latin America (4.9%), and China (4%; ascertainment bias vs. mirroring economic development and Western diet?).

"Prevalence is lower for Africans in homelands, as opposed to higher rates in the Western Europe and America.

"A Mediterranean diet increased monounsaturated olive oil, and omega-3 from fish, education and physical activity can reduce the rates.

"CBD is a neuroprotective antioxidant, more potent than ascorbate, (Vitamin C) or tocopherol, (Vitamin E), but can be given at higher doses without toxicity. CBD is an anti-inflammatory that has also been found to inhibit the formation of plaque in the brain.

"Initial trials of herbal cannabis for AD have been conducted with a more focused effort in a California nursing home. Patients were treated with a variety of preparations: THC-predominant (2.5–30 mg/dose), CBD predominant, and THCA, mainly in tinctures and confections. Marked benefits were reported: decreased agitation, increased appetite, aggression, sleep quality, objective mood, nursing care demands, self-mutilation, and pain control. Based on its components, cannabis may provide a myriad of benefits on target symptoms in this complex disorder: Agitation: THC, CBD, Anxiety: CBD, THC (low dose), Psychosis: CBD,

SHAMROCK'S STORY

Insomnia/Restlessness: THC, Anorexia: THC, Aggression: THC, CBD, Depression: THC, limonene, CBD, Pain: THC, CBD, Memory: alpha-pinene + THC, Neuroprotection: CBD, THC, Reduced plaque formation: THC, CBD, THCA."

Dr. Russo also expressed, whereas cannabis proper has been used in veterinary medicine throughout history, the use of CBD in dogs exactly parallels that in humans and has really come to the forefront in the last decade. However, there are caveats. CBD is not particularly potent and larger amounts are needed compared to lower doses of THC to do its best work, which really occurs in conjunction with other cannabinoids and terpenoids.

CBD is extremely safe. It should not be controversial but is merely through its association with cannabis. CBD is extremely versatile. While primarily employed today to treat existing problems (inflammation, pain, anxiety, etc.), its use certainly could be part of a preventive regimen. Its advantage over conventional drugs is its amazingly low toxicity, allowing chronic use without the concern of complications present with most synthetic agents.

There are however many misconceptions regarding Cannabidiol, and Dr. Russo hoped to correct some of these. In an article he wrote, "Cannabidiol Claims and Misconceptions." *** Dr. Russo stated, "CBD is frequently mischaracterized. Given its prominent benefits on anxiety, schizophrenia, addiction, and possibly even depression. CBD should be preferably labeled as 'non-intoxicating, and lacking association to cravings, and compulsive behavior that would lead to drug abuse.

"There is a misconception that CBD Is sedating. Some early literature cited a low incidence of sedation however, low to moderate doses have proven its ability to counteract sedative effects. Numerous modern studies, even those with single low doses have been free of sedative effects

"Whereas pure CBD is not sedating, many CBD-containing drugs and hemp products do display this liability. This is not attributable to CBD concentration per se, but rather to the addition of high levels of myrcene, (a naturally occurring component of plants used in commercial production of cannabis as an anti-inflammatory). Myrcene, can have a narcotic-effect at high doses. Therefore, selecting low myrcene products reduces or eliminates this liability.

CAININE COGNITIVE - Treatments & Therapies

"One current misconception is that CBD Is legal in all 50 states. CBD is an available drug in most nations, however, this is not the case in the United States, where CBD has been a forbidden agent with its own Drug Enforcement Administration (DEA) number, and designation as a THC analog. In spite of this continuing prohibition, domestic commerce in CBD in one form or another is rampant in storefronts and on the Internet; frequently accompanied by claims that its extraction from hemp refuse is a legal process. While currently tolerated without federal prosecution as of this writing, such practices may concentrate pesticides and other agricultural toxins and are explicitly illegal under the Controlled Substances Act of 1970.

"A fearful misconception for many is that CBD turns into THC in the body. This false claim has been frequently invoked online, showing that CBD could be converted into THC after prolonged exposure to 'simulated' gastric acid. While this reaction has been known for decades, there seems to be no compelling evidence that CBD undergoes cyclization or bioconversion to THC in humans."

Dr. Russo summed up with these concluding remarks. "CBD is an intriguing agent of unparalleled pharmacological diversity that is nevertheless surprisingly benign in all its observed effects. Its use has become widespread in certain geographical areas, particularly in 'legal' states in the USA, and it is on the threshold of becoming an approved pharmaceutical agent in intractable epilepsies. Given this current nouvelle richesse following its long history of obscurity, it is incumbent upon the scientific and medical communities to understand better the mechanisms of action of CBD, its limitations, and particularly the myths and misconceptions that its meteoric rise in popularity have engendered."

**Cannabis Therapeutics and the Future of Neurology by Ethan B. Russo
***Cannabidiol Claims and Misconceptions, by Ethan B. Russo
All information regarding these documents has been by permission with Dr. Russo.

Continuing Developments Regarding CBD

Dr. Bartner expressed that there are many good approaches to CCD such as supplementation with omega-3 fatty acids and possibly with cannabidiol, (CBD Oil). These are currently being looked at for their efficacy regarding CCD, as are CoQ10 antioxidants, medium chain triglycerides, (MCT Oils), and even some anticonvulsants.

The current trials being done with CBD hold a great deal of promise. One of Dr. Bartner's associates, Dr Stephanie McGrath, associate professor of neurology at Colorado State University, is pairing CBD with drug combinations that could delay, or even slow down, the progress of this disease. The trials help to determine if there is any improvement, which is great, but if not, then something else can be tried. Even when some combination of treatment is found which is fairly effective, it may need to be tweaked as things progress. In any case, CBD is definitely worth investigating.

CAININE COGNITIVE - Treatments & Therapies

The Dog/Human Connection

Possible Future Treatments- for Dogs & Humans

Dementia and Alzheimer's - Is there really a dog/ human connection? My discussion with Dr. Bartner related the realization of the pet parent "frustrations" when dealing with "Canine cognitive dysfunction." She stated, "There is not a whole lot of evidence-based knowledge available regarding dogs. The similarities between humans and dogs, may be related in some ways, but not so much in others."

My uncle's signs of dementia were exacerbated by the time he died at 96 with full blown Alzheimer's. But the progression in his behavior, spatial and physical issues seemed somewhat similar to Shamrock's. I wanted to understand how closely the two: CCD and Alzheimer's, were connected.

One thing that stood out for me was that our pets live in our environment and, generally, what we get, they can get. I also wanted to learn if we could better understand what happens to our dogs, and what can be done about it, by examining the current information for humans.

I raised these issues with veterinarians I interviewed and got mixed answers.

Dr. Gardner reaffirmed my feelings. She said, "CCD is often compared with Alzheimer's disease in humans, since the behaviors and nervous system changes associated with the two conditions are similar."

SHAMROCK'S STORY

I was encouraged to hear her mention "Alzheimer's" as that confirmed the way I figured out what was happening to Shamrock, (before I had all this valuable information). When I saw my uncle, in a room and he didn't know why he was there, or his inability to back out of places he had gotten himself into, the constant sleep disturbances, not eating, aggressive behavior, (he was normally very quiet and calm), his confusion and a constant need for movement, this triggered the feeling in me that what Shamrock was going through mirrored what I saw in my uncle.

I told Dr. Brugliera about the days when the disease seemed to be totally taking over Shamrock, and I would spend 16 to 20 hours a day devoted to her care... and didn't have anywhere to turn. The only reference I had was what I saw in my uncle as he went through dementia to Alzheimer's.

So, my big question was how Dr. Brugliera felt about the human/dog connection of this disease.

She did agree that human studies may help the way we treat our pets, but she stressed that human recommendations of MCT oils, coconut oils, keto based foods etc. need to be looked at first, as each pet patient is different. Dr. Brugliera did not feel the keto diet, which is currently on the "go to" list in human treatment of dementia and Alzheimer's, should be prescribed for every pet patient.

Dr. DePorter spoke about other cognitive enhancers that are utilized in human patients which may be beneficial for canine patients. She said these include: memantine and amantadine, (used to treat moderate to severe Alzheimer's in humans). Drugs that may enhance the noradrenergic system, which regulates cognitive function, such as adrafinil and modafinil, might be useful in older dogs to improve alertness and help maintain normal sleep/wake cycles, by increasing daytime exploration and activity. However, dose and efficacy in dogs has not been well established, or widely utilized. *(Note: All medications should be discussed with your veterinarian).

I also asked about human dementia and Alzheimer's versus, what is termed "Canine cognitive dysfunction syndrome in discussion with Dr. Tynes. She said, "CCDS is the equivalent of

CAININE COGNITIVE - Treatments & Therapies

Alzheimer's in humans. The term canine cognitive decline would be used to refer to changes associated with the normal aging process."

She also explained, "The differences are not clear cut in animals, because dogs don't usually live long enough to progress from normal age-related dementia to Alzheimer's. There is a lot we don't know about the predisposition in dogs, but when compared to humans, we can extrapolate data from Alzheimer's testing that indicates as the brain ages there are fewer chemical messengers because of a decrease in dopamine, acetylcholine, serotonin, and other chemicals which show a decline in cognition and memory, therefore, the brain struggles."

Dr. Landsberg stated, "Canine cognitive dysfunction syndrome is analogous to early Alzheimer's with similarities in signs, a decline in learning and memory, and changes in pathology in the brain. However, most dogs develop other medical issues and do not live long enough to advance to the life ending stages of dementia or Alzheimer's."

Thinking about all that these veterinarians have said regarding the similarities of dementia and Alzheimer's in humans and canine cognitive dysfunction, I suspect that information may become more available as veterinarians and pet parents gain more awareness of this disease in dogs.

Dr. Dennis Thomas, who combines alternative and complimentary forms of medicine, with Traditional Chinese has made available to my readers two articles he wrote. These articles give more depth of information and help explain more about what CCD really is and its relationship to dementia and Alzheimer's.

Article:
Canine Cognitive Dysfunction (Part One)
Posted on November 3, 2019 by d thomas

"This is the first in a two-part series about canine cognitive dysfunction. Canine cognitive dysfunction (CCD) has been recognized in dogs for many years, but like many idiopathic diseases (unknown cause), there has been little information gained as to the cause, treatment or prevention. Due to the increasing number of dogs reaching their life expectancy, the incidence of this degenerative disease is on the rise.

CCD is often referred to as doggy dementia, but in actuality, the two are not the same. From the perspective of clinical symptoms and the fact that both are idiopathic, it is easy to see why they would be considered the same. CCD is actually very similar to Alzheimer's disease in people, so we can glean the information from human studies and see if we can find similarities between the two species.

CCD and Alzheimer's both have the same pathophysiological changes that occur in the brain. Both have the presence of beta-amyloid plaque buildup in the brain that contributes to brain dysfunction and clinical symptoms whereas dogs and people with dementia, do not.

CCD is a degenerative disease affecting the brain found in senior dogs. Unfortunately, little research has been done regarding this condition, so we can only hope to use human studies to gather information that will help our affected pets. Symptoms that often occur with CCD include confusion, memory loss, neurological dysfunctions such as urinary and fecal incontinence, hearing and vision loss and others. CCD is not a normal aging process. It is an abnormality and a disease.

Many clients tell me that they initially find that their dog exhibits odd behavior. Perhaps they find them in odd places in the house. As the disease progresses, the odd behavior patterns continue. They might go outside and walk around, seem confused and return inside the house and immediately urinate or defecate. They seem to forget why they went outside. In time, they may find themselves in a corner of the room, unaware of how to get out of the corner. They may begin to circle and pace. In time, there may be incontinence, hearing and vision loss.

Recent research among leading brain specialist around the world has helped us to understand more about CCD and Alzheimer's. It is good to know this, not only to aide our senior pet, but to help ourselves and our human loved ones who might be affected by this disease. For the past 30 years or so, it has been recognized that all human patients with

CAININE COGNITIVE - Treatments & Therapies

Alzheimer's disease had accumulation of beta-amyloid plaque in the brain. Once this was determined, the focus changed to finding a drug that would eliminate or remove the amyloid plaques. Many drugs were tried and all of them failed. Alzheimer's was deemed irreversible and non-curable.

A group of neurologists and brain specialist decided to change their focus to looking for the cause of the disease. They jokingly referred to this as 21st century medicine, which begins to focus on the cause instead of finding a drug as treatment. Their findings were amazing Basically, they found that there were three groups of people with Alzheimer's, according to the causes. Two of the three groups were determined to have nutritional imbalances that were the cause. The third group were determined to have toxic causes affecting the brain. This included infections, heavy metal intoxication and others. Once the cause was determined, specific treatment was started, and many Alzheimer patients responded favorably. Some of them were cured. If we look at these causes, perhaps we can find the same thing is happening in the dog.

The first thing to understand is that CCD and Alzheimer's are an end stage process of an insidious disease that has been occurring for many years. This long-standing process usually has many variables which would explain the difficulty in identifying an exact cause. Another finding that is pertinent is that the beta-amyloid plaque buildup in the brain is a byproduct of the immune system's response to the disease affecting the brain. It is a response to a disease, not the cause of the disease.

CCD is a degenerative disease that continues to alter brain and nerve function. Once degeneration has occurred to a point, acetylcholine (a vital neurotransmitter chemical) levels are reduced which adds to further neurological dysfunction. These symptoms are usually caused by loss of function of the peripheral nerves causing weakness, urinary and fecal incontinence.

Another key factor to know is that the central mechanism for neuronal (brain) degeneration is

inflammation and tissue oxidation. If we understand this and work backwards, we can start to identify what could cause this. Potential causes include:
- inflammation
- infection
- decreased antioxidant nutrients
- decreased omega 3 fatty acids
- decreased B vitamins
- malabsorption/maldigestion of the gut
- poor liver detoxification
- excess aluminum, mercury and copper
- prolonged cortisol levels due to stress."

"In the second part of this article, I will discuss the factors that cause the potentials for CCD and look at what can be done to prevent this disease and how to treat it naturally, if it has already begun."

Article: Part Two

Canine Cognitive Dysfunction (Part Two)
Posted on November 3, 2019 by d thomas

"In the first part of this article, I discussed canine cognitive disease and its similarity to Alzheimer's disease in people. You saw that using the latest research by renowned brain specialist, we can use their findings to extrapolate the potential causes, treatment and prevention for this degenerative disease of the brain and peripheral nervous system. I listed the most common potential factors that will bring out this disease.

If we look at this list, and again work backwards, we can start to connect the dots and get an idea as to how this degenerative condition may have occurred. Inflammation, as I have said many times, is the underlying problem of almost every chronic disease in pets and CCD is no exception

Inflammation in dogs (and people) primarily is the result of an inappropriate diet. In dogs, heat-processed pet foods create inflammation. Starch in all kibble is converted to sugar and sugar causes inflammation. Inflammation occurs in the gut, leading to leaky gut syndrome, which allows undigested and unprocessed material to pass through the gut and into the blood stream, triggering a response by the immune system. This creates a hypersensitivity to the immune system that persists throughout the individual's life causing various diseases. As mentioned, the beta-amyloid plaque buildup in the brain in CCD and Alzheimer's is an over-reaction by a hypersensitive immune system.

When chronic inflammation of the gut persists, the gut becomes inefficient in its normal function and secondary deficiencies occur such as B vitamin deficiencies and folate deficiencies, both found in Alzheimer's patients. These deficiencies are common in both dogs with chronic bowel inflammation. As the inflammation persists, malabsorption and maldigestion occurs leading to more and more nutritional imbalances and deficiencies affecting both antioxidant rich nutrients as well as processing omega 3 fatty acids.

Everything that is converted chemically in the gut enters into the portal system and goes to the liver. Many of the impure and harmful chemicals are stored in the liver instead of being removed from the system. These toxins are released throughout the individual's life adding to further health complications. It is not surprising that poor liver detoxification is on the list of Alzheimer's potential causes.

If we look for sources of heavy metals in the dog's body, we don't have to look far. Mercury is found in rabies vaccine and aluminum is found in almost all of the other vaccines. Copper can be found in our drinking water. These heavy heavy metals enter into the system, cross the blood-brain barrier and accumulate in the brain, creating symptoms and diseases, such as CCD.

Infections such as Lyme disease has been found in many Alzheimer patients. In searching for causes for CCD and Alzheimer's disease, we clinicians need to be doing diagnostic blood test to detect the presence of these potential infections.

Another major factor found in people with Alzheimer's disease is prolonged elevated cortisol levels which occurs with chronic stress. Stress is an energetic imbalance that in time affects the physical body and causes disease. If our personal or environmental stress levels are high and prolonged, not only will we be more predisposed to degenerative diseases like Alzheimer's, but our dogs will also be affected the same way, which may contribute to CCD.

What can we do to prevent this disease? Prevention is always best. Feeding a non-inflammatory, specie-specific, balanced diet that is fresh and not heat-processed is critical in preventing this degenerative disease. Supporting the immune system with probiotics and digestive enzymes is recommended. Do not allow over-vaccination of your dog and if you need to vaccinate, make sure that the vaccine does not have a heavy metal preservative. Make sure that your dog has a source of omega 3 fatty acids and natural antioxidant nutrients. Minimize environmental stress. The goal is to feed a non-inflammatory diet, keep the gut and immune systems healthy and avoid toxins that affect the nervous system and to minimize environmental stress.

What can be done in regard to treatment once the disease has been detected? Like most degenerative diseases, if we catch the disease early, the better chance we have at reversing the changes. The drug that is recommended by many vets is Selegiline (Anipryl®). I do not recommend this drug due to its potential harmful side effects that include death. I like to treat these dogs with a natural approach. Here are my recommendations:

1. Diet modification if needed (see above comments)
2. Filtered water (old pipes often have lead and copper in them)
3. Multivitamins that include B6,12, folate and zinc. (Adult human=80-pound dog)
4. Cholidin (chewable supplement for pets that supply precursors for acetylcholine). This can be purchased online and every dog with CCD should be on this no matter where they are in their progression).
5. Ginkgo biloba. This human supplement for brain function and memory loss has been researched and proven effective at diminishing CCD symptoms. The dosage is 4mg/kg body weight daily.

CAININE COGNITIVE - Treatments & Therapies

6.Turmeric. This Ayurvedic herb has been shown to reduce inflammation in the brain as well as have an anti-amyloid effect. I like using the Golden Paste Turmeric formula.

7.Coenzyme Q10 is a powerful antioxidant that benefits the brain as well as the heart.

8.Tian Wang Bu Xin Dan. This Chinese herbal formula addresses the imbalances that create the symptoms associated with the brain from a Chinese medicine perspective. This formula supports cerebral blood flow and energy by supporting the kidney, liver and blood. Dosage: human adult dosage=80-pound dog.

9.Pulsed electromagnetic (PEMT). I love pulsed electromagnetic therapy for any disease that affects the nervous system. The brain and peripheral nervous system are electrical in nature and PEMT is designed to balance electromagnetic energy.

10.SAMe. SAMe is a supplement that is used in people and pets for supporting the liver and brain function. It been shown to reduce symptoms in dogs with CCD.

11.Milk Thistle: Milk thistle is a good herbal remedy to detox the liver. I recommend doing a 3-day detox with milk thistle once every 2-3 months to regularly detox the liver.

12.Eliminating stressful energy in the home environment, person and dog. I like to smudge the home regularly. Smudging with white sage will neutralize negative energy in the home. Google how to smudge your home. For personal energy, diffusing calming essential oils is beneficial for both pet and caretaker. Essential oils such as lavender, rose, vetiver and Ylang Ylang are very effective for anxiety and stress relief. (I do not recommend smudging or diffusing with cats in the room)."

Reprinted Canine Cognitive Dysfunction (Part One) (Canine Cognitive Dysfunction (Part Two) with permission from Dr. Thomas-

SHAMROCK'S STORY

Doctor's Currently Working On Human Alzheimer's

I spoke with Dr. McKinstry about the relationship between humans and animals regarding dementia and Alzheimer's. We discussed that to better understand the disease in dog's, we can learn a lot from studying the disease in human terms. She mentioned a good resource would be Dr. Bredesen's book, *The End of Alzheimer's.*

I knew about this book and Dr. Bredesen because of my communications with him regarding advances he was making in human Alzheimer's.

He is an internationally recognized expert in neurodegenerative diseases. His research explores previously uncharted territory in explaining the physical mechanism behind the erosion of memory seen in Alzheimer's disease and has opened the door to new approaches to treatment. This work has led to the identification of several new therapeutic processes that are showing remarkable early results. Dr. Dale Bredesen is a prodigious innovator in medicine, with over thirty patents to his name. Notably, he put much of his findings and research into the 2017 *New York Times'* Best-Seller, *The End of Alzheimer's,* and has recently published, *The First Survivors of Alzheimer's: How Patients Recovered Life and Hope in Their Own Words.*

The "Bredesen Protocol" is based on over three decades of Dr. Bredesen's laboratory research, resulting in hundreds of peer-reviewed publications that have uncovered the biochemical mechanisms behind the erosion of memory associated with Alzheimer's disease.

The following is the information I received from Dr. Bredesen about human Alzheimer's and what I learned from his work and his books:

I had heard him speak about Alzheimer's and felt we might have a mutual goal. I wanted to know if what we learn about Alzheimer's in humans, might help our dogs and vice versa. He told me, "You are right that dementia and Alzheimer's are under-appreciated and very common problems for dogs. There has been a fair amount of research showing that many dogs, not only develop dementia, but also have the pathology associated with Alzheimer's disease, with amyloid plaques in their brains. So, I agree there is a need to spread the word."

CAININE COGNITIVE - Treatments & Therapies

This statement gave me the desire to dig further into the similarities of this disease in humans and dogs.

My next question was, "It seems to be so difficult to diagnose and treat, what can we look forward to for people who develop Alzheimer's?"

Dr. Bredesen responded, "You are also correct that there is so much to be done on the human front. Unfortunately, many of the currently living Americans will die from Alzheimer's if we are not successful in gathering more concrete information for optimal prevention or reversal."

Recent statistics show, Alzheimer's has become the third leading cause of death in the United States and the problem for our dogs is they are susceptible to many human diseases. Understanding that, it is so important to pay attention to the science regarding prevention and treatment, and the possibilities of a reversal of this disease.

"Alzheimer's disease is one of the most significant global health threats we face today. It is an ailment that, as our population ages, is forecasted to become a worldwide epidemic. To understand the magnitude of the problem, the COVID-19 pandemic as of this writing has claimed over 900,000 Americans, and over 6,000,000 ultimately; however, nearly 100 times more of the currently living Americans, nearly 50 million, will die of Alzheimer's disease, if effective prevention and reversal are not implemented. Mainstream medicine would have you believe that it can't be prevented, is untreatable, and progressive, with most patients not surviving beyond three to eleven years post-diagnosis." With the partnership between Dr. Bredesen and Apollo Health, all of that is being challenged.

He disrupted the mainstream in 2014 with a peer-reviewed medical publication entitled, "Reversal of cognitive decline: a novel therapeutic program." In this paper, he shared his multi-step precision medicine approach that demonstrated reversal of cognitive decline in nine out of ten patients, for the very first time. He's continued to refine his clinical work and several years later published *Reversal of cognitive decline: 100 patients,* in which he outlined one hundred case studies, detailing documented patient improvements, fundamentally changing the way we understand and approach cognitive decline. Dr. Bredesen is also very highly respected in the study of Alzheimer's, and he is a *New York Times* Best Selling author. In his book *The End of Alzheimer's he* deals with a specific plan of prevention and reversal of cognitive decline.

After reading his books, I believe his information might also help us to better understand and deal with this disease in our dogs.

He presents a detailed program which he has used with his own patients, and he documents how this program can enhance cognitive ability at any age.

"Alzheimer's disease is actually a protective response to a wide variety of insults to the brain: inflammation, insulin resistance, toxins, infections, and inadequate levels of nutrients, hormones, and growth factors. Once we understand these insults, we need to address and continue by laying out a personalized lifestyle plan."

From there Dr. Bredesen's program targets diet, sleep, exercise, and brain training. He also examines the tricky question of toxic exposure. He told me, "The takeaway is that we do not need to do the program perfectly but will see tremendous results if we can do it well enough. The good news is each of the causes are treatable. The problem is the 'Perfect Alzheimer's Drug,' would have to be all things, but 'one size,' cannot fit all!

"The 'vaccine' for Alzheimer's will be a very different program from that for diseases of the past. It will be a personalized program gathered from personal input that examines contributors of cognitive decline. There are different classes of this disease, and it is important to properly identify them to be able to create the optimal plan."

Dr. Bredesen explained, "Instead, personalized precision programs look at all the contributors and address what is needed to correct the problems. Using the 'Bredesen Protocol' with my patients, I have seen, 'reversals of cognitive decline and sustained results."

The Bredesen Protocol is based on over three decades of Dr. Bredesen's laboratory research, resulting in hundreds of peer-reviewed publications that have uncovered the biochemical mechanisms behind the erosion of memory associated with Alzheimer's disease. The Bredesen Protocol offered through PreCODE (for prevention) and ReCODE (for reversal) has opened the door to innovative approaches to prevent and treat Alzheimer's disease.

"Recognizing that this disease can be caused from insulin resistance, zinc and vitamin C deficiencies, infections from tick bites or herpes, exposure to toxins, such as mold and finally a genetic disposition; gives us a better understanding of how this disease develops. Therefore, Alzheimer's becomes a 'protective response' to these issues. With Alzheimer's the brain is in protection mode and begins to shut down and close off areas, especially memory, to protect itself.

"The best treatment is to identify each person's causes and then map out a reversal of those issues. This is called, 'ReCoding'. Instead of masking symptoms with medication in traditional medicine, functional medicine digs much deeper to determine the 'root cause(s)' of disease to reverse chronic illness. The ReCODE protocol is successful for this very reason. In addition, the beauty of ReCODE is that it addresses EACH of the neuro-terrorists from having any chance of destroying your brain! This process can start with changes in diet, removal of toxins from the environment, adding brain exercises and important nutrients; vitamins and minerals and supplementation to boost the immune system and restore the brain to a normal mode."

In speaking with veterinarians, I have found that many agree with these "ReCoding" suggestions, and many are recommending these methods for dogs with cognitive decline.

Recognizing this, pet parents can utilize DISHAA for their dogs to better understand what their possible contributing factors might be and speak with their veterinarians about how to go about "ReCoding."

Based on all I learned, I turned to Dr. Bredesen and asked, "Even though you are not a veterinarian and do not treat animals, can you suggest ways to use your program that might be helpful for pets?"

He responded with suggestions of some tests he felt could be beneficial for dogs that might be predisposed to, or have been diagnosed with, cognitive decline. (These suggestions are based on tests for humans and need to be discussed with your veterinarian as to whether they, or others, are available for dogs, and whether they would be beneficial for determining these disease contributors in dogs). "These tests relate to: Inflammatory Markers, Glucose and Insulin Markers, Nutrient Markers especially for vitamin D, homocysteine, vitamin B12, folate, vitamin E, omega-3, Toxicity Markers such as glutathione, heavy metals, BUN or creatinine, ALT or AST and basic lab works like a CBC," (Complete Blood Count).

"Depending on the results, the suggestions would be to reduce any inflammation and treat any pathogens, using omega-3 (DHA especially), fish oil and, or curcumin. To heal the gut, a non-toxic diet, and probiotics and prebiotics. To reduce insulin resistance, a diet high in good fat, low in simple carbs, and intermediate in protein, high in fiber, low glycemic, while supplying nutrients as above."

*(Note: All the above recommendations are based on human supplementation and should be discussed with your veterinarian as to whether it is appropriate to give to dogs, also to ascertain dosages based on the dog's weight).

To sum up. Dr. Bredesen offered, "I do hope that a similar approach to what we have developed for humans with cognitive decline, or risk for decline, might be effective for dogs, especially in the early stages, but as you know, I am not trained as a veterinarian. My training is in neurology and neuroscience. So, I wonder whether it may make sense for a veterinarian to learn about our protocol? We have all sorts of practitioners taking our training now, from neurologists to dentists, to health coaches, to primary care physicians, etcetera, then hopefully they can develop something appropriate for dogs!"

This information has been provided by agreement with Dr. Bredesen and permission regarding his books, *The End of Alzheimer's,* and *The End of Alzheimer's Program.*

I just wanted to add that after all I learned from Dr. Bredesen, I hope we can examine the new findings about this disease and apply as much as possible for our dogs with the hope to prevent, reverse, and eventually eradicate this disease once and for all, for both humans and dogs!

The knowledge of Dr. Bredesen's work established a better understanding for me and during my talks with Dr. McKinstry we continued to discuss both humans and animals regarding this disease. She concluded, "It is so important to properly choose a diet

CAININE COGNITIVE - Treatments & Therapies

for ourselves and for our pets, especially when we are trying to prevent a future that may include dementia and Alzheimer's."

In other conversations with veterinarians, as well as neurologists, I learned that MCT oil was having wonderful results with cognitive issues and is even recommended by many of the veterinarians I spoke with.

My research also found studies that were done with dogs that were looking at MCT oil and whether it was viable when treating age-related canine cognitive decline.

Therefore, it seems that something that has had reliable results for humans is now being recommended and used to help our dogs with cognitive decline.

That information led me to a colleague of Dr. Bredesen's, Dr. Mary Newport, an author and international speaker, and her experiences with MCT and coconut oil. She had great success with these in her trials during her husband's battle with Alzheimer's.

In her book, *Alzheimer's Disease: What If There Was a Cure*? she referred to studies about elderly dogs that did show improvement when MCT oil, extracted from coconut oil, was used. Even though she had not done work specifically with dogs, she did have a pet parent contact her and at her suggestion, use coconut oil for an elderly dog. Dr. Newport suggested starting with a child amount; a quarter teaspoon of coconut oil per ten pounds of weight and waiting to see the results; which, in fact, turned out to be very encouraging. "The Welsh terrier that responded to coconut oil was 14 years old and was able to find her way around the house again and find her food bowl. "

Dr. Newport also feels that diabetes and or insulin resistance can contribute to Alzheimer's. "This could be another valuable area for the dog's veterinarian to check.

"When we see improvement on the human side of this disease, it can be a positive direction for dogs. So, after speaking with your veterinarian, coconut oil just may be a good try!"

I was curious how Dr. Landau felt about the human/animal connection. I told him that the research for humans with this disease is showing that MCT oils, coconut oils, keto based foods, etc., can help to stop and even reverse symptoms, and I wanted to know his feelings.

"When it comes to dogs, using these essential fatty acid supplements are ways to help stop the progression, not how to necessarily do away with the disease. To do that we need to do so much more, and even then, reversing the damage is usually not possible. However, slowing progression is possible."

My research further found that as with human's a recent study looked at MCT oils and found that they might help dogs with cognitive decline as they showed some improvement of memory and attention span.

I wanted to check out the veterinarian side of Dr. Newport's statement about diabetes. When I spoke with Dr. Tynes I told her that neurologists, like Dr. Newport have told me diabetes and or insulin resistance can contribute to Alzheimer's, and that research had revealed that human dementia is sometimes referred to as, "Diabetes 3!"

Dr. Tynes responded, "Reduced brain glucose metabolism in aging dogs contributes to brain energy deprivation, leading to a decrease in brain function."

That statement made another dog/human connection...blood sugar, diabetes and insulin resistance.

What Can We Learn From Human Dementia & Alzheimer's?

So, what is the conclusion regarding the connection between dogs and humans when it comes to cognitive decline? And, when we know that, the next question becomes, "Is there enough information to help our pets?

Dr. Kangas explained, "There is evidence that Alzheimer's disease is only genetically predetermined by three percent of the genes that are identified to be associated with this disease syndrome. While ninety-seven percent of the involved genes and DNA, have been affected by other causes that influence the expression of how the genes respond and subsequently lead to this disease. This influence is termed epigenetics and involves many

CAININE COGNITIVE - Treatments & Therapies

lifestyle factors that affect the expression of genes such as dietary choices, heavy toxin exposures, stress, etcetera. This information gives doctors hope that lifestyle choices and changes that are made early enough can help to prevent Alzheimer's disease and many others."

Dr. Bartner sees enough similarities between dogs and humans and feels this can guide trials, therapies and designs for what can work. "Diet as a factor has been shown in people who eat a lot of red meat and processed food, but with dogs it is harder to determine."

But there is still the other side of the issue and I asked Dr. Katz about the connection between human dementia or Alzheimer's, and pets getting this disease. She stated, "It has not been 'documented' that dogs experience Alzheimer's, and that this is also not typically a condition from which pets die, so when the disease begins to advance, and little is known what to do, that may be a reason that pet parents consider euthanasia."

Until there is more documented information regarding dogs and cognitive issues, my hope is that the information provided in this book, by these veterinarians and other doctors, will give more understanding of this disease, and in turn, more options to consider...long before euthanasia has to be one of the choices.

Dogs In Studies

Veterinary neurologist Dr. McGrath and her colleagues are studying canine cognitive dysfunction syndrome or "doggy dementia," which affects 35% of canines over eight years old.

As a companion species, dogs share everything about their environment—from sleep to food to exercise—with their humans, and therefore offer an ideal opportunity to study neurodegenerative diseases. With funding from CSU's Translational Medicine Institute, Dr. McGrath and associates are studying the disease evolution and attempting to develop an early, non-invasive diagnostic tool that could be translated to human medicine.

SHAMROCK'S STORY

"We're looking at etiology and biomarkers for this disease, but it's also broader than that," she explained. "We're also looking at how aging in cognitively impaired dogs compares with human aging, and then how healthy aging compares with cognitive decline."

"Dr. McGrath and her colleague, Dr. Julie Moreno, have combined forces to leverage basic science using translational clinical research to better understand and treat this incurable disease. That means by studying how animals like dogs age, we can gain a better understanding of Alzheimer's disease and other dementias!"

I was recently sent information about a new study that Dr. McGrath is involved in, "A new study at the James L. Voss Veterinary Teaching Hospital at Colorado State University is looking at three different medications in the treatment of canine cognitive dysfunction syndrome (CCDS) in aging dogs, with the long-term hope of advancing Alzheimer's disease treatments in humans.

"The study is being led by principal investigators Dr. Stephanie McGrath, a veterinary neurologist at the Veterinary Teaching Hospital, and Julie Moreno, Ph.D., an assistant professor in the Department of Environmental and Radiological Health Sciences.

"One of the challenges to discovering a treatment for Alzheimer's disease is identifying a good model for research, which is where canine cognitive dysfunction syndrome comes in. CCDS is a neurodegenerative disease affecting dogs with many similarities to Alzheimer's disease."

Here is the *TRAC Study Information*

"TRAC Study: investigating the effect of trazodone, rapamycin, and cannabidiol on cognitive dysfunction in dogs

Background and Purpose of the trial

With the advancements in modern medicine, both humans and canines are living longer and we're now seeing a greater percentage of dogs suffer from cognitive decline. currently, there are no approved treatment methods for cognitive decline in either humans or dogs. this study aims to find a safe and effective therapeutic agent for reducing progression of cognitive dysfunction in dogs. cannabidiol (CBD), trazodone, and rapamycin have shown beneficial

CAININE COGNITIVE - Treatments & Therapies

effects on brain aging, which means they may be effective therapeutic options for dogs. all three drugs will be tested in order to determine if one, or all, may be a safe and effective medication for reducing the progression of cognitive dysfunction in dogs, with the hope of being able to translate this to humans with Alzheimer's disease.
Study Design

We will be enrolling a total of 48 dogs into 4 separate groups: trazodone, rapamycin, cannabidiol, or placebo. after an initial diagnostic assessment consisting of a thorough exam, bloodwork, radiographs, ultrasound, MRI, and spinal tap, all clients will go home with a liquid medication to be given twice daily and a capsule to be given once weekly. this study is double-blinded, so owners and the clinical trials staff will not know which treatment group each patient is in. all clients will be expected to bring their pet back every 3 months over the course of two years with an MRI being conducted every 12 months (3 total) and a spinal tap being conducted every 6 months (5 total). in addition, some dogs will be randomly assigned to wear an activity-tracking monitor so it's important that your dog is comfortable wearing a collar at all times!"

"Our hope is that by studying the process of aging and dementia in dogs, we can start finding ways to prevent or even reverse some of the devastating changes that occur in older animals," McGrath said. "The ultimate goal is not only to help our furry companions, but as this disease in dogs closely mimics human dementias, including Alzheimer's disease, to also set the foundation for future success in dementia research in humans."
Information reprinted with permission by Dr. McGrath

If you are interested in having your dog evaluated for enrollment in the study or supporting these trials *(Note: See Recommendations - pg 250).

SHAMROCK'S STORY

The Dog Aging Project
Dogs Helping Dogs...& Maybe Even Humans

Many of the veterinarians I spoke with mentioned the "Dog Aging Project," but I hadn't heard of it before that and was intrigued to find out more.

The more I dug into the topic, the more I realized how incredible this project is. I found the following information on their website: "The Dog Aging Project, or DAP, is a multi-institutional endeavor funded by the National Institute on Aging and is the most ambitious canine science initiative in the world.

"This project is an innovative initiative that brings together a community of dogs, owners, veterinarians, researchers, and volunteers to carry out the most ambitious canine science project in the world. Their work is centered on two fundamental goals, first, understanding how genes, lifestyle, and environment influence aging and second, intervening to increase health-span, the period of life spent free from disease. The Dog Aging Project is a community science project that is committed to advancing our understanding of aging and to accelerating medical breakthroughs for dogs and humans. We will integrate our findings about dogs with other scientific and medical programs around the world to power research on health and aging in a way never before possible.

"Led by researchers at Texas A&M and the University of Washington, the Dog Aging Project team will follow tens of thousands of companion dogs for 10 years in order to identify factors that maximize healthy longevity and help future generations of dogs live the best lives possible."

Next, I reached out to the Dog Aging Project and was fortunate to speak with Dr. Amber Keyser, an evolutionary biologist, and member of their communication team. I wanted to know what the project is, what it does and how it will help dogs.

Dr. Keyser gave me more information about the project; its goals and an understanding of why it is essential to better understand dogs. She also explained how this research may help scientists understand illnesses that affect humans. "To that end, the members of this project are in both health fields, human and veterinary research. This ten-year project has just passed its second year." *(Note: as of this publication date).

One distinction Dr. Keyser made is that in human medicine there is a field called "gerontology," the study of the elderly, however, there is no such gerontological specialty in veterinary medicine. "The Dog Project is trying to create this specialty. Currently one of the biggest issues is that this field is not incorporated into veterinary education and training," and Dr. Keyser admits, "that needs to happen!"

She continued, "Human medicine has been studying dementia and Alzheimer's disease for many years and have tests to access cognitive decline through mind and physical parameters. One of the projects goals is to have the same ability for cognitive decline in dogs. The project is building these tests now. A key part of the Dog Aging Project is to study changes over time; physical and cognitive, make assessments on an annual basis, and observe what changes occur. Observational means not interfering in the dog's lives, but over the years in the program, gathering information, and just watching and recording changes.

"The areas the project is looking into are regarding data from providers, including diet, supplements, nutritional, preventative, behavioral and environmental. For example, when looking at environment, the consideration is examining different areas; north versus south, urban versus rural, etcetera. Where the dog lives, gives better information about the air, water, greenspace, and other factors that may contribute to illness. The goal is to get a picture of what illnesses dogs are getting as they age, and how these diseases are associated with each of these factors."

I was fascinated that the project study includes about 30,000 dogs. Before I began my research for this book, I had never heard about the project.

Dr. Keyser let me know, "The project has used traditional outreach and targeted recruitment through social media. The project works in partnership with universities, and seven teaching hospitals to raise awareness."

I had asked her if dogs like Shamrock, at 16 years of age, would be accepted into the project? Dr. Keyser replied, "The project is taking dogs of all ages, and only exclude dogs if their actual age is unknown. "We ask participants to answer surveys based on how their dog is right now. So, if a dog was 16 at enrollment, then their data would begin at age 16. We don't want people to answer 'retrospectively' because that data can be less accurate.

"For DAP the information derived from puppies, especially regarding spayed or neutered dogs, fits into the project goals. By looking at the ages of the puppies when these procedures were done, they may be able to understand their patterns of health. The project can learn the most from puppies, as it can collect data throughout their lives, but any age can provide information that is important.

"Currently the project has enrolled many Labs, Retrievers and Shepherds, so the outreach is to attract other breeds to the project. Pure breed and mutt's, which are termed as mixed breeds, alike help to give a good cross-section of information. They are looking for more hounds, and dogs from more urban and rural areas."

Even though the project is currently funded with a grant from the National Institute on Aging for a 10-year period, Dr. Keyser believes this project will be ongoing; primarily because dogs share our environment. It is simpler to study dogs and reach new discoveries that then can be extrapolated for humans.

"There is also an at home double-blind clinical trial of about 500 dogs of 'invited member dogs' participating in the project. The study is testing rapamycin versus a placebo. Rapamycin is a medicine used to prevent organ transplant rejection in human patients, which may regulate an enzyme that plays an important role in the progression of the cell cycle.

"The testing facilities will collect biological samples, which allow them to study the genetics and biochemical makeup of each dog and observe the changes over time. They can perform fur analysis and metal testing, look at chemistry, toxicology, and other bodily functions. Essentially, this is a wide-reaching study of many physiological processes. This belief is that this drug may have anti-aging properties.

"Rapamycin in low doses has currently demonstrated no negative side effects. Because this drug is currently in a clinical trial and results are not confirmed, it is very important to stress that we do not recommend the self-administering of rapamycin at any dose. This is an experimental medication." *(Note: This medication is not recommended for people to self-dose for themselves or their pets).

CAININE COGNITIVE - Treatments & Therapies

Here is some background information about the Rapamycin study that I received from the Dog Aging Project:

Key Facts about TRIAD

"The *Test of Rapamycin in Aging Dogs* (TRIAD) is **a double-blind, placebo controlled, clinical trial of the medicine rapamycin** being conducted by the Dog Aging Project.

Rapamycin has been shown to **increase the lifespan** and **delay or reverse many age-related disorders** in mice

The primary purpose of this project is to determine whether rapamycin increases the lifespan of companion dogs. A secondary purpose is to determine whether rapamycin improves various measures of health in aging dogs.

The **lead researchers on TRIAD** are:

- **Dr. Kate E. Creevy**, DVM, MS, DACVIM (SAIM), Professor, College of Veterinary Medicine & Biomedical Sciences, Texas A&M University
- **Dr. Matt Kaeberlein**, PhD, Professor, Department of Laboratory Medicine and Pathology and Department of Biology, University of Washington School of Medicine
- **Dr. Audrey Ruple,** DVM, MS, PhD, DACVPM, MRCVS, Associate Professor, Department of Population Health, Virginia Tech, Virginia-Maryland College of Veterinary Medicine

Dr. Daniel Promislow, PhD, Professor, Department of Laboratory Medicine and

Pathology and Department of Biology, University of Washington School of Medicine

TRIAD is funded by the National Institute on Aging, a part of the National Institutes of Health.

TRIAD is overseen by the Institutional Animal Care and Use Committee (IACUC) and the

Clinical Research Review Committee at Texas A&M University College of Veterinary

SHAMROCK'S STORY

Medicine & Biomedical Sciences, and an NIH-constituted Data and Safety Monitoring Board, to ensure that **all study activities are conducted legally, safely, and ethically**.

Eligible dogs must be **healthy dogs at least 7 years of age and at least 44 pounds** (20 kg) in weight whose owners are willing to bring their dogs to one of our participating veterinary teaching hospitals regularly.

Dogs must be cooperative for examination, including blood collection and ultrasound of the heart without sedation, and must have normal diagnostic findings at the time of enrollment.

Each enrolled dog will receive either **rapamycin or placebo for a period of 1 year**. Dogs will be monitored twice yearly during that year and for an additional 2 years after the study medication (rapamycin or placebo) is stopped.

Our participating veterinary teaching hospitals include Texas A&M, University of Georgia, Colorado State, Iowa State, Washington State, and North Carolina State."

Reprinted with Permission –Dr. Amber Keyser Dog Aging Project | University of Washington | Texas A&M University | dogagingproject.org

Dr. Keyser also pointed me in the direction of YouTube for more information. By watching "Science To Save The World," I listened to participant veterinarians in the Dog Aging Project explain that the project is a "longitudinal study of aging," meaning that it follows dogs throughout their life span. "As dogs age more rapidly than people, it is feasible to follow thousands of dogs to better understand the factors of aging."

Dr. Matt Kaeberlein, PhD University of Washington and Co-director of the project also stated that this project is "two-fold," to understand the biological process in dogs, but also the knowledge garnered from laboratory experiments to increase dog's longevity. He further explained that age is thought of in chronological terms, but biology sees aging at a different rate. Changes in aging do not happen at the same rates.

CAININE COGNITIVE - Treatments & Therapies

The project is using tests similar to human testing, such as mobility, changes in gate, walking speed, climbing steps, organ functions, weight loss, activity levels, and cognitive abilities.

Because this is a 10-year project, at this time, they are not able to make any definitive recommendations, but they are making ongoing studies available during the 10-year period. Even though these studies are not likely to be of benefit for dogs currently, their findings will benefit all future dogs.

Bringing the conversation back to canine cognitive dysfunction, Dr. Keyser said, "Because early intervention for conditions like CCDS is crucial in delaying disease progression, finding new and better ways to recognize and diagnose this disease could greatly improve our dogs' health span, the period of life during which the dog is active, healthy, and feeling good. Here at the Dog Aging Project, we're hoping to revolutionize our understanding of cognitive function and aging in dogs in order to accomplish this very goal!"

She then referred me to an article on the Texas A&M University website, specifically about "Canine cognitive decline," in which a member of the Dog Aging Project spoke about this disease.

Article:
Cognitive Decline In Aging Dogs: What To Know
April 15, 2021,
Featured In *Pet Talk

"Just as humans may develop neurodegenerative conditions such as Alzheimer's disease as they grow older, our aging canine friends also can develop dementia, also referred to as canine cognitive dysfunction syndrome (CCDS), a complex of behavioral and neurological symptoms the prevalence of which increases with age.

Dr. Brian Gray Barnett, a veterinary research fellow in the Texas A&M College of Veterinary Medicine & Biomedical Sciences and member of the Dog Aging Project research team, says that as the level of veterinary care we are able to provide canine companions improves, the number of dogs affected by CCDS rises as well. This is because the biggest risk factor for developing CCDS is age, with onset usually occurring between 12 and 15 years old.

'One study found that 28% of 11- to 12-year-old dogs and 68% of 15- to 16-year-old dogs have CCDS,' said Barnett. 'A similar study found that 22.5% of dogs over the age of 9 years show cognitive impairment.'

SHAMROCK'S STORY

CCDS can present itself in many ways, so it is important for owners to familiarize themselves with all possible signs. Many symptoms associated with CCDS may also be indicative of other conditions, so owners should seek veterinary advice to rule out other diseases before concluding that their dog is affected by CCDS.

Barnett says owners can use the acronym DISHAL to remember specific signs to look out for. This stands for disorientation, interactions, sleep-wake cycle changes, house soiling, activity changes, and learning difficulties/memory loss:

'While any of these signs could be seen as a first sign of CCDS, one study found that disturbances in the sleep-wake cycle were more prevalent in the early stages of CCDS than altered interactions and disorientation,' Barnett said.

Barnett stresses that each dog is different and may have a different progression of symptoms. The first symptoms will typically be milder and worsen as the disease progresses. If an owner suspects that their dog is presenting any of these symptoms, they should bring their concerns to the attention of a veterinarian.

'Their veterinarian will have the best plan to identify the underlying cause of the behavioral changes and find the best intervention,' he said. 'This can include treating a contributing medical condition, maintaining a consistent routine, reducing environmental stress factors, introducing enrichment activities, changing diet, and recommending specific supplements and medications when appropriate."

CCDS is unfortunately a progressive disease with no effective treatment yet developed to significantly reverse its effects. As such, the current standard of care aims to delay progression.

Luckily, veterinary researchers, such as those working with the Dog Aging Project, are hard at work studying the aging mechanisms of our furry friends with the goal of understanding the underlying cause of CCDS to develop better strategies for diagnosis and treatment.

The Dog Aging Project looks to identify factors that maximize healthy longevity and help future generations of dogs live the best lives possible.

CCDS is one of many conditions that will be helped by this research.

CAININE COGNITIVE - Treatments & Therapies

'We are learning more and more about the changes that happen in the nervous system in dogs with CCDS,' Barnett said. 'Further understanding not only might allow us to better diagnose and treat CCDS, but we may be able to apply these findings to Alzheimer's disease in humans.'"

This article was referred to by permission through agreement from Dr. Keyser – Dog Aging Project and is being reproduced in part with permission from Dr. Keyser- Dog Aging Project.
*Pet Talk is also a service of the College of Veterinary Medicine & Biomedical Sciences, Texas A&M University. *(Note: To read the full article See RECOMMENDATIONS-pg 250).

If you are interested in being part of the Dog Aging Project and learning how to Nominate your dog, including what the project is looking for, *(Note: See Recommendations-pg 250).

DEMENTIA AND ALZHEIMER'S LATTER STAGES

Give your dog...your baby...

your patience...

your time...

and all your love

to get them through this final phase

DEMENTIA & ALZHEIMER'S – Latter Stages

END OF LIFE CARE

This chapter was very difficult to write, and the questions were even harder to ask, but the hardest part was hearing the answers. I realize in the real world, the questions need to be asked and if this book is to help, even one dog, and or one pet family, it needs the honesty and realizations of this Chapter!

Here is Dr. Gardner's statement about end of life, "Sometimes pet parents need a 'trained eye' to help them manage 'in home care'." She suggested contacting a service that uses veterinarians who can come to the home to help evaluate the environment. "These visits can provide a number of enrichment activities, but especially, safety!" She stressed, "Safety should be the first concern. Pets with cognitive dysfunction can get lost, turned around, trapped in places they can't get out of and get caught in unsafe situations and become very anxious. Making sure they are safe and comfortable is a priority."

Because we love our dogs and want them to have the best, I had to take into consideration a difficult question and asked, "How can dementia affect a pet's quality of life?"

SHAMROCK'S STORY

Dr. Gardner was very open about her real concerns. "Before your dog's condition becomes unmanageable, or they begin losing their quality of life, beginning end-of-life care discussions are vital. It is important for the pet parent to understand what they want for their dog and then know whether or not that can be possible, for the pet, as well as for the family." She added, "At that stage there also needs to be a serious understanding of what happens next...keeping the dog and the pet parent comfortable and safe, throughout the remainder of the dog's life."

Her suggestions for end-of-life care are: try to keep your dog safe and comfortable, ensure they get adequate nutrition and hydration, monitor for pain or discomfort, evaluate your dog's quality of life with our scoring tool, (available at the end of this chapter), and track progression of your dog's health.

However, it is important for the pet parents to understand what to do in a crisis and be prepared for such things as: if your dog suddenly collapses, loses consciousness, has seizures or difficulty breathing, behaves aggressively, or vocalizes in pain. "Don't Wait! Contact your veterinarian immediately."

This advice may sound strange...of course you contact your veterinarian, but I know that at times like those described; especially when things are happening to your "baby," as a pet parent, you may not be able to think clearly and time may be of the essence, so being prepared to act, is the key!

Dr. Gardner went on to explain, "Pets with dementia act in unusual ways, and may become irritable, anxious, or withdrawn. Many people welcome pets into their lives for loving companionship, but dementia may destroy the bond between pet and owner if the pet retreats. If your dog fails to take joy in everyday life because they have decreased cognitive function or are unable to interact normally with loved ones, their quality of life has decreased.

"However, if things worsen and your dog stops eating or drinking or your pet displays an abrupt behavior change, immediately contact your family veterinarian, who may have additional management tips, prescribe cognitive-boosting medication or supplements, or recommend a prescription diet."

I also learned from watching Shamrock, that it is also extremely important that during this time the pet parent is in contact with the

DEMENTIA & ALZHEIMER'S – Latter Stages

veterinarian as to any issues the dog is having, as they may or may not be related to cognitive issues. The dog may have something new going on, like pain, or many other factors that are making, or appearing to make the dementia worse.

Next, we began to discuss the difficult decisions. Dr. Gardner advised, "If it can be determined that there are no diagnosable causes and the pet starts to decline further, for example the parent starts to see their dog having fifty percent or more of their day in this state of cognitive decline, then it is time to discuss end of life care."

I didn't really want to go further, but I knew I had to, so I asked, "Exactly what does end of life care involve?"

Dr. Gardner was very straight-forward with her answer, "End of life care includes hospice consultations, quality of life discussions, either in person and, or teleadvice mode, and euthanasia."

That last word, "euthanasia" sent chills down my spine. I have had to use that procedure with three of my nine dogs, but it has never been an easy decision. In each case the decision came down to, after trying everything possible; not wanting my beloved "baby" to suffer.

But Dr. Gardner broke it down in an easier way. She told me there are three end of life decisions that pet parents need to think about...

"Not time yet – but there needs to be a clear understanding of what changes that decision and what will define when it will be time

"Family issues– the family can no longer deal with the disease - what it is doing to the dog ...and to them

"Dog issues – when the dog becomes unable or just not wanting to deal with its symptoms

"It is important to point out," Dr. Gardner emphasized, "at the end of life both the pet and the family need care and support.

"When things get to that stage, it may be time for a hospice visit and, or a consultation. That visit includes a physical examination, a full assessment of the pet's quality of life, and a custom treatment plan to help care for the pet and monitor their condition. The 'Care Plan' may include medical recommendations, nutritional changes, and most often environmental suggestions to ensure the comfort and safety of the pet. The veterinarian will also learn what is most important to the family and any of their concerns or fears. We want to ensure that the family is also supported during this time and understands that caregiving can be challenging."

Dr. Gardner clarified, "Unfortunately at that time many dogs had not been seen by a veterinarian for over a year. Again, that is why it is so important to be aware of the signs of the disease and not wait to schedule a visit. Another aspect of veterinary hospice is 'Caregiver Support'. When we focus on the care of the pet, we also need to make sure the family has the tools they need, feel supported and also empathize with them, 'it is A LOT to care for a sick pet!'"

I really agreed! In the latter stages of this illness, the hours and the emotions, the pet parent may need to devote to their dog's care will be long, tiring, frustrating and very upsetting. But the main issues revolve around keeping your dog safe, comfortable, and happy, and to see that they eat and sleep as much as possible. But the pet parent also needs to understand that there probably will be times, many, many times, no matter what you do...it just may not be enough!

Dr. Gardner understood exactly what I was feeling, and she suggested, "Quality of Life assessments can be very helpful for a family to decide on a care plan and to provide things to watch out for as their pet comes closer to the end. If euthanasia is the next step, the goal is for a peaceful euthanasia for both the pet and the pet parent."

Resources for this interview were also obtained from the following articles and blogs appearing on the *Lap of Love Website.: What is cognitive dysfunction (CDS)?
Dementia Does My Senior Dog Have Canine Cognitive Dysfunction?
And with permission from Dr. Gardner- *(Note: See Recommendations -pg 250).

Dr. Gardner and Lap of Love provided the following form to help parents better understand care, choices, and how to navigate and make decisions regarding end-of-life care.

DEMENTIA & ALZHEIMER'S – Latter Stages

Lap of Love
Pet Family Concerns

SCORE EACH ITEM ON A SCALE OF 0-2:
- 0 = I am not concerned at this time
- 1 = There is some concern
- 2 = I am concerned about this

I AM CONCERNED ABOUT THE FOLLOWING THINGS:

___ Pet suffering

___ Pet dying alone

___ Not knowing the right time to euthanize

___ Concern for other household animals

___ Desire to perform nursing care for your pet

___ Ability to perform nursing care for your pet

___ Coping with loss

___ Concern for other members of the family (i.e. children)

RESULTS

0-4: Your concerns are minimal at this time. You have either accepted the inevitable loss of your pet and understand what lies ahead, or have not yet given it much thought. If you have not considered these things, now is the time to begin evaluating your own concerns and limitations.

5-9: Your concerns are mounting. Begin your search for information by educating yourself on your pet's condition; it's the best way to ensure you are prepared for the emotional changes ahead.

10-16: Although you may not place much value on your own quality of life, your concerns about the changes in your pet are valid. Now is the time to prepare yourself and to build a support system around you. Veterinary guidance will help you prepare for the medical changes in your pet while counselors and other health professionals can begin helping you with anticipatory grief.

DISCUSS THE QUESTIONS BELOW, AND THE ENTIRE QUALITY-OF-LIFE SCALE, WITH YOUR VETERINARIAN

Below are some open-ended questions that assist gauge your family's time, emotional, and (when appropriate, financial) budgets:
1. Have you ever been through the loss of a pet before? If so, what was your experience (good or bad, and why)?
2. What do you hope the life expectancy of your pet will be? What do you think it will be?
3. What is the ideal situation you wish for your pet's end of life experience? (at home, pass away in her sleep, etc.)

Suggestions on using this quality-of-life scale:
1. Complete the scale at different times of the day, note circadian fluctuations in well-being. (We find most pets tend to do worse at night and better during the day.)
2. Request multiple members of the family complete the scale; compare observations.
3. Take periodic photos of your pet to help you remember their physical appearance.

Resources:
1. AAHA/AAFP Pain Management Guidelines for Dogs and Cats. www.aahanet.org/Library/PainMgmt.aspx
2. Online hospice journal and quality of life scale: www.PetHospiceJournal.com

Content may not be reproduced without written consent from Lap of Love Veterinary Hospice.

"Lap of Love Pet Family Concerns," has been provided by agreement and permission from Dr. Gardner and Lap of Love.

SHAMROCK'S STORY

Quality Of Life (QoL)

This may be one of the hardest determinations pet parents have to weigh when caring for their beloved dogs and deciding their Quality of Life.

The Quality of Life for a dog is as important as any other way we measure a dog's life.

Quality of life can be looked at in terms of happiness, comfort, and health. The information provided here can be used at any stage of disease from diagnosis to latter stages; and it is an incredibly important tool.

Deciding Your Dog's Quality Of Life

Dr. Bartner told me, she suspects that, similar to a seizure where the dog's awareness portions of the brain temporarily shut off, dogs with advanced CCD behave compulsively and probably don't have any recollection of what is happening. They may have periods of disconnect and pace aimlessly. It is hard to know if they are "zoned out" or just forgetting what they are doing. She doesn't believe the dogs feel pain during these times, but their quality of life may not be good. They are basically going through the motions without any real involvement, or interaction.

QoL Scale -Introduction/Summary

Alice Villalobos, DVM, DPNAP, a renowned veterinary oncologist, introduced "Pawspice," a quality-of-life program for terminally ill pets. Pawspice starts at diagnosis and includes symptom management, gentle standard care and transitions into hospice as the pet nears death. Dr. Villalobos developed a scoring system to help family members and veterinary teams assess a pet's life quality, *The HHHHHMM Quality of Life Scale*. The five **H**'s stand for: **H**urt, **H**unger, **H**ydration, **H**ygiene and **H**appiness. The two **M**'s stand for **M**obility and **M**ore good days than bad. The QoL scale is also a helpful decision-making tool to assist pet parents in the difficult process of making the final call for the gift of euthanasia to provide a peaceful and painless passing for their beloved pet.

DEMENTIA & ALZHEIMER'S – Latter Stages

Quality of Life Scale
(The HHHHHMM Scale)

Pet caregivers can use this Quality of Life Scale to determine the success of Pawspice care. Score patients using a scale of: 0 to 10 (10 being ideal).

Score	Criterion
0-10	**HURT** - Adequate pain control & breathing ability is of top concern. Trouble breathing outweighs all concerns. Is the pet's pain well managed? Can the pet breathe properly? Is oxygen supplementation necessary?
0-10	**HUNGER** - Is the pet eating enough? Does hand feeding help? Does the pet need a feeding tube?
0-10	**HYDRATION** - Is the pet dehydrated? For patients not drinking enough water, use subcutaneous fluids daily or twice daily to supplement fluid intake.
0-10	**HYGIENE** - The pet should be brushed and cleaned, particularly after eliminations. Avoid pressure sores with soft bedding and keep all wounds clean.
0-10	**HAPPINESS** - Does the pet express joy and interest? Is the pet responsive to family, toys, etc.? Is the pet depressed, lonely, anxious, bored or afraid? Can the pet's bed be moved to be close to family activities?
0-10	**MOBILITY** - Can the pet get up without assistance? Does the pet need human or mechanical help (e.g., a cart)? Does the pet feel like going for a walk? Is the pet having seizures or stumbling? (Some caregivers feel euthanasia is preferable to amputation, but an animal with limited mobility yet still alert, happy and responsive can have a good quality of life as long as caregivers are committed to helping their pet.)
0-10	**MORE GOOD DAYS THAN BAD** - When bad days outnumber good days, quality of life might be too compromised. When a healthy human-animal bond is no longer possible, the caregiver must be made aware that the end is near. The decision for euthanasia needs to be made if the pet is suffering. If death comes peacefully and painlessly at home, that is okay.
*TOTAL	*A total over 35 points represents acceptable life quality to continue with pet hospice (Pawspice).

Reprinted with Permission from Dr. Villalobos

SHAMROCK'S STORY

Veterinarian's Final Words

Preparing for this book, I have conducted over 50 interviews, read more than 25 research documents, and engaged in hundreds of emails. There was so much information that I thought I would never be able to get it all into one book.

But I could not get to this point without providing you, the reader, with all the tidbits I was given. Each section relates to issues and stages of this disease. Here are the Veterinarians "Final Words!"

Before Diagnosis

My extensive research revealed that I wasn't the only one hitting the web for answers. Many times, pet parents have already researched what is happening to their pet, even before they visit their veterinarian.

Dr. Landau expressed, "With the internet there is so much information that many pet parents want to get an idea of what they are dealing with before seeing the veterinarian." He went on, "They will then bring that information to the visit." That can save time because then he can research their findings. "This is a win-win situation as the parent begins to understand the disease and yet they make sure to get the veterinarian involved ASAP, which is very important." Dr. Landau also realizes there is so much out there about this disease, which is changing every day, therefore, no doctor can totally keep up, so this collaboration with pet parents is vital in helping our pets get the best treatment,

Dr. Tynes said, "Preventing illness and disease should begin with your dog as a puppy. When visiting a behaviorist, they will discuss information about how to focus on good socialization and good positive experiences with people, places, surroundings…and for training."

Dr. Rivera reminds us, that in the long run the best method is, "Early prevention! Keeping the dog's body in balance, with harmony; physically, mentally and socially, prevents the immune system from being overwhelmed."

DEMENTIA & ALZHEIMER'S – Latter Stages

Dr. Villalobos confirmed, "As with so many diseases, early detection is still so very important! If you notice signs do not wait to make that appointment!"

Dr. Bartner stated, "When confronted with behavior and personality changes, don't overlook 'cognitive dysfunction', and definitely don't delay diagnosis... find out! Early recognition and early action are key to preserving good quality of life, and always talk to your veterinarian."

Dr. Katz told me, "The message is that every disease progresses at a different rate for different dogs, so the earlier the pet is seen, the better."

Dr. Tynes articulated, "The problem for Veterinary Behaviorists is that they usually don't see cases of cognitive decline until the general practitioner is struggling to manage the problem in a way that is satisfactory to the pet parents. Ideally screening and prevention should begin when dogs are six to eight years old, depending on their breed, and pet parents should not hesitate to ask their veterinarians for more information about CDS before it becomes a problem for their pet."

Dr. Gardner explained, "Rather than attributing your pet's changed sleep-wake cycle or excessive vocalization, to old age, ask your family veterinarian if dementia could be the cause."

There are two main points being made over and over again. "Early Prevention!" and "Early Detection and or Diagnosis! These are probably the best ways to get a jump on this disease. The best advice: start when your dog is a puppy and if your dog is older watch for signs and don't wait to visit the veterinarian.

You may wonder why I have listed so many veterinarians who make similar statements, such as the need for early detection. The main reason is to instill in pet parents the need to not delay...when you first start to see signs, don't wait; make that appointment to see your veterinarian. No matter how many times it is said, it is one of those things that we tend to forget or even ignore...we either are not sure about the signs or don't think they are important enough to bother the doctor, or waste time or money with a visit. But worse than that, we believe the problems will just go away! We don't want to hear any bad news about our precious babies. Unfortunately, these are just a few of the many, many reasons we delay!

"I have lived this! I have done this! I know all the reasons we tell ourselves…. PLEASE, PLEASE Do not ignore signs! SEE YOUR VETERINARIAN ASAP!"

Using DISHAA To Recognize Signs

In the long run, Dr. Landsberg said, "It is most important to recognize and identify signs and changes as early as possible. The best first defense against CCDS is the pet parent. They are with the dog on a regular basis and are best able to see any changes with increasing age. The point is that no change is too little nor too insignificant, and instead of ignoring the signs, make a point of discussing these changes with your veterinarian, and even take a video to get them checked out. They may be due to a medical problem including pain or discomfort, cognitive dysfunction or even related to new stresses in the home. The earlier they are diagnosed the better the chances of improving welfare, controlling the problem, and slowing decline both for pet's quality of life and maximum longevity. 'DISHAA Cognitive Dysfunction Evaluation Tool,' would help pet parents understand what to look for and then be able to discuss these signs with their veterinarian." To sum up his advice, Dr. Landsberg concluded, "Pet parents must be proactive and report signs of what their dog is doing."

Dr. Bartner suggested, "Fill out the *DISHA forms – complete them weekly or biweekly. The biggest service we can provide is to open people's eyes to getting on the rehab train earlier as that might be the biggest help for now, and it certainly won't hurt."
*(Note: See The DISHAA form -pg.50).

After Diagnosis

Dr. Kass said, "The best we can do for our beloved pets is to give them good sourced nutritious food and healthy supplements." She reminds us, "Let Food Be Thy Medicine!"

DEMENTIA & ALZHEIMER'S – Latter Stages

Dr. Landau summed up our discussion by saying, "Get your pet on the right food, on the right supplements and on the right treatments, from the very start, and ask questions in order to understand the correct course of any new treatment, along with the associated risks.

"The earlier we start our pets in the right direction the less problems we may have, but if problems arise, see a veterinarian as soon as possible to assess the situation and make a plan...and never be afraid to ask questions."

Dr. Bartner recommended, "With this disease it is good to seek out a behaviorist and a neurologist to make sure nothing is being overlooked, nor over interpreted."

Depending upon what she finds, Dr. Katz may suggest speaking with a neurologist to decide whether it might be helpful to have an MRI. "This could be another diagnostic tool which may or may not lead to a greater understanding of the disease."

Dr. Bernard expressed, "Combining holistic practices such as the use of Chinese herbs with conventional medicines, like using Gabapentin and Melatonin, when required to help ensure sleep, give the ability to help both the pet and the parent get through this horrendous disease."

I told Dr. Brugliera that I wish I had known all that I have learned from my research, during the hardest nights with Shamrock. But for pet parents I have spoken with, that feeling of being alone, and trying to cope with the traumas; especially at night, is a horror!

She told me that is why her practice offers email consultations that can help pets and pet parents. Each patient is looked at individually and depending on their stage of the disease, there are Chinese herbal medications, prescribed through telemedicine, which can be extremely helpful.

Dr. Mar said, "There are also other resources pet parents can turn to. Many veterinarians now offer online clinics. They can answer questions, and are wonderful, especially for new dog parents or when pets are experiencing a problem. They can also provide information about what happens at different stages in your dog's aging process. These virtual veterinary professionals offer telehealth and teleadvice and in some states, telemedicine. But keep in mind that based on where you live, they may not legally be able to diagnose conditions or prescribe medications for your pet."

Dr. Kangas advised, "If your veterinarian is not giving this type of information there are many veterinarians available through online services or telemedicine options, giving pet parents the opportunity to work virtually with vets anywhere in the world."

I was pleased to hear about services like telemedicine and online-clinics, teleadvice, and forums. I also heard from many other veterinarians that they have, or are considering, offering more services via email, text and the internet, during and after hours. These services are so helpful for the pet parent and do reduce the feeling of being in this, "All Alone!" With this disease and the way problems seem so much more traumatic during the night hours, this becomes a wonderful resource.

I know first-hand when you have been through the stages of cognitive decline, sometimes there is a built-up frustration, and a desperate need to try and do more. It is so good to know that instead of the only resource being emergency care or waiting the long hours until your veterinarian's practice opens in the morning; there are services to help. I have also since learned that these telemedicine services are becoming increasingly available...so check with your veterinarian.

Finally, Dr. Mahaney felt that by observing these dogs in their environment he can help the pet parent structure habits around their CCD, such as exercise, play, meals, elimination and other habits that can counteract signs of the disease.

Dr. Fraser also reminded me, "House call practices" are very, important especially when your pet needs care from your home, so veterinarians like her practice are becoming more needed in the veterinary world.

DEMENTIA & ALZHEIMER'S – Latter Stages

Dr. Mar, commented, "It is also vital for pet parents to be educated about their pet's health. Ask your veterinarian to go over what is normal, how to avoid problems, and also, what you should be aware of.

"It is okay to inquire about setting up a time solely to have a question-and-answer session regarding your pet's health and, or recent exam. That way, both the pet parent and the veterinarian are on the same page and ensure they are looking out for the same concerns."

Dr. Tynes said, "If your veterinarian does not feel diet changes, supplementation or limiting vaccines or other treatments is advisable, don't be afraid to ask for a referral to another veterinarian to get other opinions about these topics."

Finally, I asked Dr. Gardner, what else pet parents can do when they are in the midst of this disease, and she advised, "Socialize them with other people and animals, but always, where and when you know they will be safe, and provided they enjoy interaction. Engage your dog in daily training sessions to keep their mind sharp and avoid changes in their normal routine or your home's layout."
The main points here are that a diagnosis of CCDS is not the end. There are so many possibilities and with each passing day the medical and veterinary communities are continually learning more and more information to help with causes and remedies. There are so many possibilities: diet, supplements, therapies and treatments, which can help your dog, but again the biggest point is, "Early Treatment is Key!"

What Can Be Done? Veterinarian's Mixed Responses
Regarding Shamrock, I had tried everything I knew, including prescription drugs, but nothing made a lasting difference. So now I wanted to know what else could be done in the battle against this disease.

Dr. Jensen reassured me, "It is also understandable to ask the question, considering all the things you did to help Shamrock, cooking her food, giving her supplements and doing "Doga;" even without the long-term results. However, all those things were probably extremely helpful in dealing with her signs. The deeper problem was what had manifested over all the years and surfaced now, which had probably never been resolved."

Dr. Haghighat believes there are many treatments available, but in the end the best way to treat these patients is by being "proactive," and by using a "holistic approach". He said the best way is to "Focus on and treat the entire animal, the guardian and the environment together."

Dr. Fallek said, "If you work with a holistic veterinarian from the beginning, your pet will less likely develop this terrible disease."

Dr. Feinman stated, "Healthy and happy pets have the freedom and flexibility that lets them have the best lives possible. Therefore, it is so important for pet parents to have the tools, support, and resources for making this a reality for their pet. Once they feel empowered, they can help their dogs to live healthier, happier and longer lives."

To conclude he said, "Everything is based on hard science. Physics laws don't change, gravity is gravity, conservation of energy is a law of physics that governs the bodies molecular vitality.

"Understanding the role of individuality and happiness is absolutely essential for moving beyond merely treating dis-ease and instead focusing on creating true health. All living creatures, animal or human, want to thrive and flourish, to feel loved and to feel free, to feel energetic and at ease, to safely experience new things, and so much more."

Dr. Frick reminds us that spending a little more money on good food and better choices, may alleviate spending even more money in the long run-on veterinary bills... and having to deal with the heartbreak of your dog's illness.

Another important preventative Dr. Landsberg suggested, "Have frequent checkups, twice yearly after age seven or eight to be sure any changes are identified, reported, looked at, and treated

DEMENTIA & ALZHEIMER'S – Latter Stages

early. This disease can cause declining mental health and distress, which when combined with other age-related health disorders such as the heart, brain and diseases causing pain, can contribute to the pet's demise."

I wanted to investigate if prevention was possible, would reversal also be possible?

Dr. Bassingthwaighte told me, "In the case of prevention, if an animal has a strong genetic bias toward this disease, doesn't get other diseases and lives a long life, it is inevitable that some will develop dog dementia to some degree, so the answer is you cannot necessarily prevent it in all cases.

"But he continued, "You can have improvement in symptoms, but changes in the brain, in terms of the protein collecting buildup within the neural structure, which is the cause of this disease, no, I don't believe you can reverse the degenerative changes. However, I have seen symptoms improve particularly with using CBD and with a full spectrum of all other cannabinoids. But to continue improvement of symptoms, you must continue with treatments. If they are stopped the dog will regress."

He summed up by stating, "Another thing I have discovered is that with this disease, if there is pain, then treating the pain makes an enormous difference. Even old dogs with undiagnosed severe pain from arthritis and other pain in the body, made significant improvement when they were treated for the pain. Using any type of pain relief, including prescription drugs, or adding anything, 'The whole kitchen sink,' is appropriate. Give the dog relief with anything non-steroidal, gabapentin and even opioids, if needed." He also added, "Whatever is needed is appropriate! Stop thinking about side effects and just think about managing the pain, even by using strong pain relief, if needed."

Throughout this book some veterinarians have suggested ways to reverse signs, but Dr. Bassingthwaighte, and other veterinarians felt there is no way to reverse the signs, or to cure the disease.

Dr. Mahaney admitted he does not believe this disease can be reversed, but he does feel that some of the causes can be remedied; like diet and environment, and that could make symptoms improve.

SHAMROCK'S STORY

Dr. Landes said, "In very short summary of my experience, cognitive dysfunction in dogs is a frustrating condition that tends to progress despite intervention. The biggest frustration is that it is not a fatal condition, but quite debilitating for the dog and overwhelming for the caretaker. It significantly affects the quality of life of the pet and the caretaker. There is no 'cure'."

Dr. Jensen summed up, "Pet parents should know that the optimum care is to achieve good health and quality of life, not just elimination of signs and symptoms." She also suggested pet parents consider, "Your pet's life force helps the dog know what to do...they just need your help!"

Dr. Katz pointed out, "Disease usually starts as external, and then the body internalizes the causes, and many internal anti-inflammatory diseases can develop.

"But unfortunately, sometimes it is too late!" She once saw a beagle who was 15 that was having some signs of dementia; especially no longer being social. She tried some treatments, but by the time she saw the pet, it was too late for any of the possible changes to have any real effect.

"Some animals just can't be cured, and genetics might play a part, but remember diet, home situation, history of vaccines chemicals in their environmental all contribute. Stress can also be a big part, so all these causes need to be looked at.

"The hope for all pets and pet parents is to become more aware of what needs to be done long before that point.

Dr. Katz concluded by stating, "Pet parents need to be more proactive and before making decisions, they should seek out other opinions, such as from holistic vets. They should also not have blind faith but be willing to ask questions and discuss their situation to arrive at the best care for their pet."

But she also said it was good to know that there is a growing amount of evidence being sought for how this disease occurs and what if anything can be done to prevent it or limit the signs and symptoms if it does develop.

I asked Dr. Gardner, based on these situations and all the possible treatments, what is the prognosis for dogs that get CCD?

DEMENTIA & ALZHEIMER'S – Latter Stages

She replied, "Cognitive dysfunction is a progressive disease that will eventually lead to a decreased quality of life for your dog."

I held my breath and hoped for some good news and then it came...

She followed up by saying, "The prognosis depends on early detection and intervention to slow further decline, and your dog's response to a multi-modal treatment plan."

This gives the pet parent so much to work with.... They can begin to immediately use this information to not feel as "HOPELESS," "LOST," "ALONE," as I did, but instead, "HOPEFUL!" that there are so many different aspects of this disease to understand, starting with preventions, recognition of early signs and starting treatments early so your precious dog has the best chance for a good quality of life!

Most of the veterinarians I spoke with, expressed to me, whether it is diet, supplementation, or therapeutics the consensus is that the best treatments and most hopeful answers are those that approach this disease proactively; veterinarians working with the pet parent to stop the advance of the disease.

Human Alzheimer's and dementia are at the forefront of medical research. What they learn in combination with the projects being conducted for dogs, will allow canine cognitive dysfunction to become more of a topic of awareness for both the veterinary community and pet parents. This book proves the enormous information already available, so hopefully in time, the answers to dealing with this disease will be right around the corner!

Until then...the consensus seems to be 'EARLY PREVENTION IS KEY!"

When The End Is Near
Dr. Tynes related that her job is to make sure the dog's quality of life is as good as possible and maintain any needed pain control.

Dr. Gardner's final thoughts, "Consult your family veterinarian, or a teleadvice service for guidance. Learn more about pet hospice and in-home euthanasia. Be prepared so you can feel fully ready for this progressive disease. Pet loss support groups are also especially important at that time, and many are available on-line."

SHAMROCK'S STORY

From her experience dealing with CCDS dogs and with her own Cocker Spaniels, Dr. Torraca believes, "They train us, and they drive the situation." But she encourages pet parents to take control even though it is tough to handle. She concluded by stating, "EVERY dog deserves to live the best quality of life for the longest time possible, pain free, happy and strong. Be patient with your dog and yourself, which she admits is easier said than done."

Dr. Radosta spoke about "The Five Freedoms," which are the pillars of animal welfare. These are freedom from: hunger and thirst, from discomfort, pain, injury and disease and from fear and distress. Her belief is that if your pet doesn't have all 'FIVE' freedoms in their life, then they do not have a good quality of life." She further clarified, "The Freedoms are a good judge for deciding if treatments are working or if at some point the pet parent should think about it being time to let go!"

But her final thoughts were, "DON'T STOP BELIEVING! Keep pushing for answers, as long as you understand the line, as guided by the FIVE FREEDOMS "

Dr. Mar told me, "There are many procedures and treatments, especially for geriatric pets in order to give them a good quality of life, let them have life in their years. But the parent's commitment of time and even money, needs to be in line with this plan and its goals and possible ramifications."

I told Dr. Tynes that many times I was told by veterinarians and even the neurologist, "Be grateful Shamrock has lasted so far to 16, that is old age in a dog." I felt like I was being told, don't worry she's going to die soon, so just make her comfortable and let her die. I was grateful at least that our veterinarian, Dr. Faust, didn't treat her that way and always tried to find ways to deal with what was happening to her.

Dr. Tynes emphasized, "OLD AGE IS NOT A DISEASE!"

My Final Statement

After nine dogs, I realize all I didn't know. From puppy to senior hopefully is a long journey and there are many things to be aware

DEMENTIA & ALZHEIMER'S – Latter Stages

of along the way. These realizations and understandings may help your dog and you to better navigate the life stages.

I felt it important to summarize certain questions we can all pose regarding this disease. Writers are taught to be sure a story is accurate and comes full circle. Here is a list of questions to ponder

"Who" is the best veterinarian for your dog?

"What" to feed from puppy and beyond? "what" are the benefits and risks, and are there any alternatives?

"When" is it important to discuss spay and neuter, if you have a choice, and also vaccines?

"Where" you live, does your location need to be looked at for determining how the environment affects your dog?

"Why" elderly dogs need to continue certain vaccinations and treatments?

"How" treatments like heartworm, flea and tick, help and how they harm?

I have added these for more clarification:

"Which" vaccinations are really needed and "which", can be tested for, or stopped?

"Whether" there are diseases that breeds are predisposed to and those that become possibilities for your dog?

"All these factors should be considered and discussed with your veterinarian. It is so much easier to be pro-active than to try and fix what is already broken! Being an informed pet parent can give you better control and your dog a better life. Yes, there will always be diseases we can't prevent, no matter what we do, but it is so much better to know how to be aware of the issues long before they become problems.

"Start with new thinking, even if you've had many dogs, like I have! Don't confuse 'old age' with nothing you can do!

"I have learned so much about canine cognitive dysfunction syndrome, dementia and Alzheimer's throughout this journey, and am grateful to all the contributors, but one of the most important things I learned was not about the dog or the disease...it was about the pet parents need to not only be heard and understood, but also to be informed and well educated. If the relationship between the pet parent and their veterinarian is good, it should accomplish all that, and in turn be the best medicine for the dog!

SHAMROCK
THE FINAL STORY
I have no words....

SHAMROCK'S STORY

Mommy?

August

By the middle of August Shamrock was not having good days. I decided with her veterinarian that it was time to try the Xanax. Dr. Faust explained that I should give Shamrock one at bedtime, and then we should wait and see the effects. He told me, "If the medicine is metabolized in her liver quickly, she should have better nighttime sleep.

The first few days, I would stay up well into the night to see how she was reacting to the pill and if we could get her to sleep for more than four hours at a time. At first, the pill did seem to really help, but that too was short lived.

By August 21st. I was not happy with what I was seeing. Shamrock had lost more weight and was down to 18.8 pounds and having more days when the medications didn't seem to be working. I called Dr. Faust again, and he said he could see her that day.

My husband and I took her over to his office, but because of Covid, it was the first time we couldn't go in with her. Waiting outside in the parking lot was so difficult, but finally the nurse came out. We didn't get to see or talk to her veterinarian directly but were told that Dr. Faust recommended changing her medication to

SHAMROCK's Final Story

clonazepam, a drug for anxiety and seizures, and to call if there were any changes.

This was the very first time, that we left his office, with Shamrock, feeling very unsure! That night I watched the clock and waited for 12:45 AM to give her the final pill. I took her out and hoped that within the hour, she would have exhausted herself enough to go to sleep and stay asleep. I hoped this pill change would have positive results!

Initially the pill seemed to make a difference, she slept longer and better, and if she woke during the night, she would purposely bang into the bed to get my attention to take her out. But, once she got outside, she would just walk around in circles or just stand in one place and not move.

Even though her sleep was a bit better, other things were not. We weren't getting good overall results, and everything for Shamrock became a fight: eating, sleeping, walking, going in circles not wanting to be held or calmed, etc.

Her issues became progressively worse. Nothing could get her to eat a full meal, naps became almost non-existent, and any other sleep was erratic.

We tried everything to stop her from continually walking in circles, but the more we tried, the more her circles got tighter and faster. Holding her became impossible, walking her to go out became a tug of war and doing anything with her was a fight. The only thing that made her happy was peanut butter and, or vanilla ice cream.

Tuesday night, August 25th, she totally refused to eat. Anything I could get into her was completely by force feeding her food through a syringe. After a while I couldn't even get her to stop her circles, at all... it was an impossibly long day.

By 2:00 in the morning, I was totally spent and needed to close my eyes for a moment. I took her into the bedroom and tried to lie down with her in her bed, but she refused. Finally, I gave up and just let her walk. Suddenly I heard a loud noise and ran to her side. She had gotten stuck behind a table that there was no way she should have been able to fit behind, and she couldn't find a way to get out. I freed her and took her outside, thinking she was looking for a way to find the back door, but again all she wanted to do was walk in circles. This time, however, she seemed more disoriented than ever before.

At 3:00 in the morning my husband came outside and said he would stay with her while I tried to get some rest.

SHAMROCK'S STORY

By 8:00 AM, he came in and woke me saying that she wasn't doing well, and I should get up. When I went outside, he was sitting on the deck holding her. He said she seemed to be blind, and her bladder had let go. I asked him to put her down so I could watch her and agreed that she didn't seem able to see or walk properly. He said that when he laid her on the deck, she would try to get up by clawing at the deck, but she just couldn't get up. He carried her inside and laid her in her bed and we covered her with a blanket.

While he stayed with her, I went to call Dr. Faust, but he was in surgery and called me back around 11:00 AM. He told me that he would be in surgery until 2:00 PM and said I should keep her warm and call him then.

We sat with Shamrock for those hours. Talking to her, holding her, and never leaving her side, but by now her breathing had become labored. She seemed to be more unresponsive, but by that time we were sure she couldn't walk or see. She didn't moan or indicate in any way that she was in pain, she just remained very quiet....

By 2:00 PM, when we were supposed to talk to her veterinarian, Shamrock was very still, in a coma like state, and something just made me wait to call Dr. Faust back. I just sat on the floor stroking the blanket wrapped around her, thinking, and hoping she would just let go and die at home with us.

But by 3:00 PM, my husband and I agreed we shouldn't wait any longer with her in this state. At that moment the phone rang, and it was Dr. Faust; he had just gotten out of surgery. I told him everything that had gone on and we started to make arrangements to bring her over to his office to be euthanized.

As we were finalizing the arrangements, my husband came in and said her breathing had stopped.

I advised Dr. Faust who expressed his sadness for our loss. He had known Shamrock and cared about her for many years. I thanked him and expressed how grateful I was for the care he had always given her and her sister Clover. I told him I really believed that some doctors might not have devoted the time and effort he did to an elderly dog with dementia.

I got off the phone and joined my husband. We hugged her and cried. We consoled each other and agreed she lived a great life, was incredibly loved, and died at home with her loving parents... the way we believed Shamrock would have wanted it to be!

My husband got another blanket and we carefully wrapped her in this shroud, and he carried her to where she would be buried, next to her sister, Clover. Later that day we had a service to memorialize

SHAMROCK's Final Story

the life of Shamrock, our baby whose journey from Hurricane Katrina to doggy dementia and Alzheimer's... had now ended...but would never be forgotten!

EPITAPH FOR SHAMROCK

The last picture of Shamrock sleeping peacefully in her bed

Shamrock's journey made clear to me how this horrible disease could go from simple changes in normal behavior to consuming your dog, but unfortunately, it was too late for my beloved-baby...

In Memory of Shamrock, I have spent almost two years gathering as much information as I could to help other pet parents. I hope her story and the step by step understanding generously provided by the over 50 contributors, will help pet parents be armed with the tools needed to prevent and if necessary, fight back against, canine cognitive dysfunction, doggy dementia and Alzheimer's in dogs.

Shamrock gave so much love and asked for so little in return. If even one dog, and, or one pet family, can be helped, or gain some guidance from this book, then her Love will keep on giving!

SHAMROCK'S STORY

Recommendations, References, Resources

No book is complete without acknowledging all that goes into its creation and providing the reader with good sources that help you go beyond this book

Recommended Resources-Products, Services & Websites
Recommendations From Our Veterinarians

Books:

Dr. Landsberg – for more detailed information and guidance on senior behavior care: "Decoding your Dog," written entirely by the American College of Veterinary Behaviorists also included chapter by Dr. Landsberg, "Growing old with Grace."

Dr. McKinstry suggested reading Jeffrey M. Smith, a leading consumer advocate promoting healthier non-GMO choices, and author of the world's bestselling book on GMOs," Seeds of Deception." He has also penned a short award-winning film called, "Genetic Roulette – The Gamble of Our Lives," which shows evidence that genetically engineered foods are a major contributor to rising disease rates in the US population, especially among children. He discusses many problems in humans, and pets that eat genetically modified soybeans and corn.

Products- Calming Aids

Dr. DePorter -Adaptil® Diffuser

Dr Torraca - Rescue Relief drops, Calmer Canine for anxiety

Products - Dog Food

Dr. Buchoff – raw dog food - "Dr B's Longevity." full line pet food. For more information visit: *https//www.drbslongevity.com/*

Dr Fischer recommends for base mix foods, examples such as Honest Kitchen and Dr. Harvey's.

Dr. Mahaney recommends - Pure – Whole food For more information visit: *https://hellopure.com/*

Several of our veterinarians have recommended, Hills, Purina, and Royal Canine

Products Supplements

Recommendations, Resources, References

Dr. Brugliera - CAS mushroom antioxidant blend, Ellevet CBD, Standard Process Whole Body supplement as well as Standard Process calamari oil. "All of these supplements and more can be purchased through her practice." For more information visit: *www.atlantaholisticvet.com*

Dr. DePorter - SAMe is available in canine formulations: Novifit® by Virbac and both Denosyl® and Denamarin® (a combination of SAMe and Sibylin) by Nutramax Laboratories.

Dr. Kangas - B12 supplementations: RX Vitamins Amino B-Plex, Standard Process Cataplex B and B Complex liquid Vitamins for Dogs & Cats by Veterinarian's Apawthecary.

Dr. Kass – LifeVantage Petandim for all older pets to lower oxidative stress more effectively than antioxidant supplements.

Dr. Landes - dietary/herbal supplements formulated by Dr. Clemmons, to help slow the progression of CCDS

Dr. Mallu - VRS Omega Cognitive FA Oil and AyushPet Bacopa Plus also Jing Tang Chinese herbs based on their TCM diagnosis. (Sold solely through veterinarians,).

Product-Senilife

Dr. Baker - Senilife® has resveratrol, phosphatidylserine, pyridoxine, gingko biloba, vitamin E. This is a popular supplement, and one I give my own dog. Research has not been done on the effect of this supplement combined with some of the others. While generally regarded as safe, interactions may be present that have not been discovered. It is very important to discuss the supplements with a veterinarian.

Dr. DePorter - Senilife® (CEVA Animal Health) includes a combination of antioxidant ingredients: phosphatidylserine, pyridoxine, ginkgo biloba, resveratrol, and natural vitamin E which may reduce the effects of neurodegenerative aging and the associated behavior changes. Phosphatidylserine, a membrane phospholipid, has been shown in canine clinical trials to reduce the severity of clinical signs associated with CDS. CanCog, a research facility conducted a clinical trial with an earlier formulation of Senilife which found the performance accuracy was improved in the treated group compared with baseline, and dogs receiving the supplement in the first portion of the study maintained their improved performance. Gingko biloba extract contains flavonoids and ginkgolides which are active as antioxidants and appear neuroprotective.

Dr. Kangas - other brain support, herbs and nutrients such as ginkgo biloba, and resveratrol. These types of nutrients are included in products like Animal Essentials Senior Support and Senilife®.

Dr. Mar-Senilife® is a type of supplement which can promote brain health and aid in protecting brain cells.

Dr. Tynes - Senilife® from Ceva Animal Health contains phosphatidylserine, ginkgo biloba, antioxidants, and vitamin B6 and has been shown to improve cognition in dogs in both clinical and laboratory studies.

Services:

Dr. Bassingthwaighte -information on "WEBB," (Whole Energy Body Balance) *(Note: See Treatments – Body Works-pg 145). For more information, and on-line training visit:
https://www.wholeenergybodybalance.com/

Dr. Buchoff also believes in addition to a good food regimen, care of dental issues is another top priority. He recommended non anesthetic dentistry provided by Houndstooth Non-Anesthetic Veterinary Dental Service (NAVDS). *(Note: See Dental-pg173).

Dr. Frick suggested *www.checkpup.com* for analyzing your dog's functional and nutritional health.

Dr. Gardner suggested services like "Lap of Love," that provide veterinarians who come to the home to evaluate end of life issues. *(Note: See End of Life -225).

Dr. Overall advises to help with dog breathing *(Note: See Dog Breathing-pg 161), a professional, (trained, certified dog trainer or trained veterinary professional who uses only force-free techniques) can help you to desensitize your dog to food moving towards his nose. For more information visit the Pet Professional Guild site: *http://www.petprofessionalguild.com*

Websites:

Dr. Dodds said there are acupressure points throughout the body and any pet parent can go to TALL GRASS INSTITUTE: *www.animalaccupressure.com* to find charts that show the different acupressure points to use.

You can also google animal acupressure points for other information and sites.

Recommendations, Resources, References

Dr. Feinman recommends all the benefits of Holistic Actions, *https://www.holisticactions.com*. *(Note: See my experience below).

Dr. Frick - online nutrition courses available for anyone, *www.e-trainingfordogs.com*

Dr. Gardner referred: *https://www.lapoflove.com/blog/common-pet-diseases-and-symptoms/does-my-senior-dog-have-canine-cognitive-dysfunction*

Dr. Keyser recommended, Pet Talk which is also a service of the College of Veterinary Medicine & Biomedical Sciences, Texas A&M University. Stories can be viewed on the web at *https:/vetmed.tamu.edu/news/pet-talk/cognitive- decline- In- aging- dogs/*

Dr. Landsberg advocates *www.fearfreehappyhomes.com* for valuable information Old Dogs should learn new tricks check out the senior care resources at Fear Free Happy Homes.

Dr. Radosta also suggests *https://fearfreepets.com/*

Dr. Overall suggests this YouTube video: link that will help you to see how breathing and relaxation can help: *http://www.youtube.com/watch?v=DIxELL4FkWI*. This video was made by a client who taught the technique to her dog, and here he is using it to calm himself when she is not available to give him cues. Also, *Humane Behavioral Care for Dogs: Problem Prevention and Treatment, The Protocols for-Breathing and Behavior,* including tier 1 and all the tier 2 -and *The Protocol for Deference*, are available at: *www.KarenOverall.com* *(Note: See Dog Breathing -pg 161).

Dr. Mar recommends sites for the following – Teleadvice at: *whiskerDocs, ask.vet;* Telemedicine at: *Anipanion, Airvet, BabelBark, GoFetch Health (Canada), GuardianVets, My Virtual Veterinarian, PetDesk, Petriage, Pawzy (Canada), PetPro Connect, PetsApp (UK), Medechat (Australia), Milo Plans, TeleTails, TeleVet, Vet2Pet*

More Resources

Animal Communicators- Recommended were Laurie Wolf, an animal communicator who can be reached through, Equestrian Spirits *www.equestrianspirits.org.*, and the other was Stacy Krafczyk at All Sprit Healing, *www.allspirithealing.com (I have no personal knowledge regarding either of them).*

Dementia And Alzheimer's In Humans - The connection between human dementia and Alzheimer's helped me see the possibilities of what was happening to Shamrock. My uncle was the key for me...but if you have no concept of how this disease manifests

SHAMROCK'S STORY

itself in people, I suggest reading books by neurologists like Dr. Bredesen and Dr. Newport to better understand this horrible disease.

TRAC Dog Study – This study might well benefit both dogs and humans. If you are interested in having your dog evaluated for enrollment in the study, email: csuneurotrials@colostate.edu or call (970) 297-4405.*(Note See TRAC -pg 214). To support the neurology and neurosurgery service at the James L. Voss Veterinary Teaching Hospital, including research and clinical trials like this study, give to the Neurology STAND fund. For more information visit: *https://cvmbs.source.colostate.edu/could-treatment-for-doggie-dementia-yield-clues-for-alzheimers-disease-in-humans-csu-clinical-trial-aims-to-find-out/*

Help Your Dog -Help Other Dogs - The Dog Aging Project. The more that can be learned about dogs and their illnesses and needs, the more we will be able to help all dogs.

The information I currently receive from The Dog Aging Project about their studies after only being in existence for a short time; tells me just how important this will be over the entire 10 years of the study...and hopefully beyond.

If you want to be part of that information, you can even nominate your dog. They are actively looking for "Dogs of all ages, from all around the U.S., including purebred and mixed breed dogs, are invited to join the Dog Aging Project."

If you want to support this effort, you can also make a donation. For more information visit:

https://dogagingproject.org   *(Note: See Dog Aging Project-pg 216).*

Pet Parents Forums. - I heard from Dr. Feinman and other veterinarians about HOLISTIC ACTIONS, *www.holisticactions.com.*

Thanks to help from Dr. Feinman, I joined their group when I started doing research for this book. I didn't get into all the bells and whistles they offer; the pet forums I joined were just one of their many perks. I do get emails with a lot of pet information and that has been incredible.

I also started a feed asking "*Doggy Dementia - Does your dog have signs?*" I received lots of responses and good information with resources and suggestions.

Holistic Actions offers a Free membership if you want to try this out, but they offer other levels that provide one-on-one guidance, weekly support, ability to ask questions of VETS and homeopaths, the FORUMS and so much more. I wish I had known about Holistic

Recommendations, Resources, References

Actions at 2:00 AM when I was walking the floor with Shamrock and not knowing how to help her.

You can Google any of the recommendations in this section and I also suggest you speak with your veterinarian before doing or trying anything.

I know there are so also many more resources available, if you would like to suggest something, please email: *info@goldenquillpress.com, subject: suggested resources*

Thank You

Thank You to our incredible contributors, experts in their fields, for their time and essential information regarding this disease...

Thank you from us and our beloved dogs.

And We Present for You, the reader, their

Biographies

We hope you will take your time to explore the Accomplishments, Experience and Expertise of these incredible contributors and appreciate, as I do their sharing their knowledge to help you, the pet parent, navigate this disease.

Their Credentials Will Blow You Away!

Biographies, Practice, & Company Information

The following biographies, practice and company information have been graciously supplied by each veterinarian, doctor, researcher, web site or business.

I am humbled and cannot even begin to express my gratitude for their insightful information which has helped to make this book an important resource for pet parents and others alike.

I am extremely happy to introduce them and their information to you, the reader:

Dr. Cindy Baker is a 1990 graduate of Purdue University College of Veterinary Medicine. In 2003, she founded Bargersville Veterinary Hospital in Franklin, Indiana. She also graduated from the then Chi Institute, now the Chi University, in veterinary acupuncture. Incorporating acupuncture, Chinese herb, rehabilitation techniques, and treating the entire pet has been a focus of her practice. She plans to retire next year and have four veterinarians carry on at BVH. For more information visit: *www.Bargersvillevet.com*

Thank You & Biographies

Dr. Lisa Bartner is an Assistant Professor of Neurology at Colorado State University College of Veterinary Medicine and Biomedical Sciences and is board-certified in neurology by the American College of Veterinary Internal Medicine (ACVIM). She completed her BS, MS, and DVM degrees at Michigan State University, followed by internships on the East coast and a residency at CSU in 2017 after which, she has stayed-on as a faculty member. She has strong interests in neurosurgery, novel drug therapy (i.e., CBD in the treatment of seizures), and clinical neurology. For more information visit:

https://vetmedbiosci.colostate.edu/vth/services/neurology

Dr. Edward Bassingthwaighte BVSc (Hons) is a holistic veterinarian. He graduated from the University of Queensland in 1995. Dr Edward is passionate about helping pet parents give their pets the best life possible using natural, holistic treatments, and is the founder of the Whole Energy Body Balance method, a healing bodywork modality for pets, people and horses. For more information visit: *www.wholeenergybodybalance.com*

Dr. Clay Bernard received his undergraduate and veterinary medical degrees from Louisiana State University and has been practicing small animal medicine since 2005. Having practiced several years in both Las Vegas, NV and Southlake, TX, he has now settled comfortably in Austin, where he has thoroughly enjoyed helping pets and people in the community since 2010.

During his years in private practice, Dr. Bernard has become increasingly amazed at the innate, natural healing tendencies of the animal body, and he has recognized the importance and value of the Holistic approach to treating and managing disease. He began studying Traditional Chinese Veterinary Medicine (TCVM) under Dr. Shen Xie at the Chi Institute in Florida and is now certified in veterinary acupuncture, while continuing to study Chinese herbology, food therapy, and Chinese Medical Manipulation (Tui-na). Dr. Bernard understands the powerful healing effects our animal friends have on our own lives, always reminding us to live in the present moment and to "wag our tail" in all weathers. It is that endearing quality that makes them, too, deserving of a comprehensive wellness plan. For more information visit: *www.evenflowholisticvet.com*

SHAMROCK'S STORY

Dr. Dale Bredesen, an internationally recognized expert in the mechanisms of neurodegenerative diseases, has had a career guided by a simple idea: that Alzheimer's as we know it is not just preventable, but reversible. The Bredesen Protocol is based on over three decades of Dr. Bredesen's laboratory research, resulting in hundreds of peer-reviewed publications that have uncovered the biochemical mechanisms behind the erosion of memory associated with Alzheimer's disease. Thanks to a dedicated pursuit of finding the science that makes this a reality, this idea has placed Dr. Bredesen at the vanguard of neurological research and led to the discoveries that today underlie the ReCODE Report.

Dr. Bredesen earned his MD from Duke University Medical Center and served as Chief Resident in Neurology at the University of California, San Francisco (UCSF), before joining Nobel laureate Stanley Prusiner's laboratory at UCSF as an NIH Postdoctoral Fellow. He held faculty positions at UCSF, UCLA, and the University of California, San Diego. Dr. Bredesen also directed the Program on Aging at the Burnham Institute before joining the Buck Institute in 1998 as founding President and CEO. He is a prodigious innovator in medicine, with over thirty patents to his name. Dr. Bredesen is also a New York Times Best Selling author and has written many books, including, *The End of Alzheimer's, The End of Alzheimer's Program"* and he has also recently published, *The First Survivors of Alzheimer's: How Patients Recovered Life and Hope in Their Own Words*. Dr. Bredesen regularly lectures and provides educational seminars all over the world to share his approach to end the global burden of dementia. For more information, email *media@ahnphealth.com,* also visit: *https://www.apollohealthco.com*

Dr. Julia Brugliera has 12 years of experience treating animals and in 2013 she founded Happy Tails Holistic Veterinary Care as a way to bring the best in holistic and traditional care to your pet.

As a native Georgian, she loves being able to treat the animals of a community she holds so dear. She's created a team of vets and technicians that are there to provide the best care to you and your pet. We strive to give you the best in holistic and alternative pet care to help treat your pets naturally! Her practice also provides supplementation. For more information visit: www.atlantaholisticvet.com

Thank You & Biographies

Dr. Gerald Buchoff is the Director and owner of Holistic Pet Care, a veterinary hospital in Little Falls, NJ. He is also the CEO and President and owner and dietary formulator for Dr B's Holistic Pet Products, also in Little Falls, New Jersey.

Dr. Buchoff graduated from Rutgers University with his Bachelor of Science in 1975, and Master of Science in Immunology in 1976. He received his doctorate degree in veterinary medicine from G.B. Pant University in India in 1980.

Dr. Buchoff has served as President of the American Holistic Veterinary Medical Association and President of the Northern New Jersey Veterinary Medical Association.

He has been featured in newspapers, magazines, and on television and radio, and was the Co-host of the TV program "The Pet Stop" on News 12 New Jersey for 50 episodes.

He is the loving husband of Geri, proud father of 3 boys, and proud grandfather of 4 grandchildren. For more information visit: *https://holisticpetcarenj.com*

Dr. Lindsey Bullen earned her BA in Chemistry and BS in Zoology in 2007. She remained at NC State for her post-baccalaureate training where she received her Doctor of Veterinary Medicine in 2012, completed a medical and surgical internship in 2013, a residency in 2016, and a fellowship in 2017. Immediately following board-certification in veterinary nutrition, Lindsey created the Clinical Nutrition Service at the Veterinary Specialty Hospital of the Carolinas, which is now a Blue Pearl Specialty and Emergency Pet Hospital and in 2022, brought clinical nutrition to Friendship Hospital for Animals in D.C. Dr. Bullen is particularly interested in clinical nutrition application, specifically: critical care, multi-disease state, and assisted feeding. Though she is no longer in academia, Dr. Bullen brings experience and a strong passion for teaching. When she is not actively working in clinics or speaking at conferences, Dr. Bullen acts as an industry advisor and consultant through her company, Bullen Veterinary Consulting, PLLC.

Lindsey grew up in a small town near Asheville, North Carolina. Though not quite a full native of this beautiful state, she is happy to still call it home. She currently lives in Apex with her husband, Nathan, and their two boys, 6-year-old, Arthur and 3-year-old, Rowan. For more information visit: *https://www.friendshiphospital.com/*

SHAMROCK'S STORY

Dr. Stanley Coren is Professor Emeritus in the Department of Psychology at the University of British Columbia. Although best known to the public for his extremely popular and award-winning books on dogs, he is also a highly respected behavioural researcher, a Fellow of the Royal Society of Canada, and was named as one of the 2000 outstanding scientists of the Twentieth Century.

Dr. Coren's many books on dog behaviour and human-canine interactions have been international bestsellers and include: *The Intelligence of Dogs, How to Speak Dog,* and *How Dogs Think, Why Do Dogs Have Wet Noses?* and *Do Dogs Dream?* These books have brought him many awards such as the Maxwell Medal of Excellence from The Dog Writers Association of America and being named as *Writer of the Year* by the International Positive Dog Training Association.

Dr. Coren is popular with the media and his been featured on numerous television programs including Oprah, Larry King, and many more. He even hosted his own nationally broadcast television show *Good Dog!* in Canada. He is a regular contributor to *Modern Dog Magazine* and the American Kennel Club's *Family Dog* magazine. You can connect with him at his award-winning blog Canine Corner which is hosted by Psychology Today. His newest book is *Gods, ghosts and black dogs: The fascinating folklore and mythology of dogs.* For more information visit:
https://www.psychologytoday.com/ca/blog/canine-corner

Dr. Theresa DePorter is a board certified diplomate in the American College of Veterinary Behaviorists (ACVB) and the European College of Animal Welfare and Behavioural Medicine (ECAWBM). She received her Doctor of Veterinary Medicine degree from Purdue University in 1992. She has been seeing behavior consultations at Oakland Veterinary Referral Services in metropolitan Detroit, Michigan, since 2004. For more information visit:
https://www.ovrs.com/specialty-services/veterinary-behavior.html

Dr. W. Jean Dodds, DVM has spent five decades in hematology and immunology research and diagnostic veterinary clinical pathology. Dr. Dodds has over 150 research publications and holds 25 patents. She started Hemopet in 1986, the first non-profit national animal blood bank. Our canine animal blood bank is

Thank You & Biographies

licensed and inspected annually by the California Department of Food and Agriculture; Biologics License # 84.

Today, Hemopet's range of nonprofit services and educational activities include providing canine blood components and related services; adopting retired Greyhound blood donors as companions; and the worldwide Hemolife specialty diagnostic division focused on hematology and blood banking, immunology, endocrinology, nutrition and holistic medicine.

Hemopet Holistic Care referral clinic is staffed by Dr. Dodds and two holistic veterinary colleagues.

Dr. Dodds has a longstanding association and committee membership with the AHVMA and AHVMF.

She has written two popular award-winning pet health books together with Diana Laverdure; with a new one on vegan diets for dogs which is in press. For more information visit: *www.hemopet.org*

Dr. Marcie Fallek, D.V.M, C.V.A. has been a practicing veterinarian since 1988. She transitioned from conventional to holistic modalities in the early 1990's. She runs two practices, one in Manhattan and one in Fairfield, CT, Worldwide phone consults are also available. She is a certified veterinary acupuncturist and well versed in many other holistic treatments, but her passion is Classical Homeopathy a method that successfully treats a wide spectrum of disease, such as cancer, diabetes and immune-mediated disease to emotional conditions such as separation anxiety and aggression. She is the proud mother of two 17-year-old Persian cats, Tessa and Sienna and an Aussie/Border Collie mix, Kyra, recently rescued from a construction site in Russia. For more information visit: *www.holisticvet.us*

Dr. Jeff Feinman is a certified veterinary homeopath and molecular biologist devoted to creating a healthier, happier, brighter world for pets and pet parents through research into and clinical application of the principles of Vitality and Balance. Jeff is a past president of the Academy of Veterinary Homeopathy and a current board member and chairman of the research and education committee. He is the founder and Chief Empowerment Officer of the online platform holisticactions.com, and some of his peer-reviewed papers can be found on the site's blog. Jeff's personal experience with his own 40 years of Medically Unexplained Symptoms, and chronic genetic dis-ease are the driving force behind his passion for helping the world unlock and unleash the innate healing power of each individual.

Dr. Jeff and his wonderful wife, Amy, currently reside in picturesque Connecticut and happily share their home with rescue pup Archie and a Rex cat named Tigger. For more information visit: *www.holisticactions.com*

Dr. Kenneth Fischer after graduating from LSU School of Veterinary Medicine in May 1991, completed a 13-month rotating internship in small animal medicine and surgery at Oradell Animal Hospital in Oradell, New Jersey. He purchased Hillsdale Animal Hospital in Hillsdale, New Jersey in 1996 and that has been his home ever since. Around the time of taking over Hillsdale Animal Hospital, Dr. Fischer found himself frustrated by the limitations of conventional medicine. After a series of serendipitous events, he started down the holistic path.

He studied animal chiropractic in 1997 at Options for Animals, then affiliated with the American Veterinary Chiropractic Association. In 1998, he became certified in veterinary acupuncture through IVAS, the International Veterinary Acupuncture Society. Dr. Fischer has studied various holistic modalities since then, including herbal medicine, homeopathy, homotoxicology, and various forms of energy medicine. The most important foundation for health in animals is the application of principles of species appropriate nutrition, something he feels is lacking in veterinary medicine. This is why he continues to learn about fundamentals of veterinary nutrition and encourages pet guardians to apply these principles with their pets.

Dr. Fischer also seeks to minimize the downside effects of medications and chemicals on our pets as well and continues to try to blend the best of what both worlds of medicine have to offer conventional Western medicine and traditional Eastern medicine, offering the best care to our animal friends. For more information visit: *www.healingvet.com*

Dr. Rebecca Fraser grew up in Winterport, Maine and then attended undergrad at Elon College (now Elon University) in North Carolina. After undergrad she worked in neuroscience research at

Thank You & Biographies

UNC-CH before attending vet school at NCSU-CVM. Dr. Fraser graduated from vet school in 2007 and has worked as a small animal associate, relief veterinarian, and finally started her integrative house call practice, Fraser Veterinary Services. She spent nine years in Baltimore while her husband was doing a fellowship at Johns Hopkins. In 2019 they moved from Maryland to Massachusetts and so she re-established her house call practice in MA. Dr. Fraser shares her life with her husband and three amazing children. They have three cats, a dog, chickens, and bees. For more information visit: *www.fraservetservices.com*

Dr. Ava Frick graduated from veterinary college in 1980, starting out in a traditional-style practice. Then, after her son was born in 1996, she transitioned to a more holistic approach. Chiropractic, rehabilitation, exercise, and nutrition has been her keen focus ever since. Early on, even before laser was popular, Dr. Frick designed the first Laser Spinal Pad® for animals. She is positioned as the world's leading authority in veterinary microcurrent therapy spending over 20 years of research and publications in this field with Alpha-Stim® technology and was a pioneer in the area of animal rehabilitation. Dr. Frick has also consulted for Standard Process® and developed the Clinical Animal Nutrition Survey© to help doctors prioritize organ system function via input by the dog and cat parent.

Educating others and sharing her wealth of knowledge has been the impetus for her books; starting with *Fitness in Motion®, How to Interpret Hair Tissue Mineral Analysis, How to Customize Nutrition in Dogs & Cats, Tai Chi-huahua®* a low impact exercise video for dogs (and other critters), *Dog Stretching Exercises* video, contributions to online learning as an instructor at e-trainingfordogs.com, and many journal publications. She has been a guest lecturer at many national and state veterinary conferences. Ava was honored with the Hartz Veterinarian of the Year Runner-up, Franklin County Humane Society Visionary Award, and was one of the first inductees to the Animal Chiropractic Hall of Fame. Her biography, *Conversations with Animals – From Farm Girl to Pioneering Veterinarian*, was released in 2021. She now lives in Cave Creek, Arizona continuing her passions. For more information visit: *www.LifeExtendMethod.com*

SHAMROCK'S STORY

Dr. Mary Gardner is a University of Florida graduate, who discovered her niche in end-of-life care and is the co-founder and CIO of Lap of Love which has over 200 veterinarians around the country dedicated to veterinary hospice and euthanasia in the home.

There is nothing better to Dr. Gardner than a dog with a grey muzzle or skinny old cat! Her professional goal is to increase awareness and medical care for the geriatric veterinary patient and to help make the final life stage to be as peaceful as possible, surrounded with dignity and support for all involved.

Dr. Gardner and Lap of Love have been featured in Entrepreneur Magazine, The New York Times, the Associated Press, The Doctors, and numerous professional veterinary publications.

Dr. Gardner recently published her new book, *It's never long enough: A practical guide to caring for your geriatric dog.* The book covers aging, ailments, tips for home environment changes/products to use, nutrition, quality of life decisions, goals of care, euthanasia, memorializing your pet. She also won VMX Small Animal Speaker of the year in 2020! For more information you can contact: *drmary@lapoflove.com*

Dr. Sasan Haghighat, is the owner of Holistic Vet clinic in Newmarket, Ontario. After graduating from vet school and additional training in Germany he passed his licensing exams in Ontario in 2003. Having a family background in natural healing methods, he soon developed a new passion; the belief that healing starts from inside. The more he practiced veterinary medicine, the less medication he prescribed. His mantra soon became: Let Food be your Medicine and Medicine be your Food.

In the spring of 2006 he met Dr. Autumn Drouin, a leading naturopathic doctor and veterinarian; they immediately became good friends and started working closely together. This led him to attend the world-renowned Chi Institute in Florida where he studied veterinary acupuncture and food therapy (including herbs) based on traditional Chinese medicine. He has certifications in both disciplines and also over 350 hours of hands-on training in veterinary chiropractic, canine rehabilitation, and matrix repatterning.

Thank You & Biographies

He is also certified in postural rehabilitation and holds a post-graduate diploma in Bio-Regulatory Medicine through BioMedic in the United Kingdom.

He and Dr. Drouin successfully combined their treatment modalities, including naturopathic medicine, homotoxicology, biological medicine, herbal medicine, acupuncture, and conventional medicine.

His training both as an emergency veterinarian and a holistic veterinarian gives him a deep understanding of health and has given him the ability to have a full spectrum approach when treating his patients.

He believes, as long as there is no immediate medical risk, that all the healing should come from inside and that his role is to support the body by using natural means. He sees that patients with seemingly hopeless medical conditions can benefit tremendously from natural medicine.

In his free time, Dr. Haghighat enjoys cooking, travelling, and spending time with his dog Tessa and two cats Teddy and DJ. For more information visit: *https://holistic-vet.ca/*

Dr. Wendy Jensen has been practicing 100 percent homeopathy since 1992. She graduated from Cornell's College of Veterinary Medicine in 1987, before being certified by the Academy of Veterinary Homeopathy (AVH) in 1994. Dr. Jensen served as Executive Editor for the AVH's Journal (JAVH) for 12 years. She lectures extensively and also teaches for the Pitcairn Institute's Professional Course in Veterinary Homeopathy. Her writing has appeared in JAVH and the Journal of the American Holistic Veterinary Medical Association, as well as in other journals.

Together with Dr. Richard Pitcairn, Dr. Jensen wrote the New World Veterinary Repertory. Her own book, *The Practical Handbook of Veterinary Homeopathy: Healing Our Companion Animals from the Inside Out,* is required reading for the Professional Course. This text was also written to help clients understand what to expect when working with a homeopathic veterinarian to improve the health of their companion animals.

She lives in New Hampshire, volunteers at her local crisis center, and plays violin whenever she can take time out from her busy house call practice. Dr. Jensen along with Dr. Pitcairn and program director Dr. Sarah Stieg, now help other veterinarians take the

SHAMROCK'S STORY

Homeopathic journey. For more information visit:
https://www.goodreads.com/author/show/14783270.Wendy_Thacher_Jensen

Dr. Katie Kangas owns and operates Integrative Veterinary Care, a private practice in San Diego, California, offering holistic and integrative health care options for pets.

Dr. Kangas achieved her CVA certification at the Chi Institute in 2008, followed by additional training in Advanced Acupuncture, Food Therapy, Herbal Medicine and Veterinary Orthopedic Manipulation (VOM).

Her areas of special interest include nutrition, functional medicine, dental health, and pain management. Dr. Kangas has authored several articles published in veterinary journals and pet magazines and shares her passion for pet wellness education by lecturing and presenting locally, nationally and internationally.

Additionally, Dr. Kangas has a background in shelter medicine, with more than 15 years of contribution to the homeless pets in her community. She spent many years working with the San Diego County Department of Animal Services and also served as the medical director of the San Diego Humane Society & SPCA from 2002-2007. For more information visit: *www.intvetcare.com*

Dr. Evelyn Kass also known as the "Pet Nutrition Doctor, is an integrative holistic veterinarian with over 35 years of experience in both traditional and holistic medicine. She has a passion for nutrition which has led her to create a nutritional consulting business for pets. Her website provides information on choosing pet foods to optimize health through food choices. She includes topics ranging from the dangers of obesity to the concerns about genetically modified foods. Her goal is to prevent many of the chronic conditions that now appear in our pets, by providing information to help pet parents choose the proper food and supplements for optimal health.

Dr. Kass has been featured *in Reader's Digest* and has been a guest on *Your Vital Pet and Holistic Actions for Animals.* Dr. Evelyn as she is known, is an expert contributor on *Dream Dog CBD* and on the advisory boards of Animal Essentials and Ion*Biome.

She provides nutritional consulting directly with pet parents to help them understand their pet's current condition and the ways they can

Thank You & Biographies

improve it through diet, supplements, and environmental adjustments. When needed she formulates individualized, balanced, whole food diets for those pets with serious illness or significant food intolerances; and sometimes for pet parents who want to do everything to avoid chronic disease in their furry family members.

Dr. Kass currently has courses available to help pet parents feed their pets for health. These can be found here: *http://bit.ly/PNDcourses*. For more information visit: *http://petnutritiondoctor.com*

Dr. Elisa Katz grew up in Connecticut and attended the University of Connecticut where she obtained a B.S. in Pathobiology in 1995. Later she attended The Ohio State University College of Veterinary Medicine. She obtained her Doctor of Veterinary Medicine in 2000. Dr. Katz returned to her home state where she practiced for the next 13 years. After the first seven years of strictly conventional medicine, she became disenchanted with the limitations of using pharmaceutical drugs exclusively. In 2008 she became certified in veterinary acupuncture through the International Veterinary Acupuncture Society. In 2012 she obtained certification in Veterinary Chinese Herbal Medicine.

In 2013 she moved to northeastern Illinois to purchase a holistic practice. The following year she became a Certified Canine Rehabilitation Therapist through the Canine Rehabilitation Institute. Three years later she completed the intensive course through the Pitcairn Institute of Veterinary Homeopathy.

This has since become her preferred treatment modality.

Most recently in 2020, Dr. Katz became a Certified Veterinary Spinal Manipulative Therapist. This is equivalent to veterinary chiropractic treatment.

In practice Dr. Katz uses natural treatments and substances whenever possible and very few pharmaceutical drugs. She has helped many pets for whom conventional medicine had failed. She plans to help many more pets over the coming years. For more information visit: *www.holisticvetservices.com*

Dr. Amber J. Keyser is an evolutionary biologist with an MS in zoology and a Ph.D. in genetics. She is a science communication specialist who enjoys making complex scientific information accessible to the general public. She's a member of the communication team at the Dog Aging Project and serves as the media liaison for the project. For more information visit: *www.dogagingproject.org*

Dr. Douglas Knueven earned his veterinary degree from Ohio State University in 1987 and is the medical director of Beaver Animal Clinic in Beaver, Pennsylvania. He has earned certification in veterinary acupuncture, veterinary Chinese herbal medicine and veterinary chiropractic. He also has advanced training in many holistic therapies including Chinese food therapy, homeopathy, osteopathy, and nutrition.

Dr Knueven has been practicing holistic, integrative veterinary medicine since 1995. He is a longtime raw pet food advocate with over two decades of experience counseling pet caregivers on how to do it right. Over the years he has worked for several pet food and pet supplement companies and is currently the Chief Veterinarian for Kure Pet Food.

Dr. Doug (as he likes to be called) has written two books about holistic medicine; *Stand by Me: A Holistic Handbook for Animals, Their People and the Lives They Share Together*, and *The Holistic Health Guide: Natural Care for the Whole Dog*. He lectures on holistic medicine topics, in at national and international veterinary programs. In 2018, Dr. Doug was recognized as the American Holistic Veterinary Medical Association (AHVMA) "Holistic Teacher of the Year." He was also chosen to be the keynote speaker for the 2021 AHVMA Annual Convention. For more information visit: *https://drdougknueven.com*

Dr. Ronald Koh received his veterinary degree in Taiwan in 2006 and later completed a specialty internship followed by a Master's program in acupuncture/integrative medicine at the University of Florida College of Veterinary Medicine. Prior to joining UC Davis School of Veterinary Medicine in 2020, Dr. Koh was an assistant clinical professor at Louisiana State University School of Veterinary Medicine and the service chief of the Integrative Medicine and Rehabilitation since 2013. He is certified in acupuncture, rehabilitation, herbal therapy, food therapy, and medical manipulation. He completed his residency in Veterinary Sports Medicine and Rehabilitation in 2019. Dr. Koh is an experienced and internationally recognized speaker and mentor on integrative

Thank You & Biographies

medicine, rehabilitation, and traditional Chinese veterinary medicine. His clinical focus has been on providing patient-centered care and treating a patient as a "whole" individual instead of focusing on an illness or diagnosis. He also utilizes available evidence and *therapies* for pain management, neurological disorders, geriatric conditions, hospice care, and chronic medical conditions. In spare time, he enjoys spending time with family, hiking, and traveling places. For more information visit: *https://www.vetmed.ucdavis.edu/hospital/small-animal/ integrative medicine*

Dr. Kevin Landau (He, Him, His) graduated from the University of Pennsylvania School of Veterinary Medicine in 1994. He then completed an internship at the Mid Atlantic Equine Medical Center, a medical and surgical referral hospital in Ringoes, New Jersey. For the next three years, Dr. Landau was a primary care equine veterinarian with Burlington Equine in Vermont. It was during this period that Dr. Landau began his foray into holistic medicine, receiving his certification in animal chiropractic by the American Veterinary Chiropractic Association in 1996.

Dr. Landau followed his chiropractic certification with a certification in animal acupuncture in 2001 with the Chi Institute of Chinese Medicine in Reddick, Florida. Dr. Landau continued with studies in Low-Level Laser Therapy, Applied Kinesiology, Autonomic Response Testing, and Bioregulatory Medicine. He has advanced acupuncture training for both small animals and horses from the Chi Institute. In 2009, Dr. Landau received his certification in Traditional Chinese Herbal Medicine under the tutelage of Dr. Steve Marsden from A Time To Heal in Illinois. Dr. Landau has also pursued advanced training in chiropractic and Traditional Chinese Herbal Medicine as he always strives to attain the best possible results for his patients.

Landau Veterinary Services is Belchertown's holistic veterinary clinic and Doctor Kevin Landau and his team have extensive experience in using non-traditional treatment methods to enhance a pet's overall health and well-being. From Acupuncture to low-level laser therapy, from Tradition Chinese Herbal Medicine to comprehensive cancer care, they help horses, cats, and dogs with so many health issues. Doctor Landau has years of education and experience and will utilize a wide variety of holistic veterinary medical disciplines to help you honor the love and commitment that you have for your animal. For more information visit: *www.landauvet.com*

Dr. Holly Landes is a 2005 graduate of Louisiana State University School of Veterinary Medicine. She next entered the United States Army Veterinary Corps and completed a 15-month tour in Iraq in support of Operation Iraqi Freedom.

In 2009, she returned to the Augusta area and established a practice which includes chiropractic care massage, rehabilitation, and Traditional Chinese Veterinary Medicine (TCVM). She is certified in Veterinary Chiropractic and received acupuncture training at the Chi Institute of TCVM. Dr. Landes is also trained in Chinese Herbal medicine and certified in TCVM Food Therapy. She also attended and is certified in Veterinary Massage and Rehabilitation from the Healing Oasis Wellness Center.

Her goal is to address imbalances in the body, mind and environment of animals and correct them before diseased states occur, as well as to bring ill animals back to a state of balance so that they can better heal themselves. For more information visit: *https://eastviewanimalwellness.com*

Dr. Gary Landsberg is a 1976 graduate of the Ontario Veterinary College. He is a diplomate of both the American College of Veterinary Behaviorists and the European College of Animal Welfare and Behavioural Medicine. Gary has owned and operated both primary care veterinary practices and a behavior referral specialty practice in the Greater Toronto Area and is pleased to have had the opportunity to mentor several veterinary behavior residents, who are now board-certified leaders in the field. Gary is currently working in contract research as Vice President of Veterinary Affairs at CanCog Inc, and as head of Fear Free research, and a Fear Free practice certification veterinarian for Canada.

Dr. Landsberg has authored numerous behavior research papers, chapters and books in the field including *Behavior Problems of the Dog and Cat and Canine and Feline Dementia*. Dr. Landsberg has received awards for service to the profession from the American Animal Hospital Association and Western Veterinary Conference. For more information email: *behaviourdvm@gmail.com*

Lap of Love To date, Lap of Love has over 225 veterinarians in over 100 geographic locations providing families with in-home

Thank You & Biographies

veterinary hospice and euthanasia services. Comfort and quality of life is their focus. For more information visit: *www.Lapoflove.com*

Mrs. Robbin Lynn is the co-founder of The One Minute Cannabist, a consulting service that bridges the education gap between the consumer and cannabis-based products. Since 2007, she has specialized helping people understand and navigate all the latest methods for realizing the maximum benefits cannabis has to offer. She is the author of *CBD Made Simple For Pets,* the definitive guide to getting the best results when using CBD oil for your pet. She is a Certified Cannabis Advisor (CCA), Certified Senior Advisor (CSA) and has completed coursework in clinical cannabinoid medicine from the Society of Cannabis Clinicians. Robbin's main expertise of the cannabis plant is from a biochemical point of view: what compounds are present and how they interact with the human endocannabinoid system. She is an expert in CBD and highly skilled in cannabinoid therapies and products, their safe use and proper dosing and she is passionate about sharing that knowledge.

Through helping more than 20,000 people (most over the age of 50) and more than 2,000 animals, she imparts cannabis knowledge in simple to understand terms to facilitate safe use for maximizing desired results. An educator at heart, Robbin challenges herself to learn something new every single day.

Prior to 2008, Robbin spent her career as a marketing executive, building start-up technology businesses in San Diego County.

In her spare time, she enjoys spending quality time with her husband, flying with her son, and curling up with her cats to read her favorite science fiction stories or the latest cannabinoid research. For more information visit:
https://oneminutecannabist.com/

Dr. Patrick Mahaney works as a concierge-style veterinarian though his house-call practice, California Pet Acupuncture and Wellness, Inc.

He loves building personal, long-term relationships with his clients to best suit their pets' needs within the comfortable confines of their homes.

As Dr. Mahaney has followed complementary and alternative means of managing his own health issues, he sought Chinese medicine training and is a certified veterinary acupuncturist.

SHAMROCK'S STORY

To spread his message of holistic pet health on a large-scale basis, Dr. Mahaney attained a Certified Veterinary Journalist certificate and contributes to various media projects.

As he believes that effective health care providers must also walk the walk of living a healthy lifestyle, Dr. Mahaney is an avid practitioner of daily, self-care habits including weight and health management through whole food nutrition and supplements, physical activity (like yoga, cycling, hiking, running, swimming, weight training, and walking), and mindfulness practices (plant cultivation and art projects are his go-to favorites).

Dr. Mahaney's belief in the benefits of whole-food nutrition for his patients has led him to become Chief Veterinary Officer of PURE (formerly known as PURE Dog Food), a Los Angeles-based company making cooked, whole-food, veterinary-nutritionist formulated meals for dogs. PURE also has treats for both dogs and cats and has feline recipes in development. For more information visit: *www.patrickmahaney.com*

Dr. Pema Mallu knew she wanted to be a veterinarian when she was five years old. At age 14, in 1966, she started work in the first of many veterinary clinics, Now, caring for you and your pets as family is her passion and she dedicates her whole life to this purpose. Dr. Mallu graduated from The Ohio State University with her DVM degree in 1977.

After ten years of clinical practice, she became discouraged with the state of our pets' health and knew that there must be something else. In 1988, Dr. Mallu discovered veterinary acupuncture and received certification by the International Veterinary Acupuncture Society. She also became a Natural Health Practitioner; completed four years of Energy healing school, a year of Veterinary Homeopathy with world renowned Dr Richard Pitcairn, earned a three-year Master's degree in human Acupuncture and she is a certified Fear Free Veterinary practitioner.

Holistic Medicine deals with the body and mind and spirit as a whole. Dr. Mallu also brings to her practice a spiritual practice as a Tibetan Buddhist nun. Presently, she owns and practices full time at Holistic Veterinary Healing an integrative holistic veterinary clinic in Germantown, MD and lives with her two dogs Bodhi a Poochon and Jack a Yorkie Poo and two cats Loverboy and Luna and Guinea Pig

Thank You & Biographies

Boris. For more information visit:
www.HolisticVeterinaryHealing.com

Dr. Rachel Mar completed her bachelor's degree in Animal Science with a minor in photography at Cal Poly San Luis Obispo. She worked in high school ministry for one year then moved to Dublin, Ireland to obtain her degree in Veterinary Medicine from University College Dublin. Now she is an integrative veterinarian working in Santa Barbara, California. She is a Fear Free certified veterinarian and is a Certified Veterinary Acupuncturist (CVA) through Chi University. Dr. Mar is currently enrolled in the Certified Canine Rehabilitation Professional (CCRP) course through the University of Tennessee. She has a blog dedicated to improving the wellbeing of both pet parents and their pets, and also offers virtual veterinary teleadvice consults via her website. For more information visit:
www.thevitalityvet.com

Dr. Stephanie McGrath is an associate professor of neurology at Colorado State University. She treats seizure disorders, inflammatory brain diseases and spinal cord disorders. Dr. McGrath is currently conducting research in infectious etiologies and treatment options for canine inflammatory brain diseases, the use of cannabidiol in veterinary medicine and the use of stem cells in spinal cord injuries. She is one of the country's leading experts on cannabidiol research in veterinary medicine. For more information visit:
https://vetmedbiosci.colostate.edu/directory/member/?id=1701

Dr. Elizabeth McKinstry grew up on a small farm in Kennett Square Pennsylvania which her grandparents acquired during the Great Depression. She grew up with horses, sheep, dogs, cats, rabbits, gerbils and parakeets.
She knew at an early age that she wanted to be a veterinarian. Her maternal grandfather was a renaissance man being a farmer, horseman, chemist, Olympian and teacher who taught her a lot about animals and plants. Her paternal grandfather was an MD and also practiced homeopathy, while her father was an MD who practiced allopathic medicine. Elizabeth graduated from Swarthmore College with a dual major in Biology and Chemistry.
She then went on to graduate from the University of Pennsylvania School of Veterinary Medicine. She had a feline practice in

SHAMROCK'S STORY

Philadelphia and practiced feline medicine for thirty years. In 2009 she took her first course in acupuncture at the Chi Institute (Now The Chi University). Within the next few years Elizabeth got certified in acupuncture, Food Therapy, Tui-Na and Chinese Herbal Medicine. Shortly after completing all of her certifications, she then worked on her masters in Traditional Chinese Veterinary Medicine and was in the second graduating class in the entire US to get her Masters in Traditional Chinese Veterinary Medicine. The following year Elizabeth got her certification in Veterinary Medical Manipulation (the veterinary equivalent of chiropractic). Essential Oil therapy, sound therapy as well as zoo pharmacognosy are also special areas of interest. She is currently studying The Foundations of Nutritional Therapy Seminar Series by The International Foundation for Nutrition and Health. Elizabeth started her holistic practice on her farm in Kennett Square where she concentrates on food therapy, acupuncture, herbal therapy, spinal manipulation, essential oils and hair analysis for detection of heavy metals and body minerals. She has one adult son, five geriatric horses, three cats and a dog. For more information visit:

https://www.elizabethmckinstryvmd.com

Dr. Lisa Melling, DVM received a Bachelor of Science degree in Animal Science from Iowa State University in 1999 and graduated from Tuskegee University School of Veterinary Medicine in 2004 with a special interest in animal behavior and emergency medicine. In 2007 Dr. Melling co-founded Best Friends Pet Wellness, a house call practice serving the Ann Arbor area of Michigan. Frustrated by the limitations of allopathic medicine, she enrolled in Dr. Pitcairn's Professional Course in Veterinary Homeopathy in 2008. Encouraged by her personal experience with homeopathy as well as the curative results it provided for her patients, Dr. Melling became an instructor for the Professional Course in Veterinary Homeopathy in 2010 and a Certified Veterinary Homeopath by the Academy of Veterinary Homeopathy in 2011.

She has presented numerous cases at veterinary meetings across the country and was a frequent guest lecturer at the Michigan State University School of Veterinary Medicine's Integrative Medicine Club from 2011 to 2014. She has been a board member of the Academy of Veterinary Homeopathy since 2015. She has had

Thank You & Biographies

articles published in the Journal of the American Holistic Veterinary Medical Association, Integrative Veterinary Care Journal, Dogs Naturally, and Pet Wellness magazines. In 2015 Dr. Melling moved to Traverse City, Michigan and established Good Harbor Holistic Veterinary Care. In the spring of 2019, Dr. Melling completed her training and received certification in Veterinary Spinal Manipulative Therapy, better known as chiropractic care for animals. Her holistic practice provides homeopathic treatment for acute illnesses, injuries, and chronic disease as well as nutritional advice and animal chiropractic care for dogs, cats and horses. For more information visit: *www.goodharborvet.com*

Dr. Mary Newport, MD, graduated from Xavier University and University of Cincinnati College of Medicine, trained in pediatrics at Children's Hospital Medical Center in Cincinnati, Ohio, and in neonatology at Medical University of South Carolina. She is board certified in pediatrics and neonatology, the care of sick and premature newborns. She was founding medical director for two newborn intensive care units and practiced neonatology for thirty years in the Tampa Bay area of Florida. More recently, she makes home visits with people who have chronic conditions. In 2008, she implemented a ketogenic nutritional intervention with coconut and medium-chain triglyceride oil that dramatically helped her husband Steve Newport who had early-onset Alzheimer's disease. He lost his battle with Alzheimer's and Lewy Body dementia in 2016 and Dr. Newport carries on his legacy as an author and international speaker on ketones as an alternative fuel for the brain. Her latest book is entitled *The Complete Book of Ketones: A Practical Guide to Ketogenic Diets and Ketone Supplements.* For more information visit: *https://coconutketones.com*

Dr. Karen L. Overall has BA, MA and VMD degrees from the University of Pennsylvania and a PhD degree from the University of Wisconsin-Madison. She did her residency training in veterinary behavioural medicine at the University of Pennsylvania and is a Diplomate of the American College of Veterinary Behaviourists (DACVB). Dr. Overall is a Professor of Behavioural Medicine at Atlantic Veterinary College, UPEI and lectures at veterinary schools world-wide.

Dr. Overall the author of over 100 scholarly publications, dozens of textbook chapters, and the texts *Clinical Behavioural Medicine for Small Animals* (1997; Elsevier) and *Manual of Clinical Behavioural Medicine for Dogs and Cats* (2013; Elsevier) and of the DVD, *Humane Behavioural Care for Dogs: Problem Prevention and Treatment* (2013; Elsevier). She is the editor-in-chief for *Journal of Veterinary Behaviour: Clinical Applications and Research* (Elsevier).

In addition to having given hundreds of lectures to various associations world-wide, Dr. Overall frequently consults for welfare groups, governments, the entire range of working dog organizations and pharmaceutical companies.

Dr. Overall has been named the North American Veterinary Conference (NAVC) Small Animal Speaker of the Year and was named one of the *The Bark's* 100 Best and Brightest - *Bark Magazine's* list of the 100 most influential people in the dog world over the past 25 years.

Dr. Overall's research focuses on neurobehavioural genetics of dogs, the development of normal and abnormal behaviours especially with respect to early experience, assessment of behaviour, with an emphasis on working dogs, truly humane routine behavioural care and psychopharmacology. For more information visit: *www.KarenOverall.com*

Purina Institute serves as the global voice of Purina's science and represents a diverse team of more than 500 scientists and pet care experts who are located around the world. The Purina Institute is responsible for sharing the latest scientific findings in companion animal nutrition, with the goal of elevating nutrition within pet health discussions. For more information visit: *purinainstitute.com* or *purinainstitute.com/signup* - scientific updates from the Purina Institute.

Dr. Lisa Radosta is a board-certified veterinary behaviorist, owner of Florida Veterinary Behavior Service and co-founder of Dog Nerds. Dr. Radosta is a sought after national and international speaker. She has written for Blackwell's Five-Minute Veterinary Consult, Canine and Feline and Small Animal Pediatrics and is coeditor of Handbook of Behavior Problems of the Dog and Cat. She has published scientific research articles in Journal of Applied Animal Behavior Science, The Veterinary Journal and the Journal of

Thank You & Biographies

Veterinary Behavior and written review articles for Advances in Small Animal Medicine and Surgery, Compendium, NAVC Clinician's Brief and AAHA Newstat. She is the section editor for Advances in Small Animal Medicine and Surgery. She served on the Fear Free Advisory Board and the AAHA Behavior Management Task Force. Interviews with Dr. Radosta have been published in: Cat Fancy, Dog Fancy, Palm Beach Post, NAVC Clinician's Brief, O Magazine, Catster, Good Housekeeping, Sun Sentinel, Washington Post, Real Simple, WebMD and AAHA News Stat. She has appeared on Lifetime television, Laurie Live, News Channel 25 (West Palm Beach, WPBF), Mitch Wilder's Amazing Pet Discoveries, Nat Geo Wild, Animal Planet, News Channel 10 (Miami, ABC), and Steve Dale's Pet Talk. Dr. Radosta has participated in tracking, obedience, herding and therapy dog work with personal dogs--always Rottweilers. Dr. Radosta's newest book, *From Fearful to Fear Free*, is an excellent guide to living with a fearful dog. Currently, she shares her life with a wonderful husband, Scott and her daughter, Isabella as well as Maverick, her Labrador Retriever and Chewie her cantankerous black cat. For more information visit: *https://www.flvetbehavior.com*

Dr. Pedro Luis Rivera, DVM, FACFN, DACVSMR, FCOAC graduated from Purdue University, School of Veterinary Medicine in 1986. He has been practicing integrative veterinary medicine and in particular Veterinary Spinal Manipulative Therapy and Veterinary Rehabilitation with emphasis in functional neurology for the last 35 years.

Dr. Rivera is a proud Fellow of the American College of Functional Neurology and a Diplomate of the American College of Veterinary Sport Medicine and Rehabilitation.

Dr. Rivera and Michelle Rivera are the owners and main program directors of the Healing Oasis Wellness Center, a nationally accredited and recognized school (under the US Dept Of Education) providing state approved postgraduate certification programs (through the DSPS-Educational Approval Programs Of Wisconsin) and approved by the Veterans Affairs Office, among other national organizations.

The Healing Oasis has been providing post graduate state approved certification programs in VMRT (Since 1998) and VSMT (since 1999) among providing many continuing education seminars and advanced programs with an emphasis in clinical applications in functional neurology to improve patient outcomes. For more information visit: *https://HealingOasis.edu*

Dr. Ethan Russo is a board-certified neurologist, is the Founder/CEO of CReDO Science, an intellectual property-holding and formulation company targeting the endocannabinoid system for therapeutic benefit. Dr. Russo was formerly the senior medical advisor to GW Pharmaceuticals and a widely published author in many scientific journals, as well as a contributor and editor of several books. He has also been a faculty member at the University of Washington, a guest teacher at Harvard Medical School, and other academic institutions. Welcome to Cannabis Conversations. For more information visit: *https://credo-science.com*

Ms. Kathy Shafer and her sister Dali founded Houndstooth Pet Dental nearly 30 years ago, both had worked with rescues and veterinary clinics starting at very young ages; it was always their strong passion.

Houndstooth's first website was launched in 1998 and was dedicated to helping pets get the right dental care. Their information has been viewed all over the world and its content copied and used on other websites

They saw many pets whose health was devastated by dental disease and were determined to educate the guardians and veterinarians about dental wellness. Their goals were to provide care before disease impacted the pet's health. Their journey was hard and a very rough road, which turned into an amazing journey; they watched as the seed took hold and grew.

Houndstooth became a noteworthy leader in veterinary dental expansion, by offering a safe, affordable alternative to standard anesthetic-based cleanings. By combining extensive training and Houndstooth's gentle handling techniques, they were able to effectively clean both above and below the gum line and polish while your pet remained alert & comfortable. Veterinarians curious about non anesthetic/non-surgical dental procedure reached out and wanted more information and demos and joined their team approach. Kathy Shafer was determined to bring the concept of dental hygiene for pets to veterinary clinics everywhere, she knew there was a lot of work to do.

Thank You & Biographies

Unfortunately, Dali died unexpectedly in 2017. It was devastating, thousands of people loved her and embraced her as part of their family, and her loss is still greatly felt.

Kathy and Dali had logged thousands of airmiles to demo their dental procedure to everyone who would listen.

Together they proudly became known as a company based on trust, integrity, and information. "Houndstooth network of veterinarians are your pet's team for all things dental." For more information visit: *http://houndstoothpetdental.com*

Ms. Susan Thixton is a pet food consumer advocate - one of just a handful of advocates in the United States that fight to hold the pet food industry accountable to existing food safety regulations. She is the founder of Association for Truth in Pet food – a pet food consumer stakeholder organization - and the author and co-author of several books. She is also the publisher of the websites: TruthaboutPetFood.com, PetsumerReport.com, and AssociationforTruthinPetFood.com. For more information visit: w*ww.TruthaboutPetFood.com*

Dr. Dennis Thomas has taken the best practices from both the east and the west to develop his own unique brand of veterinary care that is second to none. He has outlined this approach in his 2015 book *Whole Pet Healing.*

After more than twenty years of traditional western veterinary practice, Dr. Thomas began to incorporate alternative and complimentary forms of pet health care for his patients. In addition to being trained at one of the top veterinary schools in the country he added traditional Chinese Veterinary Medicine, veterinary acupuncture, and Chinese herbal remedies to direct healing beyond the limits of traditional western veterinary care, with incredible results.

Today, Dr. Thomas takes pet health care to a new level by changing the focus from treating your pet to healing your pet. Veterinary care is more than giving vaccines, mending broken bones, and prescribing pills for your pet's illnesses. By looking past, the immediate symptoms and caring for the WHOLE pet Dr. Thomas transforms the lives of both pets and their caretakers.

Through 1-on-1 consulting calls with clients all over the world, Dr. Thomas tailors his approach to the unique needs of each individual pet. Believing that every pet's natural state of being is perfect health, Dr. Thomas works to restore and maintain the pet's energetic balance and natural state of being via the least invasive and most effective treatments available.

Dr. Thomas recognizes the importance of the healing, energetic bond between people and their pets, and utilizes this awareness to direct healing from this loving, compassionate state of mind. For more information visit: *www.drdennisthomas.com*

Dr. Debbie Gross Torraca, DPT, MSPT, CCRP, Board-Certified Orthopedic Clinical Specialist Emeritus
began her career in human physical therapy and specialized in orthopedics and pain management in both orthopedic and sports medicine atmospheres. Her knowledge enables her to translate her understanding from the human side to the animals. She has been enjoying her work with animals for over twenty-two years and is considered a pioneer in the field of canine physical rehabilitation. She is one of the founders of the University of Tennessee's certificate program in canine rehabilitation. Through the university and throughout the world, Dr. Torraca has been a well sought out speaker on a variety of subjects. She speaks all over the world to veterinarian professionals, allied health care professionals, dog enthusiasts, and owners. She is also the founder and heads the Certified Canine Manual Therapy program through the University of Tennessee. She teaches regularly at the Fenzi Dog Sports Academy, as well as any other organizations.

Her passions include sports medicine and working dogs, as well as degenerative myelopathy. Dr. Torraca focuses on the identification and treatment of pain in all of the dogs she works with. Pain is often overlooked in many physical and behavioral issues and may make the difference between success and failure. Hidden pain may often cause behavioral issues, and she has been seeing great results with the discovery of pain and appropriate treatment. She sees a variety of clients in her busy clinic, Wizard of Paws Physical Rehabilitation and Wellness center, focused on rehabilitation, wellness.

Her company, Wizard of Paws Physical Rehabilitation for Animals, LLC, focuses on that the moment an animal walks in the door whether they are eight weeks of age or eighteen years of age. For more information visit: *https://wizardofpaws.net/*

Thank You & Biographies

Dr. Valarie Tynes is a native Texan and received her DVM from Texas A&M University. She worked in private practice for 14 years before returning to academia to pursue a residency in clinical animal behavior at the University of California at Davis in 2000. She has been a diplomate of the American College of Veterinary Behaviorists since 2003 and is also Board Certified in Animal Welfare. She is a frequent speaker at veterinary meetings around the world and author of numerous articles and textbook chapters. She joined Ceva Animal Health in October of 2014 as a veterinary services specialist. For more information email: *pigvet@hughes.net*

Dr. Alice Villalobos, 2005-06 President of the American Association of Human Animal Bond Veterinarians (AAHABV), is a well-known pioneer in the field of cancer care for companion animals and a founding member of the Veterinary Cancer Society. A 1972 graduate of UC Davis, she completed Dr. Gordon Theilen's first mock residency program in oncology and has served the profession by consulting, writing and lecturing in the rapidly growing field of veterinary oncology and end of life care. She was awarded the UC Davis Alumni Achievement Award in 1994, and the Leo Bustad Companion Animal Veterinarian of the Year Award in 1999. She is Editor-in-Chief of the AAHABV Newsletter, Secretary of the Animal Health Foundation of the SCVMA and Founder of the Peter Zippi Memorial Fund for Animals, with over 10,000 rescued and placed pets.

Dr. Villalobos is serving as President of the Society for Veterinary Medical Ethics (SVME) for 2020 and 2021. She was President of the SVME in 2010-2011. She will raise discussions about the ethical obligation that veterinarians have to communicate compassionately yet frankly with clients regarding options for pets with cancer and other terminal diseases. She believes attending doctors are obligated to offer palliative and end of life Pawspice care options for terminal pets in addition to the standard options offered for either top cabin treatment, no treatment or euthanasia. She believes pet parents have the right to be informed that palliative or Pawspice care is a viable option over no treatment or euthanasia especially when the family cannot afford the cost of top cabin treatments for their pet. Veterinarians, veterinary nurses, staff and professionals from allied fields who care for animals and their families and concerned pet owners who would like to provide their input are invited to join SVME. Dr. Alice celebrates over 38 years of marriage to Ira Lifland. They live with two cats and two dogs and Dr. Alice loves walking the dogs and skiing. For more information visit: *www.svme.org*

Dr. Chris Zink DVM PhD DACVSMR is a canine sports medicine specialist with a lifelong passion for learning everything about dogs. For over 40 years, she has coached dog lovers, trainers, veterinarians, and other dog professionals via seminars, consultations, books and other media. She has won numerous teaching and writing awards and competes with her Golden Retriever and Norwich Terrier, having garnered over 150 competition titles in 12 different sports venues. Her most recent book, *Discovering Your Dog. New information on how to give your canine pal a longer, healthier life*, is available on her website. For more information visit: *www.caninesports.com*

Additional Thanks

A very Special Thank You to Georgeanne of "Soulful Hearts," for rescuing Shamrock and Clover and for taking such good care of them after Hurricane Katrina and bringing them into our lives.

Thanks to Dr. Faust regarding his care of Shamrock and Clover through all their years. No matter what I've learned in the research of this book I am very grateful for the care he provided for my babies.

When Shamrock was getting older, he didn't rush the appointments and always gave me the time to ask questions and understand the care he suggested.

Even at the height of Shamrock's illness he never made me feel like I was imposing on his time. When she was in the full throngs of the disease, he tried consistently to provide her with the best care to keep her pain free and always consulted with others to be able to get suggestions for other medications or care that might help her in any way.

I also owe an enormous thank you to the individuals who helped me obtain interviews and documents that have been so useful in this book; for permissions and providing articles and forms for reprinting

Thank You & Biographies

Also, I wish to thank the many veterinarians who I did not interview but who took their time to correspond with me and provided comments and referrals for this book:

Thanks to Incredible Resources
Organizations -
These Organizations Helped Shamrock And Clover

When Hurricane Katrina hit, rescue agencies responded but with so many dogs separated from their families, they needed homes…but had no homes to go to…

Wanting to help, an internet search led me to "Petfinder". There I found many puppies, which caught my heart and needed a home. But suddenly I found one that drew me in, and my gift was doubled, as she had a litter mate rescued with her.

That search led to "Soulful Hearts" and Georgeanne, the owner…then the process of fostering these two puppies began.

It was one of the best experiences in life….

Rescue services like "Soulful Hearts," led by amazing people like Georgeanne are truly a blessing, but especially in the aftermath of tragedies!

During their years with me, Shamrock and Clover had serious illnesses and they needed very expensive operations. I was fortunate to find companies that were willing to help, and my dogs received the care they needed. These organizations are wonderful and caring and I am so grateful they were there for me and my puppies!

Mosby Foundation For more information visit: *https://themosbyfoundation.org*

Pets Assistance – For more information visit *https://thepetfund.com:* *(Note: Ruth Krebs-Pearl of Pet Assistance has written a memoir of her journey helping pets, *What's A Nice Dog Like You Doing in a Place Like This?* Available on Amazon. All profits from this book will be donated to Pet Assistance, Inc. to benefit pets whose owners cannot afford emergency and urgent veterinary care).

Red Rover - For more information visit: *https://redrover.org*

Sergei Foundation –For more information visit: *https://sergeifoundation.org/*

Author's Biography

F. Barish-Stern is the author of *Rainbow's City* which won the ACOR prize for arts related works. She is also the co-author of *TELL IT TO THE FUTURE,* about life during the Twentieth Century, and co-author of many other books, including, *NEW HORIZON'S, FROM AN IDEA TO YOUR FINISHED STORY* and *HOW TO WRITE YOUR BOOK*. Started in 1998, Barish-Stern is the Executive Director of Golden Quill Press

She enjoys working with diverse authors, young and old, to help write, edit and publish their work, including 16-year-old, first time author, Ruth Cefola, and 90-year-old, Marjorie Struck.

She continues to teach writing and consult one on one with aspiring authors.

F. Barish-Stern is also the author of the *Code 47 to BREV Force*, trilogy, a mainstream story with a sci-fi take on relationships in the world of computers, holograms, clones and sentient beings. She continues to write short stories and articles for the internet and has more books on the way.

To My Readers & Fellow Dog Lovers

Thank you for taking your time to learn about cognitive disease in dogs and for sharing this journey with my precious Shamrock, and by extension, her sister, and our other beloved family member, Clover.

I hope that you have learned a great deal that can help you give your "baby" a better life and protect them as much as possible, from this terrible disease.

If you have found this book interesting, educational and helpful in any way, I know our veterinarians would be interested in your comments, and so would I. Please email:
info@goldenquillpress.com SUBJECT: Shamrock's Book Comment

For readers who would like to review this book, please send your comments to: *info@goldenquillpress.com* SUBJECT: Shamrock's Story REVIEW.

We look forward to giving webinars, interviews and videos. if you would like to be advised of these events, please email: *info@goldenquillpress.com* SUBJECT: Shamrock's email list. We do not sell or give your information to anyone.

Be sure to - Check out our website:
https://www.goldenquillpress.com for more information and other social media links.

One More Thing

In addition to being Valentine's Day - February 14th was Shamrock's birthday. If you fell in love with Shamrock and want her memory to keep helping other dogs, please visit our site to learn about: our "February 14th- **Love Your Dog National Canine Cognitive Dysfunction Awareness Day**". (We also honor all dogs that have been victims of this disease). To learn more visit:

Also, on our site you can find a list of Important Dog Event Dates
Thanks again for giving me your time

F. Barish-Stern

*(Note from the Publisher- We hope you have gained valuable information from this book and will check out our web site *https;//www.goldenquillpress.com* which also contains some supporting documents including an Abridged Index.

Company History

Golden Quill Press and The Write Source were started in New York in 1998, by writers, editors and publishers. These professionals had worked in the publishing field for over twenty years and saw how difficult it was becoming to get published. So how was a first-time novelist going to get noticed?

To offer writers an alternative, Golden Quill Press offered "Cooperative Publishing," a custom designed system of services writers could pick and choose exactly what services they need.

The principals, Bobbi Madry and F. Barish-Stern also provided writing classes, individual instruction, and all book services.

Bobbi R. Madry, has been the Senior Editor and Educational Director of Golden Quill Press, since 1998. She has authored numerous educational publications and programs for major New York City publishers. Adding to her long list of editing accomplishments, while working at Milady Publishing, she co-wrote and edited numerous books in the cosmetology field and even a guide for estheticians. While at Milady she also wrote *Job Seekers Guide.*

In the 1990's she was an Associate Publisher for a New York Newspaper, and also mentored aspiring writers. She has received Awards for Writing and Community Service and holds Degrees in the Arts and Behavioral Sciences.

Bobbi Madry was an editor to author William Thourlby on his books, *Passport to Power* and *You Are What You Wear.* She is also the author of *Love Makes The Difference, and* at Golden Quill Press her editing achievements include, *Compassions Lure, Challenging Messages From Beyond, Sweet Mercy,* and more.

Today Bobbi Madry remains an active voice in Golden Quill Press, still helping first-time writers. Recently she started a local focus group to help young writers find their way into the world of writing!

In 2005, Golden Quill Press combined years of experience when authors and writing teachers, Madry and Barish-Stern published a step by step, easy to follow guide for anyone interested in writing a book, *From An Idea to Your Finished Story.* Today it is in the fifth edition printing, re-designed and re-titled, *HOW TO WRITE YOUR BOOK, From An Idea to Your Published Story.*

Golden Quill Press has also partnered with Greetings on Gold, for writers who want to create their own greeting card line, and to design their own bookmarks.

Golden Quill Press - Motto: Serving the needs of creative and business writers, from an idea... to a finished story... as much, or as little as needed!

Books By Golden Quill Press

Coming Soon –Eaton's

Eaton's – The Second French Revolution By Kenneth Bray

A great department store becomes the backdrop for the revolutionary 1960's. Filled with great character's, intrigue, and love… this is a Must Read! Pre- Order yours today at *info@goldenquillpress.com* Subject Eaton's Pre-Order

***Code 47 to BREV Force,* A Trilogy** By: F. Barish-Stern

Drenched in fantasy & fictional supposition, this story echoes the reality of our world today, a world where technology rules & evil seems to lurk everywhere. Our youth are targets, their beliefs & values, family, friends, country are all being called into question. All they've been taught is being blown apart & brainwashing leaves their lives for the enemy

How To Write Your Book, BY: Bobbi Madry & F. Barish-Stern

A Step-by Step, Easy to Understand Interactive Journey. Will walk you through all the stages of writing with tips, forms, & guidelines.

Tell It To The Future BY: *Francine R. Cefola & Bobbi R. Madry

Stories about our hopes, dreams, from each decade of the 20th Century that leave personal messages with timelines. Whether witty, or filled with wisdom, they will pull at your heart strings.

New Horizons - BY: *Francine R. Cefola & Bobbi R. Madry

Poetry from the splendor of life's beauty

Books Edited And Published By Golden Quill Press

Challenging Messages From Beyond - By: Marjorie Struck
Compassion's Lure - By: Kathleen Lukens
Love Makes A Difference - By: Mary Bianchini And Bobbi Madry
Mae Sings About Short Vowels - By: Karen A. Coleman
Opening The Door To A Brighter Future - By: Daniel Windheim
Sweet Mercy By: Rebecca H. Cofer
The Granpa Spider Stories By: Granpa Spider
The Poem Book By: Daniel Windheim
There Is Hope By: Debby Paine

Books Edited, But Not Published By Golden Quill Press

Since 1998 hundreds of books have been edited by GQP for author's self-publication, or other publishing houses. For more information visit: *https://www.goldenquillpress.com*

*(Note: Previous name of author *F. Barish-Stern

SEE Actual Goldtone Metal Samples At:
http//:www.goldenquillpress.com/samples.html

ELEGANT GOLDTONE METAL CUSTOM PET PORTRAIT

THIS COULD BE YOUR PET'S CUSTOM PORTRAIT
in a black mat, ready for framing

CHOOSE FROM FINISHED SIZES

8" X 10"	OR	11" X 14"
Reg. $49.95		Reg. $69.95

Less 20% Discount To "Shamrock Book" Purchasers

Now $39.96   Now $55.96

To see our beautiful pet products in full color visit:
http//:www.goldenquillpress.com/samples.html

Also Inquire About Our Other Pet Products

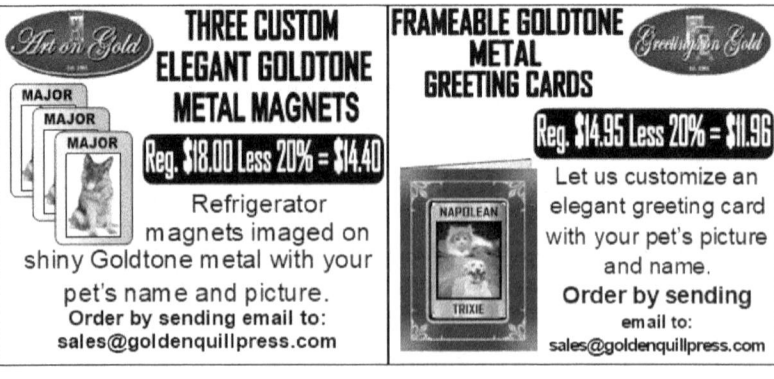

THREE CUSTOM ELEGANT GOLDTONE METAL MAGNETS

Reg. $18.00 Less 20% = $14.40

Refrigerator magnets imaged on shiny Goldtone metal with your pet's name and picture.
Order by sending email to:
sales@goldenquillpress.com

FRAMEABLE GOLDTONE METAL GREETING CARDS

Reg. $14.95 Less 20% = $11.96

Let us customize an elegant greeting card with your pet's picture and name.
Order by sending email to:
sales@goldenquillpress.com

www.ingramcontent.com/pod-product-compliance
Lightning Source LLC
LaVergne TN
LVHW021235080526
838199LV00088B/4349